Strange Death

OF

FRANKLIN D. ROOSEVELT

HISTORY OF
THE ROOSEVELT-DELANO DYNASTY
AMERICA'S ROYAL FAMILY

By

EMANUEL M. JOSEPHSON

Author of

Your Life Is Their Toy.
Rackets—Social Service and Medical.
Merchants in Medicine.
Nearsightedness is Preventable.
Glaucoma and Its Medical Treatment with Cortin.
The Thymus, Myasthenia Gravis and Manganese.
Breathe Deeply and Avoid Colds.
Roosevelt's Communist Manifesto.
Rockefeller "Internationalist"— The
Man Who Misrules The World.

[originally published by]

230 East 61st Street
New York 21, N. Y.

[Added by modern publisher.]

Dr. Emanuel M(ann). Josephson, M.D.
(1895-1975)

Reprinting of a copyright-expired work

Computer-enhanced Edition
Copyright © 2011
Sacred Truth Publishing

Facsimile Historical Reprint Series

Sacred Truth Publishing
P.O. Box 18,
Mountain City, Tennessee 37683
Christian Constitutional Republic of the United States of America
sacredtruthpublishing@mounet.com
ISBN: 1-58840-285-1

Birthday close-ups of President F. D. Roosevelt, 1938. 1939. 1940, showing growth of mole over left eyebrow. (*Press Ass.*)

President F. D. Roosevelt
showing growth over left eye.

On return from Teheran, lesion over left eyebrow showed rapid growth, indicating conversion to melanosarcoma. No subsequent close-up was released. But enlargement of distant view in "State of Nation" Broadcast picture of Jan. 6, 1945 is shown at right. The cancerous growth is missing. Distortion of left eyebrow appears to show scar of operation. Note the butterfly-like pigmentation over nose and cheeks like that of pellagra or the rosacea of chronic alcoholism. Illness, pain and emaciation are obvious. Could be picture of another, a stand-in. *Press Ass.*

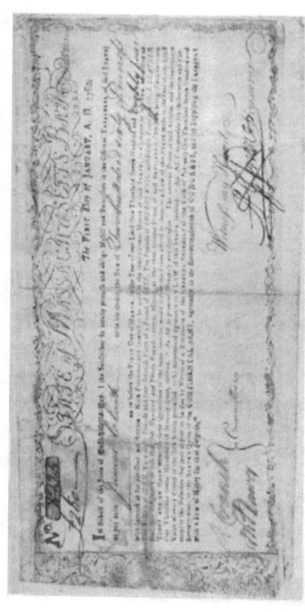

STAPLE PRODUCT NOTES ISSUED UNDER "YANKEE PLAN" FOR FIGHTING REVOLUTIONARY WAR DEPRESSION AND INFLATION Money was stabilized by defining its value in the terms of the things that people wished to purchase with it, in terms of beef, corn, sheepswool and sole leather. By incorporating these staples in the monetary base, inflation was also controlled in a direct and sensible manner. If the technology of the times had permitted of adequate production and safe storage, as is possible today, a surplus economy would have been attained by the colony, and true freedom of employment and consequently true democracy might have been effected. This plan was suggested to FDR in 1933, by the author. But under the influence of the Bank of England agent and propagandist, Maynard Keynes, of Frankfurter and German nurtured "economists", he was bent upon using the program that had failed miserably in Germany as a blind for the real monopolistic and martial plans of the Dynasty. Roosevelt had pledged revaluation of gold and maintenance of a scarcity economy to gain the delegates to the Chicago convention controlled by Hearst, and the nomination. At any rate he held in contempt homely, commonsense Yankee ideas, and preferred the New Deal (made in Germany) as a tastier bait for the sucker public. It prolonged the depression for more than a decade, but served the Dynasty's purposes well.

TABLE OF CONTENTS

ILLUSTRATIONS

INTRODUCTION TO THE REVISED EDITION

The background of the conspiracy that was the basis of the power of the Roosevelt-Delano Dynasty, and that made possible its control of the destinies of our country, is related by the author in his ROOSEVELT'S COMMU-NIST MANIFESTO (Chedney Press, 1955). It portrays the role played by the Dynasty in the Illuminist-Socialist-Communist-"One World" dictatorship conspiracy.

The second half of that volume contains what is probably the most important document in American history. It is the reprint, in full, of the 1841 publication by mentor-cousin, Clinton Roosevelt, entitled THE SCIENCE OF GOVERNMENT FOUNDED ON NATURAL LAW. It is largely an adaptation to the American scene of the conspiracy published in 1776, in Germany, by Adam Weishaupt, a renegade Catholic who had been trained by the Jesuits. He was the founder of the Order of Illuminati, which later became the Communist Party. Weishaupt is the real father, or grandfather, of modern-day Communism. And he was the preceptor of Moses Mordecai Marx Levy alias Heinrich Karl Marx.

Clinton Roosevelt was one of the group of American Illuminists, self-styled "liberals", that included Horace Greeley, Charles A. Dana, and many scions of America's "first families" who helped finance the activities of Karl Marx and his associates. His SCIENCE OF GOVERN-MENT was published as a blueprint of a conspiracy to nullify the Constitution and Sovietize the U.S.A. Published in 1841, it contains the detailed plan of the New Deal and NRA, drawn up ninety-two years before his cousin, President Franklin Delano Roosevelt, launched the conspiracy.

Clinton Roosevelt's publication is so important for an understanding of our national history, and of the ills that have befallen us, that it would have been a disaster had its well-planned blackout succeeded as a result of disintegration of the pulp paper on which it was originally published. The result would have been complete censorship and suppression of one of the most important phases of our national history and the history of the world.

The more up-to-the-minute phases of the conspiracy,

the author details in his ROCKEFELLER "International-ist", The Man Who Misrules The World (Chedney Press, 1952) and in subsequent columns.

A fourth volume is under consideration by the author, on the part played by the conspirators in the engineering of the Civil War, and on the elections and assassination of Abraham Lincoln.

Material revisions and additions have been made in the text, on the basis of subsequent researches and investigations. This is especially true in the chapter on The Odd Ailments & Strange Death Of F. D. R. It has been largely rewritten and amplified with additional data, which casts an even stranger light on this curious affair.

PREFACE

The Roosevelt-Delano Dynasty has played a far more important role in the history of the United States than is suspected even by supposedly well-informed folk. Their role in the future may be a very fateful one now that it has become an integral though subsidiary part of the Rockefeller (Standard Oil) Empire. The time has arrived when it is imperative that the nation be keenly aware of it.

An evaluation of the significance of the Roosevelt-Delano Dynasty for the past, present and future of the United States has been impossible hitherto because the data has been carefully hidden in the family records and has not been available to the public. Even in the case of one of the most publicized members of the Dynasty, Franklin Delano Roosevelt, little of the really important background is known to the public.

Apologists for Roosevelt and the New Deal implicitly acknowledge their defect and the damage they have done the nation, when they seek to evade the issue and assert with all the dialectic vehemence of the trained Marxist:

"But Roosevelt is dead. Why bring him up?"

It must be acknowledged that Roosevelt is a very pathetic object for hero worship, and they might well like to drop the subject. But unfortunately the grave injuries that were done the nation through Franklin Delano Roosevelt, as tool, agent and mouthpiece of sinister powers behind the government are not as dead as he. They live on and must be studied, dealt with and corrected where possible.

On the topic of Roosevelt, the American public fall into two large groups. There are those who venerate and adore him, and regard him in the light of a savior. The others detest him as unscrupulous, treacherous, dishonest and a thoroughgoing fraud.

To both of them, however, there is completely unknown the truly important facts with regard to Franklin Delano Roosevelt, the man, his familial background, his allegiances and interests, his objectives, and the dynastic tradition which he carried on.

More memorials have been set up for the Roosevelts, especially for Franklin Delano Roosevelt, than for all the rest of the Presidents put together. Despite this, the only facts in regard to Franklin Delano Roosevelt known to the public are those dispensed by his publicity men, some of them relatives and by the New Deal propagandists. These fall far short of the true picture of the significance of Roosevelt and his Dynasty in the past and current history of the land.

This woeful ignorance of the strongly biased public on the subject of Franklin Delano Roosevelt is best illustrated by my experience in October, 1944. I was invited to give a radio broadcast on the subject of "Know Your President". The form of the broadcast was a quiz contest consisting of twenty important questions about President Franklin Delano Roosevelt, his background, his activities and his avowed objectives. In the first broadcast on October 20 the questions were read and prizes were offered for correct replies to be received before the next broadcast, one week later. Not a single correct reply was received to the questions which I now quote:

"It is the claim of the Roosevelt-Delano clan that they have contributed twelve Presidents to the United States and have virtually ruled this country since its inception.

Question 1: Can you name those Presidents?

Three Presidents have been assassinated in the course of our history.

Question 2: How many of them have been followed by relatives of Franklin D. Roosevelt?

Question 3: Which of them narrowly escaped impeachment as President of the United States? Why?

International alliances and entanglements are of special interest to us now.

Question 4: To what reigning monarch is President Roosevelt sufficiently related to claim cousinship, and how?

Question 5: What justification is there for the statement that the Secretaryship of the Navy is hereditary in the Roosevelt family?

Question 6: Is there any justification for the idea that the Roosevelt clan have a vested interest in war?

Question 7: What United Nations leader placed the blame for precipitating the present war squarely in the lap of President Roosevelt?

Question 8: How many relatives has President Roosevelt appointed to office? Name some.

Question 9: From what sources, in addition to the German government, was the most important part in the financing of Communism in the U. S. derived?

Question 10: From what source did Senator Robert F. Wagner import the "New Deal"?

Question 11: Do you regard the key New Dealers including Nelson Rockefeller, Averill Harriman, Francis Biddle, Jesse Jones, Will Clayton and other representatives of America's largest fortunes as sincere champions of Labor? Do you think that it is their honest purpose to turn over control of the nation to Labor and thus destroy themselves and their fortunes in an act of political and economic hari-kari? If not, what is their real objective?

Question 12: What program have the Roosevelts advocated and published for the solution of the Jewish and Negro questions? Do they accord with the views advocated in the blueprint of the New Deal?

Question 13: Have any negro victims of infantile paralysis ever been admitted to President Roosevelt's business, Georgia Warm Springs? Or has an attitude of Jim Crowism been adopted, despite contributions of colored folks to Birthday Balls and despite the Roosevelt insistence that other folks must not discriminate against them?

Question 14: Has President Roosevelt a holding company of his own despite his opposition to holding companies that has been so violent that he has destroyed investments of billions of dollars held by innocent investors in holding companies? What is its name and activity?

Question 15: What has been the fate of money invested by the American public in stock issues floated under the name of Franklin D. Roosevelt? What have these issues been?

Question 16: What has been the fate of billions of dollars invested by the American public in railroad and utility stock as a result of action by the S.E.C. that supposedly was established for the purpose of protecting the investing public?

Question 17: Has Franklin D. Roosevelt ever been completely honest and straightforward in his attitude on any question that affects public interest? Has he ever kept a campaign pledge made in public interest?

Question 18: Who have been the principal ghostwriters who have thought Franklin D. Roosevelt's thoughts and written the speeches he declaims so well?

Question 19: Do you approve the New Deal policy that provides everything for foreign lands under Lend Lease, including liners for post-war trade that are thinly disguised as airplane carriers, but alleges that it can not produce enough shipping to bring our soldiers back to their homes and families from two to five years after the close of the war in Europe, as announced by the New Deal War Department? Does this not make it more apparent than ever that the true motto of the New Deal is "America Last and Least?"

Question 20: What happened to the large black mole that grew rapidly over the left eyebrow of President Roosevelt about two years ago? What is the significance of the two operations for "wens" that Drew Pearson reports he has undergone during the past year?

It is my purpose to present the facts concerning this Dynasty that has played a dominant role in the affairs of the nation that is so completely unsuspected even by those who regard themselves as well-informed. It is also my purpose to relate the factual basis of a true evaluation of the significance of that role, especially for the future of the nation.

THE ROYAL FAMILY

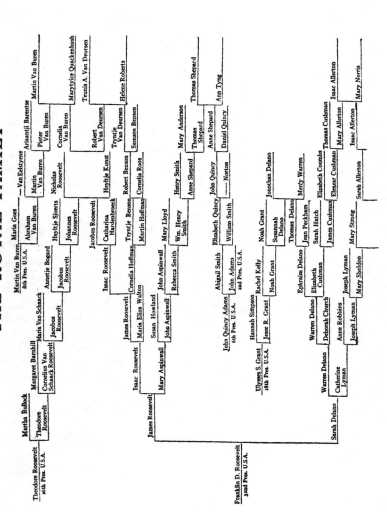

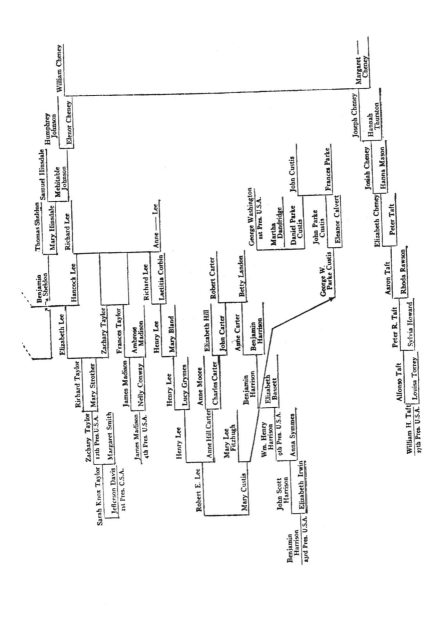

CHAPTER I

PRESIDENTS ON THE ROOSEVELT FAMILY TREE

Franklin Delano Roosevelt displayed on his family tree twelve presidents of the United States, and one president of the Confederate States, with whom he claimed direct relationship. Only four of the presidents were on the Roosevelt side of the family. Eight were derived from the infuential and powerful Delano family.

So closely has the secret been kept that it will undoubtedly surprise the reader to know that the most closely related of these presidents to F. D. R. was not Theodore Roosevelt, but Ulysses S. Grant.

On the Roosevelt side of the family, F. D. R. claims relationship to John Adams, the second president and John Quincy Adams, the sixth president, Martin Van Buren, the eighth president, and Theodore Roosevelt, the twenty-sixth president. On the Delano side he claims relationship to George Washington, James Madison, fourth president, William Henry Harrison, Zachary Taylor, twelfth, Andrew Johnson, seventeenth, Ulysses S. Grant, eighteenth, Benjamin Harrison, twenty-third, and William Howard Taft, twenty-seventh.

GEORGE WASHINGTON

The relationship of President George Washington to the Roosevelt-Delano clan is remote and not nearly so direct as in the case of the other eleven. It traces through George W. Parke Custis, a nephew of Martha Washington by her first marriage to Daniel Custis, whose daughter married General Robert E. Lee, a fifth cousin of Sara Delano Roosevelt.

An interesting sidelight on the remoteness of the relationship is cast by George Washington's rejection of an invitation to attend the funeral of the wife of the Revolutionary War veteran and New York State Senator, Isaac Roosevelt, which he noted in his diary on November 14th, 1789 in the following entry:

"Received an invitation to attend the funeral of Mrs.

Roosevelt (the wife of a Senator of the State) but declined complying with it, first because the *propriety of accepting an invitation of this sort appeared to be very questionable*, and secondly (though to do so in this case *might* not be improper), because it might be difficult to discriminate in cases which might thereafter happen." (F. D. Roosevelt's Colonial Ancestors, A. V. Page, 1933, p. 21).

The remoteness of the relationship would serve in some measure to explain the complete absence in F.D.R. of the nobler and finer qualities of George Washington—his modesty, his humility, his sanity, his absolute honesty, his high and rigid principles, his refusal to stoop to cheap expediency and politics, his passionate devotion to the cause of freedom, liberty and democracy, his loyalty to his country and refusal to sacrifice it to the interests of any foreign land, his spurning of nepotism and abhorrence of the cheapening of the office of President through exploitation for social or business advancement.

All of these characteristics definitely stamp George Washington as not a true member of the Roosevelt-Delano clan, however insistently they claim him. Affirmation of relationship to George Washington by Franklin Delano Roosevelt, who lent his support to the "Union Now" movement and had as a member of his cabinet, Harold Ickes an official of that movement, and who was instrumental in World Wars I and II in betraying the interests of his country to Great Britain and reducing it to a more subject state than the lowliest of the British colonies, is the height of irony.

Washington nobly rejected the "indispensable", dictatorial and regal status that Franklin Delano Roosevelt and other members of the Dynasty have sought.

JOHN ADAMS

John Adams was originally related to the Roosevelts through the marriage of Franklin Delano Roosevelt's grandfather, James to Mary Aspinwall, a descendant of Thomas Shepard and Ann Tyng who were ancestors also of the Adamses. The relationship was in the order of seventh cousin. But as is so common in royal families, relationships in the Roosevelt-Delano clan are intensified and made closer by inbreeding and marriage of cousins. In the present generation for instance, Frederick B. Adams married his distant cousin, Ellen W. Delano, thus enabling heir apparent, James Roosevelt to talk of "my cousin" Fred Adams when discussing sugar and insurance deals.

John Adams was an Illuminist (as the Communists were named then) a follower of Adam Weishaupt who was the grandfather of present day Communism. Adams organized the first Illuminist cell in New England.

John Adams and his second cousin Samuel Adams were moving spirits in the resistance of New England to British tyranny. Whether influenced by their interests in commerce and trade, especially with the West Indies and other British colonies, and in smuggling, as some folks allege, or not, there can be no question as to their devotion to the cause of the Revolution. Both signed the Declaration of Independence. Popular Samuel Adams is regarded as the author of most of the Bill of Rights and was instrumental in the adoption of the Constitution by the State of Massachusetts which he served as lieutenant governor and governor between 1789 and 1797.

John Adams, Harvard graduate, courageous and devoted to the cause of the Revolution, but vain, argumentative, impetuous, resentful, suspicious and in the main unpopular, member of the Continental Congress, ambassador to France and to England, got only thirty-four out of sixty votes for vice president as contrasted with the unanimous vote for George Washington in 1789. His snobbishness which impelled him to write that "the rich, the well-born and the able" members of Congress should be kept apart in a Senate did not add to his popularity. In the role of proud aristocrat he fiercely resented the failure of the electors to make him President instead of George Washington. With Alexander Hamilton, Adams became a recognized political leader of the Federalist party.

Adams secured his election to the Presidency by eliminating Thomas Jefferson. Feeling against the Illuminists ran high in the colonies in 1796, because of their involvement in the engineering of the French Revolution and its "Reign of Terror". Adams publicly betrayed his fellow Illuminist, Jefferson, who had organized the first Red cell in Virginia, in 1785, and exposed him in a letter which can be seen in the library on Rittenhouse Square in Philadelphia. As a result, Jefferson was defeated in that election.

In 1796, Washington refused to accept another election to serve a third term, because of the danger of setting the precedent of a president assuming office for life and becoming dictator or monarch. John Adams was chosen as President despite his unpopularity, because of the miscarriage of a maneuver within his own party which sought to defeat him. During his term, he fell out with Hamilton and his own supporters. By 1800 he had gained such complete control of his party that despite their distrust of him he secured the Federalist nomination for presidency. He was defeated by Thomas Jefferson. In a spirit characteristic of the clan, John Adams was so enraged at his loss of office that he refused to attend Jefferson's inauguration and instead drove out of Washington during the inaugural.

John Adams assumed the role of aristocrat among revolutionary rabble. His concept of the proper form of government for the country was domination by a self-perpetuating aristocracy that would rule, in reality, and further their interests while maintaining a pretense of democracy and popular franchise. It is his idea that now prevails in the Dynasty. The Federalist political machinery which he was instrumental in creating, served the purpose of securing his nomination to the presidency despite unpopularity in his own party. The control of the political machine which he built has been handed down more or less intact in his family and Dynasty throughout the subsequent generations. It has served to advance numerous members of the Dynasty to the top ranks of society, politics, industry and commerce. It is one of the mainstays of power of the Roosevelt-Delano clan.

It was fortunate, indeed, for the country that the interests of John Adams coincided with those of the Revolutionists. For he had the courage of his convictions and he furthered them with vigor and intensity that might have been telling if he had opposed the Revolutionary cause. But it was even more fortunate for the cause of democracy that there were such men

— 15 —

as Thomas Jefferson and James Madison to offer some opposition to his plans for setting up a hereditary oligarchic rule.

The opposition that confronted John Adams and his associates was not sufficient, however, to avert the establishment of an oligarchy that is in large measure hereditary. But it was sufficiently powerful to force the oligarchs to maintain a pretense of democracy. This pretense of adoption of the most radical, they call it "liberal", cause of the times, has come to be adopted as a screen behind which each successive generation of the Roosevelt-Delano Dynasty push their drive for establishment of absolute rule by an oligarchy and the ultimate establishment of a monarchy.

John Adams established the precedent of nepotism which has become one of the outstanding characteristics in the political activity of the Roosevelt-Delano Dynasty, and one of their strongest traditions. This was evidenced in his appointment in 1782 of his fifteen year old son, John Quincy Adams, as "additional secretary" to the American Commissioners in Paris negotiating the treaty of peace of the Revolutionary War.

JAMES MADISON

James Madison was one of many distinguished descendants of William and Margaret Cheney. These included his third cousin, President Zachary Taylor who was father-in-law of Jefferson Davis, his fourth cousin, General R. E. Lee, and his seventh cousin, President William Howard Taft. Through the marriage of his great grand uncle, Hancock Lee to Sarah Allerton, Franklin Delano Roosevelt was a seventh cousin of James Madison.

James Madison studied for the ministry at Princeton. In 1775 he became chairman of the Committee of Public Safety and in 1779 was elected delegate to the Continental Congress, where he urged that Congress be given the right to levy duties, despite the opposition of his constituency. When elected to Virginia's House of Delegates in 1784, as a Unitarian, he opposed the granting of special privileges to the Episcopalian Church and fought for religious freedom. The bill he introduced was labelled Jefferson's Bill and was passed the following year. He also opposed the further issue of paper money. His influence was largely responsible for the form which the Constitution took and for its adoption against the opposition of the Federalists and others. Though defeated in his senatorial candidacy, he was elected to Congress from his home district, defeating James Monroe.

In Congress, Madison introduced the first Tariff Bill as well as the amendments to the Constitution that were subsequently adopted as the Bill of Rights. He was an advocate of State rights and opposed Hamilton's bill to establish a national bank. He sought to limit the President's prerogative and favored France and was antagonistic to England. In 1807, Madison was elected President, as candidate of the Republican ticket. Throughout his career, Madison had advocated commercial reprisals rather than war against England to force her to recognize our neutral rights. But when seeking reelection, less than two weeks after his nomination, he sent his war message to Congress on June 1, 1812. His reelection followed, despite the suggestion of the Federalists that he forced to resign because of their opposition to war.

JOHN QUINCY ADAMS

John Quincy Adams, son of John Adams, furnished the country with the spectacle that has been uncommon in our history outside of the Roosevelt-Delano Dynasty, father and son simultaneously serving in the top rungs of the national government and succeeding each other to the presidency. At the time that John Adams was vice-president, George Washington appointed his son, John Quincy Adams, successively as Minister to Netherlands, at the age of twenty-seven, and then Minister to Portugal. Before he took the latter post he was transferred in 1797, by his father who had succeeded Washington as president, to the post of Minister to Prussia. At the end of the presidential term, his father recalled him.

In 1802 he was elected to the Massachusetts Senate and in 1803 he was appointed United States Senator in spite of the unpopularity of his father with a large group of his own party, the Federalists led by Alexander Hamilton. He resigned before his term of office ended and returned to his alma mater, Harvard, as professor of rhetoric and oratory.

In the meantime, he had bolted the Federalist Party, joined the Republicans and participated in the caucus which nominated Madison for the presidency. President Madison appointed Adams, Minister to Russia in 1809 and in 1815 to England, a position occupied by his father before him and his son, Charles Frances Adams, after him. In 1817 he became Secretary of State on the Cabinet of President Monroe.

In 1825, John Quincy Adams was chosen President by the House of Representatives as a result of a deal made by him with Henry Clay, for the purpose of defeating Andrew Jackson. In return Adams made Henry Clay, Secretary of State. This raised the cry of bribery and corruption. So great was the unpopularity of Adams and the opposition to him in Congress that his presidency proved a failure. He was renominated by his party in 1828. Another scion of the Roosevelt-Delano Dynasty, General William Henry Harrison, was his running mate as vice-president, but Andrew Jackson was elected in 1828 to succeed him.

In 1831 Adams was elected to Congress where during a period of seventen years, his energies were largely devoted to abolitionist activities.

MARTIN VAN BUREN

Martin Van Buren was a descendant of Martin Van Buren and Marytyice Quackenbush as was also his fourth cousin, Isaac Roosevelt, great great grandfather of Franklin Delano Roosevelt. Van Buren's daughter-in-law, Angelina Singleton, wife of Abraham Van Buren, who was his hostess in the White House, was a cousin of President Madison's wife, Dolly.

Van Buren was a native of Kinderhook, New York, which lies not many miles north of the bailiwick of Franklin D. Roosevelt. A successful lawyer, though possessed of a very rudimentary education, he entered politics as an adherent of the George Clinton section of the Republican party. In politics his success was signalized by his leadership of a corrupt political machine that was known as the "Albany Regency", and dominated New York State politics for decades. His nickname "Little Magician" attests to his skill at nepotism and the spoils system. The Roosevelt-Delano Dynasty has since then done its level best to live up to the tradition Van Buren set for it of dirty politics, corruption, nepotism and the spoils system. With rare exception, all these later presidents of the Dynasty have proved a credit to their vicious progenitor.

Van Buren filled the offices of Surrogate of Columbia County, New York State, State Senator, and Attorney General of New York State. In 1821 he was elected to the U. S. Senate, and in 1827 was reelected. At the same time he served as campaign manager for Andrew Jackson. In the following year he was elected Governor of New York State, and resigned from the Senate. But after less than two months as Governor of New York, in 1829, he was appointed Secretary of State by President Jackson. He courted Jackson's favor; and after an interlude in which he served as Minister to England, without confirmation of his appointment, displaced Calhoun as vice-presidential candidate of the first Democratic convention.

In 1836 Van Buren, as successor of Andrew Jackson, defeated William Henry Harrison in the presidential election. On assuming office he appointed his son, Captain Abraham Van Buren, as his secretary. Abraham's wife, who was a cousin of President Madison's wife Dolly, was mistress of the White House during Van Buren's term of office.

Van Buren's presidency was marked by two successive commercial panics in 1837 and 1839. He undertook to "follow in the footsteps of his illustrous predecessor". Though renominated in 1840 he was defeated by William Henry Harrison. He sought the nomination of the Democrats in 1844 but failed to secure it.

True to the tradition of the Roosevelt-Delano Dynasty, no loyalty or allegiance to any party could be expected of him and no party could hold him. Traditionally, they acknowledge no allegiance except to themselves. As in the case of John Quincy Adams, Van Buren bolted his party and, with Adam's son, Charles Francis Adams as vice-presidential candidate, ran for office as candidate of the "Free Soil" Party in 1848, but did not win a single electoral vote. This presents an interesting demonstration of the influence attained, the cooperation between its members and the control of political machinery developed, even at this early date, by the branches of the growing Roosevelt clan. Both candidates were members of the Dynasty, for the second time in a generation.

GENERAL WILLIAM HENRY HARRISON

The use of the Army as a springboard to the Presidency, and of war heroes as political fronts is an old one and a favorite of the Roosevelt-Delano Dynasty. Setting aside their claim to George Washington, they have contributed five of them to the role of President. Some of these hero-presidents have been real and others have been synthesized for political purposes,— created by rapid promotion through nepotism of favored individuals to the rank of general-in-command towards the end of a war so that they can claim some credit for the successful course of the war. Such an instance is still fresh in the minds of the public in the promotion of Franklin Delano Roosevelt's son, Elliott to the rank of General over the heads of thousands of professional career soldiers and officers, for his distinguished services in commuting to and from the fronts and fighting the battles of the cabarets, nightclubs and bistros on the home front. This brings to mind the old saying: "Generals die in bed with their shoes off."

William Henry Harrison was the first of the series of military presidents. He was a grandson of Benjamin Harrison, a Virginian, a signer of the Declaration of Independence, and a grandfather of Benjamin Harrison, the 23rd President. He was a third cousin of Henry Lee, father of General Robert E. Lee, as well as second cousin of James Madison, fourth President, and General Zachary Taylor, twelfth President, and a fourth cousin of General Ulysses S. Grant, eighteenth President.

Harrison graduated from Hampden-Sidney College and began the study of medicine in Philadelphia. After the death of his father, against the advice of his guardian, Robert Morris, Harrison joined the Army in 1791 as ensign, went West and fought the Indians. He was rapidly promoted to captaincy, but resigned from the Army in 1798. Shortly thereafter, he was appointed Secretary of the Northwest Territory. In 1799 he was chosen by the Jeffersonian Republicans as delegate to Congress from the Territory. In 1800 President Madison, his cousin, appointed him Governor of the Indian Territory and for a short time in 1804 he acted also as Governor of the Louisiana Territory, a tremendous expanse of territory.

In a skirmish against the Indians, preliminary to the War of 1812, Harrison engaged some Indians with a force of militia and regular troops,—the much touted victory of Tippecanoe. After the outbreak of the War of 1812, he was made brigadier-general and placed in charge of all troops in the Northwest Territory, and the following year he was promoted to the rank of major-general. At the end of the War, after Perry's naval victory, Harrison advanced on Detroit and captured the territory previously lost to the British. In 1814 he once again resigned from the Army.

Between 1816 and 1828, Harrison was successively Congressman, Ohio State Senator, and U. S. Senator. In 1828 efforts to secure for him command of the Army and Vice-Presidential election on the ticket of John Quincy Adams both failed. He was appointed first American Minister to Colombia, but was recalled within a year. Retiring he took the lowly job of Clerk in the Court of Common Pleas, Hammond County.

Defeated as Whig Candidate for the presidency by Van Buren, in 1836, Harrison in turn defeated Van Buren in 1840. He survived his inauguration by one month and was succeeded by Vice-President John Tyler.

GENERAL ZACHARY TAYLOR

Zachary Taylor was the second of the series of five Army presidents of the Roosevelt-Delano clan. He was a second cousin of President James Madison and of (President) General William Henry Harrison, father-in-law of President Jefferson Davis, third cousin of Henry Lee, father of General Robert E. Lee, fourth cousin of (President) General Ulysses S. Grant, fifth cousin of President Franklin Delano Roosevelt, and sixth cousin of President William Howard Taft.

Zachary Taylor, following in the footsteps of his father, Revolutionary veteran, Col. Richard Taylor, was commissioned at 23, first lieutenant in the Army in 1808. In the War of 1812 he participated in the defense of Fort Harrison. By 1814 he had attained the rank of major and resigned from the service. He was reinstated in the service in 1816, promoted to the rank of lieutenant-colonel in 1819. He took part in the Black Hawk War in 1832 and the Seminole War in 1836. Following the battle of Okeechobee, he was breveted brigadier-general. In 1846, he defeated the Mexicans in the Rio Grande Valley and at Saltillo, and had become the popular hero of the Mexican War.

Nominated presidential candidate of the Whig Party in 1848 at the height of his military success and popular acclaim, his Louisiana plantation, slave ownership and his family background swung the tide in an election in which the question of slavery played a paramount role. His support of slavery was not as whole-hearted as he had led his supporters to anticipate. Shortly after his entering office he had antagonized them and was bitterly attacked by them. He was stricken by illness and died while in office, July 9, 1850. Millard Fillmore succeeded him in office.

ANDREW JOHNSON

Andrew Johnson is named as one of the twelve presidents of the United States who share common ancestry through the Delanos with Franklin D. Roosevelt in an article entitled "MY COUSIN IN THE WHITE HOUSE" by Daniel W. Delano, published in "PIC" Magazine on July 8, 1941. No data is available that permits detailing the degree and manner of the relationship. The ancestry probably traces back to Humphrey Johnson. In spirit Andrew Johnson is outstandingly a true progenitor of Franklin Delano Roosevelt.

Andrew Johnson began his political career in 1828 as Alderman in Greenville, Tennessee of which he became Mayor in 1830. After a period in legislature, he was elected to Congress in 1843. On his defeat for reelection to Congress in 1853, he became Governor of Tennessee. In 1857 he was elected Senator on the Democratic ticket, in which capacity he remained until 1862 when he was appointed military governor of recaptured Tennessee. True to the tradition of the Dynasty, once in high office he flaunted his campaign platforms and violated the interests of the electorate. In 1864, to hold the votes of the Democrats who favored the war, Johnson was nominated vice-president to run with Lincoln on the ticket of the Union Party.

Following Lincoln's assassination, Andrew Johnson became President. Johnson favored a lenient reconstruction policy, opposed immediate, general negro suffrage, and personally attempted to force an antagonistic Congress to rubber-stamp his bills. But in those days men were *men*— and even Congressmen were *men*. To assert their authority, Congress passed in 1867 the Tenure of Office Act over the President's veto. The act prohibited the President dismissing from office without the consent of the Senate, any officer appointed by and with the consent of Senate; also an amendment to the Army Appropriations Bill subordinating the President to the Senate and the Chief of Staff of the Army in military matters. This wholesome move to restrict the monarchic power of the President was defiantly violated by President Johnson by his removing from office, Secretary of War, Edwin M. Stanton and replacing him *ad interim* first with Grant and then with Lorenzo Thomas.

Congress promptly brought impeachment proceedings against President Johnson, in February 1868. The charge finally voted on, rings familiar to us these days, viz: "eleventh, that Johnson had publicly stated that the 39th Congress was not an authorized Congress and *that its legislation was not binding upon him.*" Unfortunately the vote was 35 to 19, lacking but one of the two-thirds majority required for impeachment.

Johnson's victory considerably enhanced the monarchic power of the President. It prepared the way for the abuses of executive power that signalized the regime of later members of the Dynasty. The deliberate effort of Franklin Delano Roosevelt and the New Deal to eliminate the Constitutional check on the monarchic power of the President by Congress through the device of discrediting it with the nation by a constant stream of vicious propaganda and through various devices robbing it of its power and initiative and converting it into an impotent and pathetic rubber-stamp, culminate this fight for expansion of presidential powers initiated by Johnson.

There should be noted at this point, the odd "coincidence" that of the three Presidents of the United States who have been assassinated, two have been succeded in office by members of the Roosevelt-Delano Dynasty—Andrew Johnson and Theodore Roosevelt.

GENERAL ULYSSES S. GRANT

General Ulysses S. Grant was the closest relative of Franklin Delano Roosevelt among the Presidents of the United States. He was one degree closer than Theodore Roosevelt, who was a fifth cousin. Grant's great grandmother was Susana Delano, and Franklin D. Roosevelt's great great grandfather was her brother Thomas Delano.

Hiram S. Grant received an appointment to West Point under the name Ulysses S. Grant. In 1845, two years after his graduation, his regiment joined the forces of General Taylor in Mexico, where he fought in a number of engagements in the war. He emerged from the war, a captain. After marriage to Julia T. Dent, in 1848, he was stationed in California and Oregon.

In 1854, he resigned his commission amid charges of excessive drinking. During the following six years he lived in St. Louis making a poor living at farming and dealing in real-estate. In 1860 he became a clerk in the leather store of his father at Galena, Illinois.

Grant volunteered at the outbreak of the Civil War and was commissioned Colonel of the 21st Illinois Regiment by Governor Yates; and then was commissioned brigadier-general. Shortly thereafter he fell into disgrace, suffered serious military reverses, and was relieved of his command. Subsequently he was reinstated but sustained further reverses.

Despite Grant's mistakes and reverses, Lincoln and Stanton supported him. This political support served to keep him in his command. To outcries against Grant's drunkeness, Lincoln replied to the deputations that if they would find out what sort of liquor Grant drank, he would send some kegs of it to the other generals.

The fall of Vicksburg on July 4, 1863, marked the turning point in Grant's career. At Chattanooga he was placed in command of four armies that on November 25, 1863, administered a crushing blow to the Confederates. Grant then was made Commander-in-Chief of the Union forces with the rank of Lieutenant-General. In the months that followed, the war was characterized by a ruthless sacrifice of Union forces in a drive on Lee's army in Virginia. Six thousand men, for instance, fell in a useless assault lasting only one hour, at Cold Harbor; and in two months the Union Armies before Richmond and Petersburg lost seventy-two thousand men. These sacrifices were eventually rewarded with success.

To the people at large Grant appeared as a savior of the Union. His dispute with President Johnson over his appointment by Johnson in defiance of Congress as Secretary of War to succeed Stanton, contributed in some measure to his nomination as presidential candidate on the Republican ticket. He was elected against a weak Democratic candidate set up by the New York party machine, ex-Governor Seymour.

Grant during his presidency dropped to lower depths than ever Martin Van Buren had dreamed of, the level of crookedness, corruption and nepotism traditional in the Roosevelt-Delano dynasty. Cabinet positions were put on the auction block. For instance, Alexander T. Steward, drygoods merchant of New York City was repaid for many costly gifts which he presented to Mrs. Grant, by the post of Secretary of the Treasury.

Numerous members of Grant's immediate family were placed on the public payroll, including the following:

1. Frederick Dent, Grant's brother-in-law, aid to the Vice-President.

2. A second brother-in-law, (brother of Frederick Dent) United States Customs, San Francisco.

3. A third brother-in-law, Government Indian trader, New Mexico.

4. A second cousin, Receiver of Public Moneys, Oregon.

5. James F. Casey, Collector of Port, New Orleans and distributor of Federal patronage.

6. Peter Casey, Postmaster, Vicksburg, Mississippi.

7. Jesse Root Grant, Postmaster, Covington, Kentucky.

8. Michael J. Cramer, his brother-in-law, Minister to Denmark. Cramer who was a German, antagonized the Danes by telling them how inferior they were to the Germans.

9. Columbus Delano, Secretary of the Interior.

All types of shady and dishonest ventures were sponsored or aided by associates of Grant. The Fisk-Gould Gold Conspiracy manipulated the price of gold from 132 to 155 and then smashed it down to 135 and precipitated a financial panic known as Black Friday. Associated in this enterprise was Grant's brother-in-law A. R. Corbin. And Grant himself played an important part in directing the policy of the Treasury Department to make this manipulation possible.

Secretary of the Treasury, William A. Richardson, appointed a political henchman of Grant's, John D. Sanborn, special agent for collection of delinquent taxes. Sanborn received, as commission, half of the taxes collected. He soon expanded his activities to take a cut of half of all moneys pouring into the United States Treasury until a Congressional Committee stumbled onto this looting of the Treasury. The Committee urged dismissal of Secretary Richardson. Grant permitted him to resign. He was appointed immediately Justice of the Court of Claims.

Benjamin N. Bristow, who succeeded as Secretary of the Treasury uncovered evasion of Excise Tax on a huge scale by the Whisky Ring that involved bribery of Grant's principal secretary, General Orville E. Babcock. The money collected by Babcock had been used to finance Grant's campaign for reelection in 1872. Indicted with the rest of the conspirators, Babcock was acquitted as a result of voluntary intercession and character testimony by President Grant. Secretary Britow who had so courageously performed his duty in protecting the Treasury, was "cold shouldered" out of office by Grant.

Grant had the same contempt of the Constitution as characterized most of the Presidents of the Dynasty. He assumed the royal prerogative of making a treaty to annex San Domingo, disregarding the Senate's role prescribed in the Constitution in making treaties. The treaty was rejected by a Senate that had not yet degenerated to the rubber stamp state.

These and numerous other exposed cases of nepotism, bribery and corruption served to stamp Grant's two terms in office as the most shameful and dishonest in our history to that date. They have been surpassed, however, by the corruption of Franklin Delano Roosevelt's regime that was so closely patterned after Grant's in that respect.

True to the tradition of the Roosevelt-Delano Dynasty, Grant held in contempt the democratic precept laid down by George Washington who refused to serve a third term, in the interest of preserving democracy. In 1880 Grant's profligacy and incompetence left him in poor financial condition. He widely advertised among his friends that he would either have to obtain lucrative employment or get a third term as President. Whereupon he set out to secure the nomination of the Republican Party. Nomination was refused him and given to Garfield, who did not live to enjoy his office long. He was succeeded by Chester A. Arthur, leader in the fight at the Republican National Convention to reelect Grant for a third term.

Grant's financial needs were provided for by a two hundred and fifty thousand dollar fund raised by subscription by the New York Times, just as Franklin Delano Roosevelt's needs were taken care of by a subscription fund of eight hundred thousand dollars raised from the financial community to bribe him to run for office. Jay Gould repaid the service Grant and his family had rendered him in the Gold Conspiracy by contributing twenty-five thousand dollars to the fund. It was gratefuly accepted by Grant.

Not content with the provision thus made for him, Grant barged into Wall Street and engaged through the firm of Grant and Ward in a colossal swindle as stupid as Franklin Delano Roosevelt's financial flotations.

Senator Charles Sumner, in a speech before Senate, on May 31, 1872, aptly summed up the unprincipled incompetence of Grant. Several of his statements emphasize the pattern of conduct in public office that has come to be expected of the Roosevelt-Delano Dynasty such as:

1. Anyone who brought gifts to Grant's door was sure to receive favors.

2. Relatives, and friends of relatives, were appointed by Grant regardless of fitness with a favoritism described as "a dropsical nepotism swollen to elephantiasis".

3. Grant assumed monarchical prerogatives and flaunted the Constitution.

Another characteristic of the latter-day office holders of the Dynasty is exploitation of the presidency by
the sale of their literary effluvia. This stems from
their financial incompetence and inability to hold on
to money no matter how much they make. Grant sold
his memoirs to help support his family and to pay his
debt.

GENERAL BENJAMIN HARRISON

Benjamin Harrison was a grandson of William Henry Harrison whose genealogy already has been outlined. After graduation from Miami University, he
studied law and engaged in the practice of law in In-
dianapolis. At the outbreak of the Civil War he was
commisioned second-lieutenant by the Governor, raised a regiment and was promoted to the rank of colonel. He saw service with Buell and Sherman. After the
war was over, he was brevetted a brigadier-general.

Harrison was defeated in his candidacy for governorship in 1876. He was an ardent supporter of James
Garfield, who offered him a cabinet post. In 1881, he
became United States Senator but failed of reelection
in 1887. In 1888 he was nominated Republican Party
candidate for presidency, and defeated Cleveland. In
1893 he was renominated but was defeated by Cleveland.

COLONEL THEODORE ROOSEVELT

Theodore Roosevelt was a descendant of Nicholas
Roosevelt, son of Claas Martenszen van Rosenvelt (or
Rosenfeld, in the German form) and Heyltje Kunst,
early New Amsterdam settlers. He was a fifth cousin
of Franklin D. Roosevelt and through his side of the
family was more or less distantly related to the other
Presidents of the Dynasty. Eleanor Roosevelt, a niece
of Theodore Roosevelt married Franklin Delano
Roosevelt and tied in the relationship of the two
sides of the family more closely, as is so frequently
the case in the history of the Roosevelt-Delano Dynasty and other royal families. Through his first wife, he
was related to the Boston Cabots and the Lees.

In Theodore Roosevelt the Dynasty emerged from its
amateur status of crude politicians to the status of
professional demagogues and expert tricksters of public opinion and panderers to the mob. Educated at

Harvard, he came under the influence of the "liberalism" there in vogue that is richly tainted with Bismarck's subsidized propaganda of class warfare. He then began the study of law at Columbia University Law School but abandoned his studies for the avowed purpose of making professional politics his career. Thanks to the influence of the Dynasty, he was elected as regular Republican candidate to the New York State Legislature in 1881, for three successive terms; and in 1883 at the age of twenty-four, he was his party's candidate for Speaker of the Assembly. In 1883 he was a delegate to the Republican Convention in Chicago that nominated Blaine for president.

With an eye to acquiring Western background and support for his political career, he bought two cattle ranches in North Dakota where he spent two years. While he was absent in the West, the Dynasty made him Republican candidate for Mayor of New York City. He was nominated by Chauncey Depew, attorney for the Vanderbilt-New York Central interests, and Elihu Root, the Ryan-Morgan-Boss Tweed attorney. Thomas C. Platt, New York's Republican boss was ordered to support him. He received fewer votes than Henry George, the candidate of the United Labor Party.

In 1889, his distant cousin, President Benjamin Harrison appointed Theodore Roosevelt to the United States Civil Service Commission. The civil service reforms instituted during the Cleveland Administration had proved popular; and Theodore Roosevelt was demagogue enough to know how to profit from anything that was popular.

One of the outstanding features of Roosevelt-Delano Dynasty in its development, is its appreciation and effective use of all channels of publicity. Theodore Roosevelt was the first of them to court the press with the consequence that he always enjoyed the complete support of a good press. He became the prototype of the Dynasty which is now unexcelled in its public relations and self-publicity.

In 1895, Roosevelt was appointed President of the Board of Police Commissioners of the City of New York and in 1897, he was appointed by President McKinley, Assistant Secretary of the Navy. The Navy Department post is a purposefully hereditary one in the Roosevelt-Delano Dynasty, as will be related in a later chapter, because of their interest in naval armor and naval armament.

When the Spanish American War broke out in 1898, Roosevelt resigned from the Navy Department. He raised a regiment of cavalry, known as the "Rough Riders" and in spite of lack of previous military training, such is the magic of the Dynasty, became its lieutenant-colonel. As might be expected as a result of influence and favorable press, Col. Theodore Roosevelt emerged as the great synthetic military hero of the Spanish American War. In 1898, the war hero was given the nomination by the Republican party of the governorship of New York State and was elected.

In 1900, Theodore Roosevelt was nominated vice-president to run with McKinley, by the Republican Convention at Philadelphia. This convention was dominated by Mark A. Hanna who represented the major industrial combines of the country and particularly the Rockefeller-Standard Oil interests. It was public knowledge that in both 1896 and 1900 the Rockefeller-Standard Oil interests contributed $250,000 to the Republican campaign fund. Theodore Roosevelt was nominated under these auspices.

McKinley did not live to enjoy his office long. It is a startling "coincidence" that of the three United States Presidents assassinated, two of them, Lincoln and McKinley were succeeded by members of the Roosevelt-Delano Dynasty, Andrew Johnson and Theodore Roosevelt, respectively; and the third, Garfield, was succeeded by Chester A. Arthur, a supporter and campaign manager of a third member of the Dynasty, Ulysses S. Grant, who obeyed its dictates.

Succeeding McKinley in office, Theodore Roosevelt immediately proceeded to pretend to betray the very groups who had given him the nomination and supported the election campaign. He assumed the melodramatic role of Presidential rabble-rouser and "trust buster". As such he was a complete fraud. He was always accusing others of nature-faking. But never has there been done a better job in nature-faking and humbugging the public than was done by his Wall Street sponsors, through their controlled press, in the build-up of Theodore Roosevelt.

Theodore Roosevelt was completely the tool of

J. P. Morgan and Company and their associates who had sponsored him politically. He submitted to Morgan's agents for censorship all his official statements. His first message to Congress was submitted for editing to Cassatt, Aldrich, Hanna, Root, and Knox, all affiliated with Morgan. His third annual message to Congress was submitted to James Stillman, President of the National City Bank, and passages referring to currency were changed at his suggestion. He followed the dictates of E. H. Harriman in most matters.

Teddy played to the gallery by advocating a new Department of Commerce and Labor and by pretending to attack Morgan. The attacks which he made upon the Morgan interests were designed to bamboozle the voters into believing that he was a champion of the little man. But they always served Morgan's advantage, as in the Northern Securities Company case. The Panama Canal venture which he sponsored was moteivated by a forty million dollar swindle of the American taxpayer serving the advantage of Philippe Bunau-Varilla and his associates including J. P. Morgan and Company, Kuhn, Loeb and Company, August Belmont, Levi P. Morton, William Nelson Cromwell and others, according to stories published in the New York World. The Panama Canal route was less desirable than the Nicaraguan which had been chosen previously but was adopted because it was controlled by the speculators.

With the same defiance of the Constitution that characterized the Dynasty before him, viz. Andrew Johnson and Ulysses S. Grant, Teddy Roosevelt deliberately conspired to circumvent Congress. Henry Pringle, Roosevelt's biographer, states that he secretly dispatched G. M. P. Murphy, Vice-President of Morgan's Guaranty Trust Company to look over the ground with an eye to staging the Panama revolution against Colombia to force the issue. At the behest of J. P. Morgan & Co., acting on behalf of foreign creditors, Roosevelt ordered the seizure of the Dominican customs. Congress was completely disregarded in this move to use U. S. armed forces to collect private debts. Unknown to the Senate, he also entered into a secret agreement, or quasi-treaty, with England and Japan regarding the Pacific Ocean that paved the way for U.S. entry into World War I on the side of England and Japan.

An insurance investigation was motivated by Harriman's fight with Ryan for a half interest in 502 shares of Equitable Life Insurance Society he had purchased from John H. Hyde. The ultimate results benefited J. P. Morgan and Company who acquired the stock in 1910 for $3,000,000. When the insurance companies were compelled to divest themselves of control of a group of banks and stock in the First National Bank and the National City Bank, they were turned over to J. P. Morgan and Company. George W. Perkins, a partner of Morgan's emerged as the villain in the insurance scandal. He became Teddy's most trusted adviser.

The degree of the Morgan influence over President Theodore Roosevelt is indicated by the extent to which he surrounded himself with Morgan henchmen. As vice-presidential candidate, while still Governor of New York State, at a dinner which he gave in the banker's honor in December 1900, Roosevelt had reassured Morgan personally regarding his sham "liberalism" thereby clearing the way for the formation of the U. S. Steel Corporation. Further assurance was given by the inclusion by Roosevelt in his Cabinet of numerous Morgan henchmen, including George von L. Meyer, first as Postmaster-General and then as Secretary of the Navy; Paul Morton, Secretary of the Navy; Herbert L. Satterlee, Morgan's son-in-law, Assistant Secretary of the Navy; Elihu Root, Secretary of State (who resigned from the Cabinet to defend Morgan in the Northern Securities Company case, to his complete satisfaction, and then returned to the Cabinet); Robert Bacon, Morgan partner, as Assistant Secretary of State; William Howard Taft, Secretary of War, and others. Notable is the frequency with which Roosevelt changed his Secretaries of the Navy in order to retain direct control of the Navy himself.

"Teddy" Roosevelt was as antagonistic to the Rockefellers as he was friendly and helpful to his political sponsors, the Morgan group. His "trust busting" activities were designed to court public favor and to trick folks into believing him to be a champion of the common man and an antagonist of great wealth, so as to cover his partisanship. The policy of trust "regulation" which Roosevelt later advocated originated with George W. Perkins, Morgan's partner and the President's intimate and adviser. "Regulation" is selective and is admirably designed to further special interests. TR's hatred of the Rockefellers was rooted in his belief, instilled by his advisers, that Rockefellers were his enemies. He attacked them viciously and vindictively. This did not deter him, however, from seeking contributions to his campaign funds from the Rockefeller group. Around nomination time Roosevelt extended a invitation through Congressman Silbey to Archbold, President of the Standard Oil Company, to luncheon at the White House. The Standard Oil Company contributed thereafter $100,000 to the 1904 campaign fund. At the time of the contribution Archbold was assured that Roosevelt was cognizant of the contribution. Roosevelt, played to the gallery as usual, and pretended to demand the return of the money. But when the same contribution was listed as coming from H. H. Rogers, a Standard Oil executive, Roosevelt was completely content with this transparent effort to deceive the public. His campaign managers then went back to the Standard Oil Company to ask for another $150,000, but were turned down. While he railed at "malefactors of great wealth", he sought them out as friends and supporters.

Roosevelt's campaign of "trust busting" was sham. He was playing to the gallery and courting the rising tide of "liberalism", as German propagandized Marxism was then labelled. The drive on big business was aimed to destroy the "bad trusts", the Rockefeller trusts, and regulate the "good trusts", the Morgan trusts. As is usual with the Roosevelts, the criterion of "good" or "bad" was entirely personal—those who opposed his plans were "bad". This was clearly expressed by Theodore Roosevelt to the Clapp Committee:

> "I never changed my attitude toward the Standard Oil in any shape or manner. It antagonized *me* before my election, when I was getting through my Bureau of Corporations bill, and I then promptly threw down my gauntlet to it . . . "

For Roosevelt the Standard Oil dissolution decree was a tiff for the edification of his public. For the nation, it meant the deliberate precipitation of the disastrous 1907 panic, which followed a fortnight after the decree.

The panic of 1907 was deliberately engineered by Dynastic and allied bankers, as was the panic of 1929. Roosevelt himself acknowledged that it was a conspiracy started, or at any rate aggravated, for the purpose of permitting U. S. Steel Corporation to combine with Tennessee Coal and Iron Corporation in violation of the Sherman Anti-Trust Act. The dissolution decree handed down by Judge Kenesaw Landis against the Standard Oil Company and the huge fine imposed, played an important part in undermining confidence and in infuriating the Rockefellers. The Rockefeller interests, who controlled Amalgamated Copper, of which Robert Bacon, a Roosevelt Cabinet member, was director, strategically struck at a weak point in the financial structure of the country. They raided the stock of their competitor, United Copper, a low cost producer that had consistently undersold them. It was controlled by their bitter enemy, F. Augustus Heinze. The smash in the price of the United Copper stock closed the Mercantile National Bank of which Heinze was President and also closed his bank in Butte.

The conspirators closed the Knickerbocker Trust Company. They also started a run on the Trust Company of America in order to secure control of a large block of Tennessee Coal and Iron Company stock held as collateral for a loan of less than a million dollars and force its exchange for U. S. Steel Corporation stock. This was the price demanded by J. P. Morgan for helping the Trust Company with United States Treasury money which President Roosevelt had turned over to J. P. Morgan and Company for this purpose. Further pressure on the market was continued that threatened the closing of the Wall Street brokerage house of Moore and Schley, to set the stage for Roosevelt to give with apparent justification, formal consent to the merger of Tennessee Coal and Iron Corporation with U. S. Steel Corporation.

Theodore Roosevelt drove hard to enhance the monarchic power of the President and establish a dictatorship. He heartily echoed in his speech and deeds the attitude of Louis XIV, "L'état, c'est moi". He was a good actor and a shrewd demagogue. He appealed to the unthinking mob. The members of the Gridiron Club who come in close contact with the Presidents and have excellent opportunity to judge them, shrewdly portrayed and caricatured Teddy Roosevelt at their 1907 dinner as a would-be "emperor".

At the end of the second term, Roosevelt picked his heir and dictated the nomination of another member of the Dynasty, a distant relative, William Howard Taft. Taft, however, was a Rockefeller puppet and refused to take orders from Roosevelt. Instead, he authorized prosecution of the United States Steel Corporation as a Trust, for its purchase of the Tennessee Coal and Iron Company. This enraged Roosevelt because his bosses of the Morgan clique controlled U. S. Steel, and he had given his consent to the deal.

Theodore Roosevelt was not a person who would forgive the disregard of his imperial order, and he attempted to bar Taft's renomination. He found that he could not dictate to the Republican Party and get the nomination for himself, for a third term. Following the policy of the Dynasty to give allegiance to no one but themselves, to pay heed to no tradition—as had his Dynastic predecessors, John Quincy Adams, Martin Van Buren and Ulysses S. Grant—he engineered the bolting of a section of the Republican Party, organized a third party, the Bull Moose Party, and made himself its presidential candidate for a third term. He was soundly trounced. But he engineered the defeat of Taft and the election of Wilson.

In the Wilson regime which followed, the control of the Navy Department that had come to be of paramount importance to the Dynasty, was placed in the hands of another of its members, Franklin Delano Roosevelt, Theodore's nephew by marriage as well as his fifth cousin. Teddy Roosevelt used all his prestige as President to further the career of Franklin as his political heir, because of affection for his niece.

Fortunately for the nation, Roosevelt's "trust busting" was merely "nature faking" and shallow demagoguery. It was his "line", his method of attracting attention to himself and his antics and distracting attention from what he was doing behind the scenes. Characteristically, he inveighed against "muckraking", as he labelled exposés made by others, but he himself, resorted to it to attract the radical and Marxist vote. He was shrewdly aware that from the standpoint of the uncritical mob "what one says counts for more than what one does, if one shouts often and loudly enough".

He anticipated Goebbels by decades. When Theodore Roosevelt entered the White House there were only 150 large combines or "trusts". When his term ended, despite all his pretexts at "trust busting" there were over 10,000 "trusts" in the land.

The idea that large business combines are bad is obviously absurd. The larger the industrial unit, the more effectively it can serve. The damage lies not in trusts but in the suppressive misuse to which they may be put. With chicanery Roosevelt pretended to fight trusts, while actually fostering their abuse. But in this respect Cousin Franklin Delano, his heir, has far outdone him.

WILLIAM HOWARD TAFT

William Howard Taft was the son of Alphonso Taft Secretary of War and later Attorney General in the Cabinet of his kin, President Grant, and Minister to Austria and then to Russia under President Arthur, the staunch Grant supporter. Descended from William and Margaret Cheney, Taft shares common ancestry with Presidents Ulysses S. Grant, William Henry Harrison, Benjamin Harrison, James Madison, Zachary Taylor and Franklin Delano Roosevelt. His relationship to the balance of the Dynasty was more tenuous. Taft's father-in-law, Judge John W. Herron was a law partner of President Rutherford B. Hayes.

Graduating from Yale and Cincinnatti Law School in 1880, Taft became successively law reporter, Assistant Prosecuting Attorney and Assistant City Solicitor, Cincinnatti and Judge, Cincinnatti Superior Court. By 1880, ten years after graduation he had become United States Solicitor General. That was an extraordinary performance even for a man of acknowledged legal talent. No doubt it reflects the magic of the Dynasty.

In 1892, Taft was appointed by his kin, Benjamin Harrison, United States Circuit Judge. In 1896 to 1900 he was simultaneously Dean of the Law School of the University of Cincinnati. In 1900, McKinley appointed him President of the United States Philippine Commission, and in the following year, Governor of the Philippines. Theodore Roosevelt appointed Cousin Taft, Secretary of War.

In 1908, Roosevelt picked Cousin Taft as his successor and gave him the Republican nomination. The story of his tiff with Roosevelt, his renomination and defeat by Wilson has been related.

Taft was a product of Rockefeller's Ohio political machine which Mark Hanna had built up for them. His favoring of the Rockefeller interests and antagonism to Morgan might have been anticipated by anyone acquainted with his earlier career.

In William Howard Taft's son, Robert Alphonso Taft, the Dynasty seeks to give the nation another of its unique presentations—hereditary transmission of the Presidency in spite of the obstacles presented by the forms of democracy.

CHAPTER II

ROYAL COUSINS — KING GEORGE VI

Eleanor Roosevelt has placed in the Hyde Park Memorial Library a genealogical table, drawn up by P. W. Montague-Smith, assistant-editor of Debrett, that traces Franklin Delano Roosevelt's common ancestry with England's royalty through Henry II, great grandson of William the Conqueror through the Delano side. This may be fact or may be the usual dribble of social climbers who seek to justify their aspirations by claiming descent by pure line from Adam through William the Conqueror.

But the collaterals of the Roosevelt-Delano Dynasty have frequently intermarried with the nobility of Europe, forming alliances that have had a serious import for our history. Through one of the alliances, Franklin Delano Roosevelt has become a closer relative of Queen Elizabeth and King George of England than of either Presidents Ulysses S. Grant or Theodore Roosevelt.

Multitudinous intermarriages tie in the Roosevelt-Delano Dynasty with the Astors. Franklin Delano Roosevelt's granduncle married Laura Astor, John Jacob Astor's granddaughter. Generations later, James Roosevelt Roosevelt, Franklin Delano Roosevelt's stepbrother married Helen Schermerhorn Astor, daughter of Mrs. William B. Astor and aunt of Vincent Astor. Thus Vincent Astor is a step-nephew of Franklin Delano Roosevelt as well as a cousin several degrees removed.

How Princess Elizabeth Is Linked To Roosevelt and George Washington

WILLIAM THE CONQUEROR

Henry I

Matilda

Henry II

John

Henry III

Edward I

Maud m. Henry the Lion, Duke of Saxony

Henry Count Palatine of the Rhine

Agnes m. Otto the Illustrious Duke of Bavaria

Edward II	Edmund Earl of Kent	Agnes m. Hellin Marquis de Franchimont, 1225
Edward III	Joan, the Fair Maid of Kent. m. 2ndly the Black Prince	Hellin Marquis de Franchimont
Edmund Duke of York	Thomas Holland, Earl of Kent	Jean m. Mahienne de Lannoy, and assumed that surname, settling in Flanders 1360
Richard Earl of Cambridge	Eleanor m. Edward Cherlton Lord Powys	Hugues de Lannoy d, 1349
Richard Duke of York.	Joyce m. Sir John Tiptoft	Guillebert de Lannoy
Edward IV	Joyce m. Sir Edmund Sutton, son of 1st Lord Dudley	Baudouin le Begue de Lannoy, Gov. of Lille, d. 1474
Elizabeth m. Henry VII	Sir John Sutton of Aston-le-Walls, near Rugby	Baudouin de Lannoy, Gov. of Zutphen, d. 1471
Margaret m. James IV King of Scotland	Margaret m. John Butler	Philippe de Lannoy, Councilor and Chamberlain to Emperor Charles V
James V	William Butler	Jean de Lannoy, Gov. and Capt. Gen. of Hainault, 1559
Mary Queen of Scots	Margaret m. Lawrence Washington of Sulgrave Manor	Gysbert de Lannoy, a Huguenot, for which he was disinherited
James I King of England and VI of Scotland	Rev. Lawrence Washington	Jean de Lannoy of Leiden, d. 1604
Elizabeth	Col. John Washington sailed to America 1659	Philippe de Lannoy (La Noye), landed at Plymouth, Mass., on the Fortune from Leiden November 11, 1621
Sophia	Capt. Lawrence Washington	Jonathan de Lano
George I	Capt. Augustine Washington	Thomas de Lano
George II	GEORGE WASHINGTON 1st President of U. S. A.	Capt. Ephraim Delano of Dartmouth. Mass.
Frederick Louis Prince of Wales		Capt. Warren Delano
George III		Warren Delano
Edward		Sara m. James Roosevelt
Duke of Kent		FRANKLIN DELANO ROOSEVELT
Queen Victoria		
Edward VII		
George V		
George VI		
PRINCESS ELIZABETH		

Through the Astors, the Biddles, the Drexels and the Pauls, Roosevelt is related to Viscount William Astor of Cliveden and others of the British nobility. The relationship appears to be closest through the Astors. Second cousin Viscount Astor's niece, Rachel Spencer-Clay married David Bowes-Lyon, brother of England's Queen Elizabeth.

This illustrates the mode of dilution of royal blue blood. Another illustration is the marriage of Princess Elizabeth to Phillip Mountbatten, son of the former King George of Greece, whose family name of Battenberg was conferred by his great grandfather Alexander, son of the Duke of Hesse on his morganatic wife. He is related on the distaff side, through the Cassels, to Meyer Rothschild, the founder of the Jewish banking firm. It is reputedly the Battenberg strain in the Spanish royal family that is responsible for the hemophilia that curses it.

Thus it was that when King George and Queen Elizabeth on their visit to the United States to enlist its support in the war, visited Hyde Park and addressed Franklin Delano Roosevelt as "cousin", they were indeed dealing with a third cousin. This royal parley did much to bolster the aspirations of America's Royal Family. It also settled our entry into the war and the sacrifice of our men and wealth to bolster the moribund British Empire.

CHAPTER III

SIGNIFICANCE OF DYNASTY'S FAMILY TREE

Among the significant facts concerning the Roosevelt-Delano Dynasty are the following:

1. Over one-third of our thirty-three presidents have been derived from a single interrelated group of families

2. Their presidents have held office sixty-six of the one hundred and fifty-nine years of our national existence, despite the death of two of them within a short time after inauguration.

3. Thirteen of them have served fully, or in part, a total of eighteen terms as president, and additional terms as vice-president.

4. Of a total of forty presidential terms in our history, eighteen have been served by them.

5. The only two instances of hereditary transmission of presidency from father to son, John Adams and John Quincy Adams, or from grandfather to grandson, General William H. Harrison and General Benjamin Harrison, in our history has been in this Dynasty. In the person of Robert Alphonso Taft, an effort is now in process to reaffirm that tradition.

6. On a number of occasions the nation has been confronted with two candidates derived from the Dynasty, as in 1848, Martin Van Buren and Charles Francis Adams, were presidential and vice-presidential candidates on the Free Soil ticket; 1944 when Franklin Delano Roosevelt and Thomas Dewey, both of the Dynasty were Democratic and Republican candidates respectively; and 1948 when three of the Republican candidates Robert A. Taft, Thomas Dewey and General Douglas MacArthur are all derived from the Dynasty. In 1836 Martin Van Buren, Democratic Presidential candidate defeated General William Henry Harrison Whig candidate—both of the Dynasty. In 1840, in return contest, Harrison was victor.

7. The number of policy making offices in local and national government that have been filled by the members of the Dynasty are innumerable and utterly out of proportion to their number.

Apologists for the Dynasty and surprisingly enough even those possessed of intelligence, have a stock explanation for these extraordinary phenomena.

"A family that has been in this country for so
long a time is certain to be related to every other
family in the land", they explain.

It is absurd to represent that within ten to fifteen generations the half dozen families which have constituted the backbone of the Dynasty could have intermarried with the forty some million families that can not trace their relationship even remotely to any of our presidents. This apology is as false as it is insincere.

It fails to explain the fact that there is no relationship traceable between the other twenty-one Presidents. It is also very striking that there is no relationship traceable between any of those twenty one Presidents amongst themselves despite the fact that their ancestors were in this country as long, and some longer, than the Dynasty's.

To refute the apologists there is the phenomenon of intense inbreeding and intermarriage between the families comprising the Dynasty, with the occasional introduction of the scion of some commercial dynasty such as the Astors, the DuPonts and others. This follows the pattern of the royal families of Europe. It results in multiple relationships that reinforce those of direct line of ancestry. Thus Frederick B. Adams, a sixth cousin of Franklin Delano Roosevelt married Ellen W. Delano, a first cousin; James Roosevelt Roosevelt, Franklin Delano Roosevelt's half-brother, married Helen Schermerhorn Astor making a more distant cousin an in-law; and among the Delanos, it is their boast that most marriages are between cousins.

Quite as striking is the deliberate and steady enhancement by the Presidents of the Dynasty of the monarchic powers of the President with the simultaneous wiping out of the checks on that power imposed by the Constitution. This indicates a deliberately designed drive to make themselves the Royal Family of an American monarchy. The published blue-print of this drive is the theme of a later chapter.

Striking proof of the fact that the relationship that exists within the Dynasty is of a different intensity and degree than is found in the ordinary run of families, can be discerned in the publications of the Roosevelts—Eleanor Roosevelt's column "My Day" and her other effluvia and "F. D. R. His Personal Letters". These make it evident that the relationships within the Dynasty are of far different order than occur in the ordinary run of families. One finds intimacy and social contact assiduously maintained among cousins five degrees removed. Eleanor Roosevelt, though a cousin five times removed of Sara Delano Roosevelt's husband, was taken in by her; and when the need arose, married her off to Franklin. This is much the same state of affairs as exists in Europe's royalty and nobility.

A significant development for the Dynasty is its intermarriage with European royalty and nobility especially British. Their intermarriage with the British royalty make King George VI a closer relative of Franklin Delano Roosevelt than was even President Ulysses S. Grant.

Most convincing of all, however, are the appointments dictated by nepotism and the "deals" that cry of favoritism and violations of the nation's interests such as the Adams sugar deal and the Clayton cotton control deal. A few of these will be outlined later.

The clearest demonstration of the purposefulness of the transmission of office within the Dynasty is the case of the secretaryships in the Navy Department which will be detailed.

In conclusion it should be noted that there is a unanimity of opinion among the Democratic and Republican representatives of the Dynasty that "Democracy is a failure". Thus Roosevelt and his New Dealers insist upon the inadequacy of Democracy. They insist upon the improvement that could be effected by the totalitarian devices they adopted. On the other hand, Mrs. George St. George, a first cousin of F. D. R., elected to Congress on the Republican "anti-Roosevelt" ticket from Hamilton Fish's Tuxedo Park district and with his support, has been reported to have pronounced with no qualification, the same New Deal concept, "Democracy is a failure". She has issued no denial of this report. They all subscribe to the views of Hoffman Nickerson on the need for an American monarchy.

The best commentary on the peculiar quality of the relationship that exists within the Dynasty to the nth generation which is characteristic of royalty, is a statement by Eleanor Roosevelt quoted by Westbrook Pegler:

"Although we are a lucky and somewhat robustious family given to contrariness and quarreling, nevertheless, in the great crisis of life, we close up like a fist in a common defense."

Undeniably they constitute a coherent and collusive, open and "behind the scene" government.

CHAPTER IV

MARXISM—COMMUNISM, NAZISM
NEW DEALISM

MADE IN GERMANY

Two outstanding developments over-shadowed the events of the first half of the twentieth century. The first was the dissemination of Marxism. The second was the phenomenal rise of the Rockefeller Empire, the greatest the world has even known. The two developments became closely connected and interwoven.

The point of origin of Marxism was Germany. Karl Marx was the son of Heinrich Marx whose correct name before it was "Aryanized" was Hirschel Levy, the son of Rabbi Marx Levy of Trier. His mother was a Polish Jewess derived from a family of rabbis, including Rabbis Meir Katzenellenbogen of Padua, Joseph Ben Gerson ha-Cohen and Joshua Heschel Lvov. His elder brother, Karl's uncle was also a rabbi.

In order to retain his post as counsellor in the Trier court, when the Rhineland was taken over by Germany, Heinrich Marx (né Hirschel Levy) was baptized in 1817, one year before Karl was born. He retained his court job and advanced to the position of Justizrat and a leader of the Moderate Constitutional party in Trier. Karl's Hungarian Jewish mother, Henriette did not become baptized until after the death of her parents in 1825. Karl and his brothers and sisters were baptized in the National Evangelical Church (Protestant) on August 24, 1824, when Karl was a little over six years old.

Karl Marx suffered from an acute inferiority complex regarding his Jewish origin. He never could bring himself to realize that those about him regarded him with questioning, if not contempt, because he pretended to be something he was not. He held the Jews responsible for his state. His paranoia and inferiority complex were compensated by an intense hatred of the Jews. This found expression in the first works he wrote for publication. In the Deutsch-Franzosische Jahrbuch of 1844 he wrote in a review entitle "Zur Judenfrage" ("On the Jewish Question") the following:

"What is the basis of Judaism? Selfishness and greed.

"What is their faith? Swindling.

"Who is their God? Money.

"There can be no solution of the problems of the world without the destruction of the Jews and their religion, (Judenthum)."

In 1875 he wrote

"The Hebrew faith is repellent to me".

Thus Karl Marx, a neo-Lutheran, became one of the fathers of Nazism, acknowledged by Hitler and his crew.

At college, as a phase of compensation for his paranoid inferiority complex, Marx paraded as a Christian and undertook an intensive study of Canonical or Church Law. Thus he wrote to his father from Berlin on November 10, 1837:

"I confined myself to positive studies . . . some of Gauterbach's books . . . especially on ecclesiastical law."

In the Canonical Law he found sections which interpret profits in commercial transactions as usury and a cardinal sin. That meant that the Church law demanded "production for use and not for profit".

This left open only three legitimate vocations: one was to join the Church orders; the second was to labor; and the third was to assume the role of the baron who preyed on the laborers on the pretense of protecting them, as do the modern Labor Barons and their gangster henchmen, and to live by physical force or violence. This was Medievalism. The church later abandoned this doctrine except within its own orders, because it was found unsound and dangerous. It was largely responsible for the breakdown of civilization, law and order in the Middle Ages, and for the enslavement of mankind. It threw Europe into a reign of terror that lasted more than a thousand years.

But Karl Marx was not merely anti-Jewish, he was anti-religious and especially anti-Catholic. He wrote that he classed Christianity as a Jewish religion. In this respect his ideas coincided with those of Bismarck, whose anti-Catholic activities have been recalled by the Pope recently as the origin of Nazi activities in Poland. Marx attacked religion as an opiate for the masses. But he stole the doctrine, "to produce for profit is a cardinal sin", which the Church abandoned because it was proved false, and made it the basis of his new religion, Marxism or Communazism.

Marx's hatred, like that of his followers, the Nazis, extended to all non-Germanic peoples, even those that supported his movement. He disparaged the Negro and held the Russian revolutionaries in contempt.

Labor, Marx hated whole-heartedly, and he despised the individual worker. When he married he sought out a noblewoman, Jennie von Westphalen. When one of his daughters wished to marry a worker, he forbade it and ordered her to marry a bourgeois capitalist.

Karl came from an affluent bourgeois family and never did a day of labor in his life. The loss of the fortune which his father left him, as a result of his incompetence, bred him a paranoiac hatred of all who possessed property, the "Capitalists", because he regarded them as responsible for the loss of his fortune. This aligned him as a bitter supporter of the "have nots", not because he loved Labor but because he hated "the Capitalist" more.

His neurotic, paranoid character and overwhelming sense of inferiority gave rise in Marx to a compensatory illusion of superiority that insisted upon autocratic and absolute dominion and to violent suspicions that were the origin of the "purge" complex, that characterizes all his followers. Karl's sisters related that even as a boy, he was a fearful tyrant. He drove girls downhill at full gallop and compelled them to eat the cakes he made with his dirty hands out of filthy dough. His schoolmates feared him because of the satirical verses and lampoons he hurled at his enemies.

Utterly lacking in originality or capacity for lucid thinking, Marx showed faith in his concept of distribution of wealth only by plagiarizing the fallacious ideas of others. Foremost among the fallacies which he borrowed was the so-called "Law of Supply and Demand". In its converse form—"it is primarily scarcity that gives value"—he undertook to justify ethically its application to human beings and their labor. That became the basic idea underlying labor unionism.

But unionism is only a half way measure in carrying out the idea of maintaining a scarcity of human beings and their labor. The full and boldly carried program for creating a shortage of human beings is concentration camps and wholesale murder. Hitler alone carried out Karl Marx's precepts completely and to their logical conclusion. In this as in applying his anti-Semitism, Hitler was Marx's most faithful disciple. In faithfully following Hitler's footsteps, Stalin and his Communist cohorts are carrying out Marx's precepts.

Quite as fallacious was Marx's reasoning in justifying his German patriotism. As a defense against the Prussian attitude that Jews were aliens, Karl Marx developed an intense German Nationalism. Among the first words that he wrote were

"The emancipation of the German is the emancipation of Man".

His sham pacifism and internationalism vanished with the outbreak of the Franco-Prussian War, and was replaced by a martial enthusiasm and anxiety for a German victory. Expert at self-deception by dialectics, he justified his attitude in a letter to Engels as follows:

"The German working class is superior to the French from the viewpoint of organization and theory."

In a victory of Germany he pretended to discern a victory of the German working class, and most important, of his theories. Dialectics alone can match these views; or his advocacy of class hatreds and warfare, which in final analysis is the worst form of civil war, with his pretended internationalism and quest for common welfare.

But even more obvious is Marx's deception in offering his Communist program as an *improvement* on human freedom. For Communism necessarily means total loss of freedom, virtual or actual slavery. Under Communism, the government and the people who control it, own everything and everyone. They dictate all conditions of life, including wage and employment. Without freedom to earn a living, all other freedoms are meaningless. Only a dialectician trained to reason away the obvious and the truth can fail to realize that state ownership of the machinery of production also implies irresponsible ownership and neglect. For what belongs to everyone belongs to no one; and it is neglected by everyone, for a reason that is axiomatic and is clearly demonstrated by a psychological experiment on rats.

Three rats were placed in a cage that was provided with three levers which released food to them from an overhead trap. The rats rapidly learned to press on the levers and catch the food. More complex conditions were then introduced into this rat society. The levers were placed on the opposite side of the cage distant from the traps that released the food. Only one of the rats had sufficient intelligence to associate pressure on the lever with the distant release of food, and initiative and energy to do it. But this was of little avail to him. For the stupid and slothful rats learned to grab the food released by their ambitious colleague. Though he worked unremittingly he seldom managed to get the food which he released and died of starvation. Later the others died.

— 46 —

Most humans are like the stupid, slothful rats. For that reason Socialism, Communism and state ownership of machinery of production are doomed to failure. Eventually they degenerate into a dictatorship of the most forceful and most ruthless member of the community; for in final analysis the rule of the abstraction, the State, is the rule of the individual. The more absolute the power of the State, the more autocratic is the rule of that individual. Thus the Communist or Socialist State is inevitably a dictatorship. By its virtue, the dictator is owner of everything and everybody he surveys—he is a perfect feudal lord. Such over-centralization of power naturally implies the end of efficiency and initiative and the disruption or destruction of industry, commerce and social organization. For the rank and file it implies wretched slavery.

Within less than a century after mankind had attained its first legal formulation of the concepts of freedom, in the Constitution of the United States, Karl Marx undertook to lead them back to enslavement as vassals of fascistic Labor Barons and Communazi leaders. It is the very purpose of Marxism and Communism to destroy human freedom and make men the tools of an absolute dictatorship.

CHAPTER V

BISMARCK AND GERMANY PROPAGANDIZE MARXISM, COMMUNAZISM, NEW DEALISM

In the dissemination of Marx's doctrines several anomalous forces played highy important roles. Thus the New York Tribune, under Horace Greeley, employed Karl Marx as correspondent. For ten years it published articles by him that gave him a world-wide audience which he never would have reached to propagandize; and afforded him his only source of income, a pound a week. The really decisive initial force in the spread of Marxism however, was Bismarck and later, Germany.

Prince Otto von Bismarck, Teutonic Knight who was bound by the Order's thousand-year-old oath to conquer the world, originated the "welfare" and "social service" program that now parades as the New Deal.

Subsequently, he became the foster-father of Marxism and Communism. His objective in doing these things was world conquest, "Deutschland uber Alles". No one who knew the Iron Chancellor could be deceived for one moment into the belief that he had the remotest interest in the welfare of the weak or downtrodden. His mottos were "Blood and Steel" and "Might Makes Right".

The program was a recrudescence of one which was old when it was introduced by the Gracchi in ancient Rome and eventually destroyed the Empire. It was given to Bismarck largely by Professor Adolph Wagner who was reputedly an ancestor of our Senator Robert F. Wagner. It served Bismarck's quest for personal power in several manners. First, it robbed the Socialists of the planks of their platform which made the greatest appeal to the mob—Social Security, Unemployment Insurance, Workmen's Compensation, Health Insurance, and all of the other quasi-benevolent and paternalistic clap-trap.

Bismarck shrewdly saw in these plans, devices fashioned to destroy liberty and to chain the working class to his program and to any jobs to which they might be assigned. He saw in the program a snare which would deceive them into accepting submarginal wages and the surrender of adequate present existence in return for a mirage of future security. As a means of winning the favor of the workers and of gaining some measure of power over industry and entrée to its records, a part of the cost was levied on the employers. This made of what conceivably might have been a boon to the worker, a penalty on industry for offering employment; and meant a tax on industry which materially increased the cost of production. Both factors ultimately operate to increase unemployment.

Bismarck also foresaw that with the working class tied to him by this program, he could force into line the German industrialist, the nobility, and finally the reluctant Prussian king, to support his plan of a united German Empire. Junker Bismarck, who had contemptuously spurned any traffic with the working classes, whom he called a "revolutionary rabble", had grown tired of being buffeted about and shelved by his liege lord, the weakling King of Prussia. Adversity had served to make of him a diplomat who could advance from one compromise to another, from one treachery to another, to attain by a series of adroit maneuvers his ultimate goal—the consolidation of his own power by forcing his king to accept the position of Emperor of Germany. How well he planned, history reveals. With the Danish invasion, the elimination of Austrian interference in 1866, and the consolidation of his position by a treacherously conceived conquest of France in 1870, the German Empire became not only a reality, but also simultaneously a "first class Power".

But for Bismarck, this was merely a begining. With far greater vision, he planned the political and commercial conquest of the world—"Deutschland uber Alles". He placed on Germany the stamp of a national paranoia which still drives it with mad singleness of purpose and signal "success". The World Wars are mere interludes.

The conquest of world markets by German industry and commerce was planned by Bismarck. In such a struggle the burden of taxation and cost involved in the "welfare" program might have proved a severe handicap. Obviously it was necessary to overcome it by forcing the adoption of the same program and handicap on competitor nations. Resort was had for this purpose to subjugation by ideas, propaganda and "boring from within".

There was launched one of the most persistent, persevering and skilled propaganda campaigns in the world's history for the imposition of Bismarck's "New Deal" on the entire world. Now almost a century later it still continues to sway history and the world.

In this "New Deal" propaganda Bismarck found many allies. The pretended humanitarianism of the program won over many unthinking, kindly persons as well as most religious sects. These groups are the best camouflage and front for any propaganda. Throughout the world these deluded groups still ardently advance Bismarck's destructive propaganda.

Allies of unusual value were the labor movement, Karl Marx and his Socialism, and the Communist Internationale. Initially Bismarck had regarded them as the arch-enemies of his plan. He had called upon Lasalle for advice in his fight on them. On his counsel he plucked the "New Deal" from the program which they agitated, with the objective of deflating them.

But Bismarck soon came to recognize that Karl Marx

and his Revolutionary Socialism or Communism were shams. He saw that they offered no real menace among Germany's dull, plodding, intense, unimaginative, docile and disciplined workers. He discovered that Karl Marx was an intense German Nationalist who gloried in the vaunted "superiority" of the German worker and who sensed that his program offered no threat to his Vaterland. Marxian Socialism was therefore the ideal propaganda weapon with which to demoralize other lands.

The International Association for Labor Legislation was subsidized by Germany as a device to spread the Bismarxian "social welfare and labor" program. The Communist Internationale and the international and domestic labor unions were natural allies, made to order for Bismarck's purpose.

Labor unionism has played an all-important role in the Bismarxian and Communazi propagandas from the very beginning. It serves the purposes of Bismarck as a most efficient agency for paralysis of industry and commerce, and for fomenting misery and unrest.

Bismarck came to regard Karl Marx as an important ally in his Pan-Germanic propaganda. He appreciated that Communism planted in other lands would disrupt and demoralize them and would hasten the conquest of "Deutschland uber Alles". Bismarck eventually invited Marx to return from exile and offered him the editorship of his own paper, the "Acht-Uhr Abendblatt." Marx rejected the offer stating that he could serve the cause better in England. Marxist propaganda tracts printed in many languages became one of Germany's principal exports.

Germany's entire education system, as well as her diplomatic corps, was made part and parcel of the Bismarxian propaganda set-up. Subsidized learning and scientific achievement were widely advertised and publicized and lent color to claims of German intellectual superiority. Trading on this reputation, Germany was able to palm off on the world pseudo-sciences, such as sociology, social service and modern economics, which are nothing more than very thinly disguised, false propaganda.

A system of recognition, adulation and decoration of foreign educators and scientists fostered their teaching doctrines that served the purposes of the Bismarxian propaganda. Germany thus made the education system of other lands a part and parcel of her propaganda machine. The Communist propaganda machine, which has recently been exposed as dominating our entire school and university system, is but a subsidiary of the machine which Bismarck built.

Harvard University was among the first in the U. S. to succumb to this subversive propaganda. It freely exchanged professors with the German universities. The German professors sent were official government propagandists. The American professors vied for the honor of recognition of the German universities. These honors they could gain only by serving the interests of the German Government by furthering its propaganda. Thus the American universities became foci of subversive propaganda. This intensified the Illuminist-Communist "educational" strain in America.

How Bismarck's "welfare" program served the purpose of destroying both the Socialist working class whom he abhorred and the smug industrialists whom he detested, is portrayed in the petition of the Federated Industries of Germany to their Government in 1929, in which they pleaded that the so-called "welfare" program of Bismark's, fallen into Socialist hands threatened the existence of the nation and its industries. The report read as follows:

" . . . Appropriations for public undertakings . . . and increased outlays for welfare institutions offer less resistance than does an attempt to improve the standard of living through the natural process of economic development . . . The intervention of the state should be restricted and should extend only to such branches as cannot be served by private enterprise . . . The way of socialization leads to destruction of economy and pauperization of the masses, and German industry recognizes in it a danger not only to private enterprise and the workingman, but also to the nation at large . . . "

The German Republic disregarded this warning of crisis and of the dire consequences that would inevitably follow. The results of the Marxian fallacies we all know.

Bismarck and Marx were the guiding spirits of Nazi Germany. They had foreseen the docility of the German worker and the absolutism it made possible

Nazism or some other form of dictatorship and slavery were the inevitable consequences of Marxism and of the "welfare" program of the "New Deal" launched by Bismarck. Its development was guided by Hitler's "Brain Trust", Professor Haushofer and his Geophysical Institute. The class hatred of Marx was converted into another equally absurd hatred—the Aryan. Marxist "internationalism" translated itself into Aryan "internationalism". The war on Capitalism logically assumed the form of raping of other lands. For Marx's definition of "capital" in final analysis is "the other fellow's property". Restriction of the supply of labor is most effectively obtained by slaughtering workers. The philosophy of Marxism and of Nazism is obviously identical. Nazism is the active tense of Marxism. And it is but natural that Communism should take over where Nazism left off.

The first of the formidable competitors of Germany that succumbed to the propagandized Bismarxian program was England. The Fabian Society was the chief agency of the propagandists. A few years before the World War I, Great Britain was forced by the agitation among her working classes to swallow the whole bait —hook, line and sinker. German industrialists openly urged upon Parliament the adoption of the program. Thereby were set in operation forces which are now speeding the disintegration of the British Empire. Premier Ramsay MacDonald in an address before Parliament in 1929 frankly blamed the welfare, dole and health insurance laws for the insoluble economic problem presented in England by the unemployment situation.

From the point of view of American affairs, even greater significance was lent to the situation when the wholly alien ideas were given an aura of respectability in the eyes of American Tories by their adoption in England. This was accentuated by the fact that British industry was now in the same position with respect to the cost of the "welfare" program in its competition for world markets. It became of interest also to British industry that the United States should adopt an identical handicapping program.

It was not long before Sir Arthur Newsholme, representing the British Ministry of Health, began to visit this country to lecture systematically on the advantages of the "Security" and "Socialized Medicine" plans. He joined forces with the local agitators for the adoption of the program, in spite of the fact that it has resulted in England in a steadily rising death rate that culminated in 1938 in one of the highest death rates in the civilized world.

Russia was the next to succumb. In the stalemate of World War I, in 1917, Germany averted the need of fighting on two fronts by planting German made Communism in Russia. Colonel Nikitine, head of Russian counter-espionage relates with fidelity in his book "The Fatal Years", how the German General Staff transported Russia's exiled band of German-trained Communist agitators in sealed trains from Switzerland through Germany into Russia. Rockefellers financed the Communists through their banker, Jacob Schiff, with millions of counterfeit ten ruble notes with which to buy the votes of the soldiers and sailors.

Russian Communism was "made in Germany". The unity of purpose of Bismarck-guided Germany and Communist Russia was fully confirmed by the Communazi alliance. It is still further proved by Russia carrying on the Communazi program from the point where Nazi Germany left off.

France was next to succumb. That the evolution of the program in Germany and England is not an isolated accident but is a natural consequence is revealed by the experience of every country that has adopted it. The experience of France is a clear-cut demonstration. Succumbing to the propaganda, France adopted the Bismarck program in 1932, after Minister Loucheur had assured the Chambre de Députés that its costs would merely be ten per cent of the national income. At that time there was practically no unemployment in France in spite of the depression which raged in the rest of the world. No sooner was it put in force than the cost of living in France rose forty percent. As a consequence the workers, whose existence has always been a marginal one, were forced to strike to avoid starvation. As usual, the "security" program precipitated economic collapse and insecurity, as its author had designed. This is well portrayed in Van der Meersch's "When Looms Are Silent".

The earliest published record of the launching of the Bismarxian propaganda in the United States is found in the report of the German subsidized International Association For Labor Legislation (reported in the American Labor Legislation Review. V. 4, p. 511, 1914) :

"Work toward the formation of an American Section was initiated in 1902, when the Board of the International Association began to make its objects known in the United States and to form connections with interested individuals."

The formation of the American Association for Labor Legislation in 1906 marked the beginning of the United States drive for the adoption of the Bismarxian program. Among the original founders of the Association were Richard T. Ely, the economist, Edward T. Devine and Mary K. Simkhovitch, social workers. R. O. Lovejoy noted in radical circles, Mary van Kleek, Director of the Industrial Division of the Russell Sage Foundation and left winger, and John B. Andrews, Director of the Association. These were later joined by John A. Kingsbury, Charles C. Burlingham, William Hodson, and Homer Folks, social workers, Ida M. Tarbell, biographer of the Standard Oil Company and the Rockefellers, Frances Perkins, later New Deal Secretary of Labor and Harry L. Hopkins, later New Deal ringleader, and Eleanor Roosevelt.

The initial support of the Association as might be expected, was German. Acquisition of control of the Russell Sage Foundation, several years later, through Mary Van Kleek and Leon Henderson, helped to provide amply for it. The same group reorganized Illuminist Socialism as the Communist Party in the United States almost a decade before Russia was saddled with Communism. This element was sufficiently influental to carry out successfully a drive on capitalism as exemplified in the most vilified and largest of the "ogre" trusts, the Standard Oil Company and Rockefeller that culminated in a court order for dissolution of the Standard Oil Company. That brought into play the most anomalous, but most important force that has fostered Communism in the U. S., the Rockefeller Empire. Thus Illuminist Communism, the college conspiracy, completed its cycle from Germany to the U.S.A., back to Germany and then to the U.S.A.

CHAPTER VI

THE ROCKEFELLER EMPIRE

COMMUNISM, WAR AND OTHER

"PHILANTHROPIES"

The Rockefeller Empire is an outgrowth of the Standard Oil Company. Rockefeller had built up with tremendous skill the powerful oil monopoly. By 1915, the Company produced almost one third of the oil yield of the United States. Complete monopoly of the oil business in the United States and throughout the world loomed as a conceivable goal and became the objective.

The dominant position in oil had been gained by gangsterism, that would make Al Capone blush. Special railroad rates and rebates extracted from railroads also played an important role in wiping out competition. In the process there had been used the unsavory methods, ranging from theft to slaughter, which were the custom of the time in business. Those methods did not differ materially from those of the respected Morgans, Vanderbilts, Goulds and a host of others of that time. Rockefeller's chief offense was his inordinate success and his taciturnity and independence.

Rivals who were less successful in the application of the identical methods used by the Standard Oil Company, organized the "liberals" and the "socially minded," the social service cliques of that era, together with the demagogues, politicians, and crooked newspapers, for another type of battle on their successful competitor—commercial blackmail.

As resentment against the Oil Trust grew, the Rockefeller Standard Oil interests were held up by the politicians through the device of "strike bills", and badgered by investigations and court actions. The muckrakers, church organizations and social service groups exposed the ugly situation and further fanned public resentment. President Theodore Roosevelt, who had

— 55 —

succeeded Rockefeller's hand-picked ally, President McKinley, played to the gallery by attacking the Standard Oil Company while indirectly he demanded increased Standard Oil contributions to his campaign funds.

The situation reached its climax in 1907 with the decree handed down by Judge Kenesaw Landis against the Standard Oil Company imposing a fine of twenty-nine million dollars. Two weeks later the panic of 1907 was precipitated. In 1911 the dissolution of the Standard Oil Company was ordered by the Supreme Court.

Rockefeller fiercely resented what he regarded as government interference in his private business. He regarded its conduct as his own affair. It could hardly be expected that he would not fight back. He responded as keenly and as incisively to the virulent and well organized slander and persecution as he had to the other problems that had confronted him in his business. Two modes of approach to such a problem were habitual; first was to compromise with a powerful enemy and to join forces with him; the second was to engineer in the meantime to master and destroy him.

The enemies who confronted Rockefeller and who were responsible for the situation were three—the Wall Street crowd whom he had bested, the welfare and "liberal" crowd and the government. His score with Wall Street he paid rapidly. Within two weeks after the handing down of the decree, there broke loose the 1907 panic.

The effectiveness with which the welfare and "liberal" crowd had been used in the campaign against him and his Company impressed Rockefeller. They could be made to fit into the pattern of "philanthropy". They were cheaply bought off; and he took them over lock, stock and barrel. Among these "welfare" agencies were the radical church element, the Federation of Churches.

The social service and "uplift" organizations and their allies were taken in hand and later organized through the New York Tuberculosis and Health Association, under the directorship of Harry L. Hopkins, into a nation-wide Social Service Trust. The control of social service and church organizations served a dual purpose. It muzzled the sanctimonious and self-righteous elements and covered all activities thus engaged in with a cloak of respectability. But what was even more important, they tapped the pocketbook of the gullible to the tune of four billion dollars a year in normal times. That money could be put to many important uses.

Not one cent, for instance, of the money collected by the New York Tuberculosis and Health Association from the sale of Xmas seals under the direction of Harry L. Hopkins ever went to a person with tuberculosis or an institution for his care. It was spent in building up the Social Service Trust, in political activities, in building up a press censorship and for the personal use of its bosses especially Hopkins. (Your Life Is Their Toy, Chedney Press 1940, pp. 22-24). Harry Hopkins became one of the principal Rockefeller almoners. Frances Perkins also ranked high.

The Rockefeller "philanthropies" were conceived for the dual purpose of taking the curse off the Rockefeller name and enabling the Rockefeller-Standard Oil interests to carry on without interference from a hostile public or the government. One could hardly expect a man of Rockefeller's efficiency and financial ability to fail to expect to profit handsomely from the disarming advantages of a "philanthropic" front. That Rockefeller realized the profitable business possibilities of a "philanthropic" set-up is indicated by an interesting and revelatory story told of the inception of the plan to buy over public opinion and confound his detractors. It was conceived by Rev. Frederick Taylor Gates who had won John's D.'s respect by his sharpness clothed with piety. Rockefeller had profited handsomely from deals engineered by Gates through religious activities as an executive officer of the American Baptist Education Society. Especially appreciated was his aid in gaining control for a pittance of the Mesabi Mines, one of the richest iron deposits in the country. It netted many millions of dollars when later incorporated into the U. S. Steel Corporation. In *"John D. A Portrait In Oil"* John K. Winkler quotes Rockefeller Sr. as follows:

" 'Fred Gates was a wonderful business man,' says John D. with satisfaction. 'His work for the American Baptist Education Society required him to travel extensively. Once, as he was going south, I asked him to look into an iron mill in which I had an interest. His report was a model of clarity!

" 'Then I asked him to make some investigation of other property in the west. I had been told this particular company was rolling in wealth. Mr. Gates' report showed that I had been deceived.

" 'Now I realize that I had met a commercial genius. I persuaded Mr. Gates to become a man of business.' "

Mayhap one can judge with reasonable correctness that if religion helped net Reverend Frederick T. Gates inordinately large profits in his dealings with his fellow men, the manipulation of millions certainly would not fail to do so. The "philanthropies" established by this "wonderful business man" could be expected to be highly profitable, directly or indirectly. They have been more profitable than investments of identical sums in even the Standard Oil Company.

The objective that lay at the back of Gate's and Rockefeller's minds at the inception of these "philanthropies" were clearly stated by Gates in the first publication of the General Education Board, the "Occasional Letter No. 1", as follows:

"In our dreams we have limitless resources and the people yield themselves with perfect docility to our molding hands. The present educational conventions fade from our minds, and unhampered by tradition, we work our own good will upon a grateful and responsive rural folk. We shall not try to make these people or any of their children into philosophers or men of learning, or of science. We have not to raise up from among them authors, editors, poets or men of letters. We shall not search for embryo great artists, painters, musicians, nor lawyers, doctors, preachers, politicians, statesmen of whom we have ample supply. The task we set before ourselves is very simple as well as a very beautiful one, to train these people as we find them to a perfectly ideal life just where they are. So we will organize our children into a little community and teach them to do in a perfect way the things their fathers and mothers are doing in an imperfect way, in the homes, in the shop and on the farm."

It is noteworthy that the ultimate object of the "*educational* philanthropy" is the opposite of its current "windowdressing" activities.

The degree in which their objective has been attained is illustrated by the unanimity of views between all political parties aired by Assistant Attorney General

Thurman Arnold which already has been mentioned. This unanimity is traceable to the influence of the Rockefeller interests on the educational institutions of the country and to the power which their interests exercise in the councils of all major political parties.

The objective was fundamentally propaganda of the type that is now regarded as essential for the establishment of a dictatorship or a totalitarian regime, such as was the goal envisioned by Bismarck a generation prior. In some respects the goal sought was tantamount to the restoration of the caste system that characterizes feudalism and medievalism.

The school of thought which this objective represents found its fullest expression in Hoffman Nickerson's masterpiece "The American Rich," which antipated Hitler's regime and advocated a similar form of government for the United States. He suggested the abolition of universal franchise, restriction of the vote to wealthy property owners, elimination of education because of the spirit of inquiry which it creates so that there may be restored the medieval mind and its submissiveness, and ends with a plea for establishment of a de facto monarchy in the U. S. A.

Gates shrewdly realized the advantages of poisoning and perverting public opinion at its fountainhead, the schools, colleges and universities. Gates took full advantage of the cloak of piety and the support offered by his position in the Baptist Church in accomplishing his purpose. He had Rockefeller endow the University of Chicago, as the first step in gaining control of education.

In 1901, Rockefeller established and endowed the Rockefeller Institute for Medical Research. The Rockefeller interest in medicine is explainable on a number of grounds. First is the realization that there is no more vital interest for mankind than health; and those who offer to promote health are naturally regarded as benefactors. Folks are generally willing to spend all they have to recover their health. This makes the business aspects of medicine very profitable. Rockefeller was well aware of this because his father "Doc" William Rockefeller had earned his livelihood as a quack doctor selling petroleum oil as a fake patent medicine "cure" for cancer. The Rockefeller interest in oil had in fact arisen out of their interest in patent medicine.

A few benefits have accrued to mankind from the activities of the Rockefeller endowed medical research organizations. These have been surprisingly few in comparison with the large sums expended. Most of them that have had any real value have been sanitation projects that bore some relation to commercial or industrial developments. It is notable that in era of vast strides in the chemistry of medicine, no basic discoveries and few significant ones have emanated from the Rockefeller group. Some outside investigators have been subsidized, however, after they made significant discoveries.

A large proportion of the discoveries announced, on the other hand, have proved unfounded. Among them are the following:

The discovery of the organism that causes infantile paralysis.

The discovery of the organism that cause smallpox.

The discovery of the organism causing mumps.

The discovery of the organism causing measles.

The discovery of a curative serum of pneumonia.

The discovery of a preventive vaccine and curative serum for yellow fever, and numerous others.

Tremendous medico-political pressure has been brought to bear to protect the reputations of these supposed discoverers and of the Institute.

The vast funds of the Rockefeller endowed Institutions have been utilized for the purpose of gaining control of educational institutions, hospitals and other medical and research facilities. It has created vested interests and rackets in medical research. Institutional and personal jealousies, intensified by tremendous power acquired by small cliques with the funds of the Foundation, have resulted in the suppression of needed researches by really capable, independent workers. It has barred many of them from the opportunity to engage in research. It has served to enable its employees to reestablish medieval dogmatism in medicine in order to protect their reputations and interests. Their efforts to protect their jobs have served to retard medical advance and to injure the interests of the public.

The Rockefeller Institute was founded for the avowed purpose of directing medical practise in channels desired for various reasons by Gates and Rockefeller. It was designed for the purpose of control of medicine. Gates was convinced that the medical tradition built up through the ages was unsound and must be replaced by an arrogant "Medical Science" which insists that what it does not know is untrue. This ignorant dogmatism coupled with research politics has resulted in the Institute retarding the advance of medical knowledge, prostituting it to commercial interests, and has cost many lives.

Discoveries such as the improvement of the method of preparation of tryparsamide have been patented by the Institute and licensed to manufacturers. Whether the anti-pneumococcus serum processes, many of which were developed in the Institute, are patented or licensed has not been made public. But at least one of the firms which exploits the serum has been identified in the public mind with the Rockefeller interests.

The Institute denies that it receives any royalties on its patents. It does not state whether it, or its sponsor, owns any stocks in the companies involved. It also refuses to make public its stock holdings. This refusal is surprising in view of the full and detailed publication made by the Foundation of all its holdings.

The Rockefellers have large interests in the chemical and pharmaceutical industries. They also have very large holdings in the German Dye Trust, I. G. Farbenindustrie, on the directorate of which the Standard Oil of New Jersey was represented by its president, the late Walter Teagle. The Chase National Bank, with which the Rockefellers are closely identified, has floated Dye Trust securities on the American market; and its attorneys, Milbank, Tweed, Hope and Webb, headed by A. G. Milbank, Chairman of the Board of the Borden Company and the Milbank Memorial Fund, have acted for these interests.

It is reasonable to suppose that an institution operated with the efficiency and in the spirit of the Rockefeller "philanthropies" would not be so unbusinesslike as to cast to the winds the large profits which have devolved from some of the Institute's products. Gates undoubtedly was a "business genius" of the rarest foresight and perspicacity.

There is at hand evidence that profits rather than charity or humanitarianism were the prime objectives of the Rockefeller medical "philanthropies." An instance of commercial advantage of "research" endowment leading to the disregard of human values is the million dollar endowed "research" on ethyl gas and the danger of lead-poisoning that it inflicts on the nation! The U. S. Public Health Service and the U. S. Government had barred the use of ethyl-lead gasoline after a series of poisonings and deaths of workers who made the mixture.

Then a munificently endowed research led the Government and the U. S. Public Health Service to withdraw its prohibition of this type of gasoline. As a result, the entire nation is now exposed to the danger of chronic lead poisoning by lead-filled, automobile-exhaust gases. In due time the mental and physical health of the people is certain to suffer.

Another instance is the tryparsamide patent licensed to Merck and Company by the Rockefeller Institute, Tryparsamide is a dangerous drug that not infrequently causes complete and permanent blindness. Nevertheless the anti-venereal disease campaign that has been conducted by the government under Rockefeller controlled Surgeon General of the United States Public Health Service, Dr. Thomas Parran, has compelled the use of this blinding remedy in the treatment of often benign and quiescent cases of syphilis. Many persons have been totally and completely blinded by the use of this Rockefeller Institute licensed patent drug.

Enormous profits are being made in drugs and chemicals that exceed even those made from oil. In more recent years oil and gas are being used to supply the raw materials for drugs. The Rockefeller interests are known to have extensive holdings in the drug industries. They control among others American Home Products, Sterling Products, Winthrop Chemical Company, American Cyanamide and its subsidiary Lederle Laboratories, and numerous other highly profitable enterprises in the drug field. It is probably safe to say that the Rockefeller profits from drugs and chemicals match their profits from oil.

The Rockefeller interests in the medical and allied industries has been reinforced by the control which they have acquired over medical education through the agency of the Institute and their other "philanthropies".

In the field of medical education, they met with early and easy success. They joined forces with the

American Medical Association and its rackets. Medical education is one of the more lucrative medical commercial rackets which the A. M. A. bosses sought to monopolize by destroying their competitors. Alone they could not manage to put the competing schools out of business. But with the aid of the Rockefeller power they forced through legislation in all parts of the country that drove their rivals out of business, after public opinion had been prepared by a specially designed report on medical education by Abraham Flexner.

More than half of the medical schools in the country were driven out of existence; and the Rockefeller interests gained control over medical education and over medical business that eventually enhanced materially the possibilities of profits inherent in the "philanthropies". By some odd quirk the quest for profits in medicine has led them to support the cause of "socialization" of medicine. They do not seem to have stopped to consider that the "socialization" of medicine will point the way to the "socialization" of industry and of "philanthropies" as well. They have saddled on the medical school Bismarxian or Communist propagandists and agitators, in the case of Johns Hopkins University Medical School in the guise of "professor of the history of medicine."

Professor Henry Sigerist, their protegé whom they have planted in that school has signed, with Earl Browder and Robert Minor, all the important manifestoes issued by the Communist Party, including that approving of the alliance of Russia with Hitler. He is a ranking agitator for "Socialized Medicine", a key Communist program.

The General Education Board which is by far the most important of the Rockefeller propaganda agencies was founded in 1903, by John D. Rockefeller Jr. and a group that included as collaborator, George Foster Peabody. This is the same George Foster Peabody who later turned over Georgia Warm Springs to Franklin Delano Roosevelt in the maneuvers that prepared the way for his serving the Rockefeller interests as President of the United States of America. Initiated as a Baptist Church endeavor to promote education among the Negroes, the General Education Board was granted a charter by Congress through a bill introduced by Rockefeller's agent in the Senate, Senator Nelson W. Aldrich. The charter was virtually unlimited in its scope in the field of any activity that might be construed as remotely resembling education.

The General Education Board was the chief agency employed in the drive for the destruction of democracy and the establishment of a dictatorship in the United States. For this purpose it fosters, as did Bismarck, Communism as the shortest route to dictatorship in a Democracy, and has converted the U. S. educational system into Communist propaganda agencies.

The progress made by the Board was disclosed in an article in the New York *Globe* on March 28, 1919, by Dr. W. S. Spillman, formerly Federal Farm Management Chief, as follows:

". . . I was approached by an agent of Mr. Rockefeller with the statement that his object in establishing the General Education Board was to gain control of the educational institutions of the country so that all men employed in them might be 'right.' I was then informed that the Board has been successful with smaller institutions but that the larger institutions had refused to accept the Rockefeller money with strings tied to it. My informant said that Rockefeller was going to add $100,000,000 to the Foundation for the express purpose of forcing his money on the big institutions."

The Board eventually succeeded in gaining control of almost every school, college and university in the country. They found it hard to resist the lure of the jingle of ready cash. They were forced to turn over to the Board power of dictation of their personnel and curriculum. Senator Kenyon, of Iowa, reported this to the U. S. Senate in January 1917.

The Board has saddled on our educational system, in the guise of teachers and professors of the "social sciences," the high priests of class war and revolution, professional agitators and the chanters of the abacadabra of the "social philosophies" a la Bismarck and Marx. It has made them the haven of Socialists, Communists, distributors of wealth and other crack-pot New Dealers. It has helped make the foundation source of prostituted "professors" and "authorities" for the *agents provocateurs* (also known as "leaders") of labor. These professorial propagandists make most of their incomes as front-men, partners, catspaws and agents of labor union racketeers and as "neutral arbitrators" of labor disputes under the Wagner Act. To-day there are few professors in the larger American Colleges who are not thoroughly Marxist or openly Communist. Particularly the professors of social sciences, who are so often appointed by Presidents and other public officials to commissions as representatives of the *public*, can be depended upon to support the Communist or radical labor elements. The Commissions thus appointed under the New Deal, are "loaded" and biassed. They can be depended upon to betray the public. They are on the payroll of the unions.

In this respect, the General Education Board has been most damaging and dangerous. It has used its power over the schools, colleges and universities throughout the country to place on their teaching staffs hosts of advocates of radical isms and outright propagandists of alien doctrines. It has placed its resources at the disposal of enemies of our country and its government.

Senator Chamberlain of Oregon, in 1917 foresaw and sounded a warning of this danger in the U. S. Senate. He stated:

"The Carnegie-Rockefeller influence is bad. In two generations they can change the minds of the people to make them conform to the cult of Rockefeller or to the cult of Carnegie, rather than to the fundamental principles of American democracy."

His prophecy is already fulfilled.

The direct dividends derived from the activities of the General Education Board were many, including:

Favorable publicity for the founders and advertising of their interests that was worth millions.

The power to influence public opinion and the policies of the Government by propaganda distributed through the schools, colleges and universities

Control of researches and discoveries, and their application and profits.

The power of voting the stock holdings of the institutions which they control and of dictating the expenditure of their funds.

The power of appointment of personnel of the institutions which can be converted to the uses of nepotism and favoritism.

Directly following the Supreme Court decision in 1911, ordering the dissolution of the Standard Oil Company, Rockefeller sought of Congress a charter for the Rockefeller Foundation "to promote the well-being of mankind". Congress twice refused a charter to hold one hundred million dollars, on the grounds that it was a device for evasion of payment of taxes, that it was primarily intended for propaganda for seduction of public opinion and influencing politics, and that it would be a menace to the nation. The Foundation succeeded in securing from New York State in 1913 a charter to hold five hundred million dollars.

The bill chartering the Rockefeller Foundation was introduced into New York State Legislature by a man who has discreetly served the Rockefeller interests though he has never permitted himself to be too closely identified with them in the public eye—Senator Robert F. Wagner.

The Foundation has supplemented the activities of the Institute and the General Education Board and has extended them into as many quarters of the world as go the ramifications of the Standard Oil Company subsidiaries and successors. It combines the functions of a tax-exempt business relations agency and super-diplomatic corps. Through its well-advertised and publicized subsidies it has gained entry into many governmental circles from which the interests which it represents would be excluded.

Through a Director of its International Health Division, Dr. Thomas Parran, Surgeon General of the U. S. Public Health Service, for instance, the Foundation is directly represented in a division of our government that is important for its sponsors. He also interlocks the directorship of the Milbank Memorial Fund and a host of other agencies. Significant names on the directorate of the Foundation are: Arthur Hays Sulzberger, the publisher of the New York *Times*, John Foster Dulles and John J. McCloy.

The creation of the Foundation followed closely on John D. Rockefeller Jr.'s shift in religious attitude toward the "new" or "liberal" theology which pragmatically decried fundamentalism and sectarianism in Protestantism. It is interesting to note that the fundamentalist ministers such as John Roach Stratton accused him of seeking to standardize education and religion through *German rationalization*.

The Foundation supplanted the activities which had formerly occupied Baptist missions. It is the diplomatic corps that prepares the way for commercial conquests. By elimination of inter-denominational antagonisms attached to missionary work it no doubt proved more efficient. In China the medical missions prepared the way for the conquest by Standard Oil of the kerosene and oil market. They also lent impetus to the creation of modern China. The Bible-selling oil merchant, Soong, was the father of the commercial dynasty which now leads China. Oil is also an important factor in the background of the Chinese-Japanese wars.

The Rockefeller Foundation liberally supported Organized Social Service, especially the organizations that have been devoted to the exploitation of disease under the guiding genius of Harry L. Hopkins. For a period of more than a decade John D. Jr. might have been termed the "angel" of Harry L. Hopkins. This implies that the Rockefellers have sponsored the political machine financed with funds gathered for social service activities, which eventually created the "New Deal." The Rockefeller interests are well represented on the directorate of most of the more important social service agencies.

It has been related that German-born Senator Robert F. Wagner, whose name is synonymous with all the specious doctrines and the most destructive measures of the "New Deal," has been identified with the Rockefeller interests and originally secured the New York State charter for the Foundation. Harry L. Hopkins acknowledged his debt to the Rockfellers, when he was appointed Secretary of Commerce, by offering the post of Assistant Secretary to Nelson Rockefeller. This was reported by Walter Winchell, who later announced that the Rockefeller publicity staff had vetoed Nelson Rockefeller's acceptance of the post. The reason may be discerned in the quiet but persistent propaganda conducted by the Rockefeller publicity men in the press, especially in the Rockefeller controlled or dominated papers such as the Hearst publications and in the New York *Times*, to pose John D. Rockefeller Jr. as a business-men's candidate for the job of President of the United States. It is noteworthy that the "New Deal" has dealt most kindly with the Rockefeller interests.

Absurd and dangerous doctrines have been promulgated and incorporated into the law for the deliberate purpose of creating chaos for sinister ulterior motives. This explains why the resources of the General Education Board and of the Foundation have not been used to promulgate and to influence the adoption of a more rational concept of economic and social structure.

With the aid of the machinery of the Foundation it would not take much effort to teach the nation that the menace to its security does not lie in accumulations of wealth, however large they may be; that on the contrary such accumulations constitute a factor of safety for the nation as well as for the individual. The real menace lies in the stupidly conceived and irrational monetary system which so limits the amount of money in circulation that accumulation of reserves by the nation and by individuals results in paralysis of exchange; and bars the setting up of reserves of essential commodities, the raw materials of the necessities of life.

Little more than a century ago the distinguished economist Malthus enunciated, on the basis of a tremendous amount of statistical research, what was named the "Law of Malthus." The "Law" states that population increases by geometric progression and must outstrip the production of food, which it says increases only by arithmetic progression.

From this economic "Law," Malthus deduced the idea that the world would become over-populated and consequently reduced to starvation. Instead we are now ploughing under crops in order to prevent destruction of their value by supposed over-production. Man's ingenuity in improving production and in creating machinery of production was disregarded by Malthus. And they proved his "Law" an absurd fallacy.

An equally fallacious economic "law," that of "supply and demand" and "marginal utility" (a euphuism for speculation, which is the real determining factor) bars us from remedying the reverse condition of that predicted by Malthus—an apparent over-production of food for our present-day populace. If one were to resort to the practice of framing fallacious thinking into "laws," the modern version would read as follows:

"The population and commodity production of

the world grow to exceed the dimensions of its monetary system. For survival of that monetary system population and commodities must be destroyed."

And that is being done by means of wars.

In final analysis the economy of the world requires one of two choices: Either the population and material wealth of the world must be destroyed to the point of bringing it within the scope of our present monetary system by a process of war and starvation, in conformity with the above-stated modernization of the "law of Malthus;" or the currency and medium of exchange must be rationally based and soundly expanded to match expansion of population and real wealth.

It is the first plan that rules throughout the world at the present time—identically in Russia as in the United States. It is taught dogmatically and without question in all our schools and universities, whether conservative or radical. Karl Marx in his "Socialism" has justified its application to fixing the value of human beings and their labor. It is the mainspring of the so-called "New Deal" and is the fundamental premise of all social service "philosophy" and thought.

It is apparent that there has been a deliberate fostering of these fallacious views in the classroom, in the land and in the rest of the world, for the insane purpose of precipitating a smashup of the world's economy that will result in absolute concentration of all the wealth and power of the world in a single hand.

The insanity of such an objective is obvious to anyone who stops to think or to consider history. Stability or security, which, in final analysis, all men seek in the brief span of life, can never exist in the presence of a system that breeds starvation and violence. In such a system the master is as likely to succumb to the forces which he has set loose as are the mastered.

There was far greater wisdom in John D. Jr.'s Sunday School homilies which taught that wealth is not essentially evil but a blessing. They did not point out that it is the stupid economic organization to which society clings that converts that blessing into the semblance of a curse.

The General Education Fund has suppressed such views as those of the son of its founder. It has done much to crush the originality of thought that might have enunciated and popularized such rational views. Instead the Rockefeller "philanthropies" have dogmatized the teachings of institutions of learning, and they have fostered destructive Bismarxian propaganda.

It is significant that the Foundation was conceived at the time of the dissolution of the Standard Oil Company. Undoubtedly it had become apparent to the Rockefellers that in order to avoid interference with their enterprises by governments they must take them over more directly and completely than they had thus far done. Taking over governments would not insure absolute submissiveness. This required that the form of the governments of the world must be changed to absolute dictatorships and that all concepts of democracy must be wiped out. That purpose is the obvious explanation of the objective of the Rockefeller interests in giving unlimited support to Communism, Nazism, Fascism, New Dealism and any other type of dictatorship.

The international activities of the Foundation were invaluable in paving the way for the formation of a world-wide oil monopoly. Rockefeller personally directed these maneuvers. This is clear from the report made by Chairman Walsh of the United State Commission on Industrial Relations, who reported:

". . . Mr. Rockefeller is the Foundation. The testimony shows that the trustees exercised no authority that does not come from him."

The Rockefeller-Standard Oil interests have fostered dictatorships and used them as pawns on their game of international diplomacy. Their all important game since gaining control of the oil reserves of the Americas has been the play for oil lands in the East and the Near East, Caucasus, Iran, Iraq and Saudi Arabia with which to supply their European and Mediterranean markets. Their chief competitors and adversaries have been the British, the Royal Dutch and Shell Companies. The British government has been closely tied up with the companies and adamant in blocking the Rockefeller interests from the oil reserves in their sphere of influence. It was evident that nothing short of destruction of the British Empire would serve to open its territories to the Standard Oil. The Rockefeller interests proceeded to destroy the British Empire in World Wars I and II.

The objective of Kaiser Wilhelm's Berlin to Bagdad Railroad plan, that was one of the principal precipitating causes of World War I, was to wrest Near Eastern oil from the control of the British. The fine hand of Standard Oil can be seen in this move that precipitated war. It was only when the British agreed to let down the barriers to Standard Oil that the U.S. was pushed into the "War to Save Democracy"—a rather high-sounding title for oil. Following the war, Standard Oil obtained concessions in Roumania, Bulgaria, Ethopia, Sumatra, Persia, Kamchatka, Turkey and Saudi Arabia. It also obtained oil monopolies in France in which the French Government was a partner, in Czecho-Slovakia and in China.

After World War I the British took over the Baku oil fields from the Turks and Germans, who had seized them. After their withdrawal they supported the Denikin Army. In the meantime in 1920 the Standard Oil of New Jersey purchased the Baku oil holdings of Nobel Oil Co. For eight years the Rockefeller Standard Oil group battled Royal Dutch and Shell for Baku oil, in the diplomatic field. The Rockefeller-Standard Oil group came out the winner. They offered to grant recognition of the Soviet Government by the United States and the support of Communism in the U. S. in return for oil. After placing Roosevelt in office, they did effect recognition. In 1935, the Socony Vacuum announced that it had bought oil heavily from Russia since 1927.

In the meantime the Rockefeller-Standard Oil interests were busy developing another source of oil in the Mediterranean. A subsidiary, the Anglo-American Oil Company had obtained in 1933 an exclusive concession in the northern half of the Harrar Province in Ethiopia. There is no record of any effective development of the concession, no doubt due to British pressure.

In 1933 there was organized, the African Exploration and Development Company affiliated with Socony Vacuum for exploration of Ethopian oil. Sir Francis Rickett, Rockefeller-Standard Oil negotiator made no headway with Haile Selassie. He turned to Rome and offered Mussolini a deal on Abyssinian oil. In return for invasion of Abyssinia he offered the assurance of the Rockefeller Empire that no sanctions would be exercised by the Rockefeller-controlled League of Nations of which Raymond B. Fosdick, a Rockefeller employee, was executive. The Standard Oil undertook to supply Mussolini with Roumanian oil in return for a thirty year monopoly of the Italian oil market. And after the war started, Socony Vacuum built two refineries in Naples for him. After two months of war, in December 1935, peace was offered Haile Selassie in return for the cession to Italy of the oil-rich Fafan Valley and the lands west of it. The Rockefeller interests did not get complete control of Ethiopian reserves until 1947, when a concession was granted Sinclair Oil, a subsidiary of Standard Oil of Indiana.

In the Chaco in 1933 Standard-British rivalry precipitated the war between Bolivia, backed by the Rockefellers, and Paraguay, by the British. Paraguay openly brought charges against the Standard Oil Co. of New Jersey which in the meantime increased its leases in the war area from 386,000 to 2,703,000 hectares.

The invisible Rockefeller Empire is a super-government that is rapidly encompassing the entire globe. It has entered into partnership or other deals, and has dominated the governments of numerous countries throughout the world including France, Italy, Roumania, Germany, Czecho-Slovakia, Iran, Iraq, Saudi Arabia, Turkey, China, Abyssinia, Japan and Soviet Russia; and in the Western Hemisphere, Canada, Mexico, Venezuela, Colombia, Bolivia, and Argentine.

For the past thirty-five years, the government of the United States has been a completely dominated and minor dependent bureau of the Rockefeller Empire that has always done its bidding. For more than half a century, the Rockefeller Empire has controlled by its contributions the nominations in the major political parties. Under Franklin Delano Roosevelt, their agent, the Rockefeller Empire entered into open rule of the United States.

CHAPTER VII

BLUEPRINT OF THE NEW DEAL
HOFFMAN NICKERSON'S "THE AMERICAN RICH"

Monopoly of every necessity of life and of national existence, and absolute dictatorship are the basic doctriness of the Rockefeller Empire. For this purpose the Rockefeller "philanthropies" have fostered Marxism as the shortest cut to dictatorship in a Democracy. The world-wide chain of dictatorships which they seek would not be complete without an American dictatorship. In this idea of an American dictatorship, the Roosevelt-Delano Dynasty fully concurs. It was quite natural that an alliance should be formed between them.

So complete is the contempt of America's rulers for the moronic level of intelligence of its people that they sponsored the open publication of their program in the form of Hoffman Nickerson's book "The American Rich". It was published by Doubleday Doran & Company at the time that Theodore Roosevelt Jr. was its president. It was a blueprint of the New Deal subsequently adopted in the Roosevelt regime, published in 1930, three years before it was launched. Hoffman Nickerson was the prophet of the Empire and Dynasty whose counsel and blueprint were followed closely.

The schemers of the New Deal left nothing to chance but prepared to flim-flam the nation well in advance, in this matter, as well as in others. Thus the Agricultural Allotment Plan was drawn up in 1932 by a Hindu, Svirinas Wagel, Barney Baruch's Hentz & Company's economist, to appear to be a boon to the farmers,—whereas it was a made-to-order godsend for the speculators in commodities and designed to make their gambles "sure things".

The theme of "The American Rich" is a familiar one.

Democracy, the "Cult of Equality", is, always has been, and always will be a failure, it relates. It must be eliminated under the pretense of improving it. The objective to be sought and attained by finesse, is Medieval feudalism and serfdom — a masterful upper class dominating, the rest of the population reduced to slavery. And at the head there must be a king. That is the form of government the United States must have if it is to have a perfect government.

It is to the interest of the group that can be called perpetually rich, because they can always dip their hands into the pockets of the people through the Treasury, to see to it that the United States attains a perfect, feudal monarchic government. To accomplish this the rich must organize amongst themselves to fight a common cause and pick their agent, who will be made to appear to desert and betray his class. They must then undertake by sly undercover methods to "divide to rule". The people must be dealt with not as Americans, but as minorities set at each other's throats, Labor vs Capital, Black vs White, Catholic vs Protestant, Christian vs Jew, for example. Then the selected agent must be made to appear the champion of all causes, the indispensable composer of differences, while from behind the scenes he must never cease to foment.

This agent then can assume readily the role of popular leader and be elected President. Once in office, everything must be done to keep him there by repeated reelections. The government must be converted into a huge propaganda agency and perverter of popular thought. He must cater to the mob. But all the while he must discredit and break down the checks on monarchic power of the President incorporated in the Constitution—the Supreme Court and Congress. But in the process he must be made to appear to seek an improvement on democracy. The gullible, moronic public must never suspect that he seeks to wipe out democracy—"The absurd Cult of Equality".

Once elected, the President must be continually reelected. The opposing candidate must merely be a straw man selected by the same group, to be knocked down and defeated. The people must be deceived into believing that they are exercising the democratic right to vote, while they have been robbed of the right of choice, i. e. the right to vote, by restriction of nominations by the same group, to men subservient to them.

When the President will have been reelected often enough, he will have had an opportunity to appoint to the Supreme Court all the justices, who will do his bidding. The Supreme Court, packed thus or otherwise, will have ceased to be a check on the monarchic power of the President, as required by the Constitution. Instead it will have become a prostituted agency serving the President and the invisible powers behind him.

The problem of eliminating the power of Congress, of effecting "the twilight of legislature", Nickerson points out, is a bit more complicated but it must be done.

" . . . they (legislatures) must be abolished or

their bases and functions changed" (p. 259).

"The first step toward complete monarchical (Presidential) initiative is the executive budget plan now prevailing in the Federal government and in thirty-four of the forty-eight states. Even the logical second step of limiting the constitutional powers of the legislative bodies has been taken in seven of the thirty-four, Maryland, West Virginia, New York, Massachusetts, California Nebraska and Wisconsin. THE RICH THEREFORE MIGHT DO WELL TO HELP FORWARD SUCH A DEVELOPMENT". (p. 261).

Nickerson goes on to suggest:

"The resistance of legislature to the pruning of their sovereignty could easily be broken down by the imperative mandate. Candidates for legislative office might be compelled to swear that if elected they would support measures curtailing parliamentary and increasing monarchical initiative. In this way the executive budget laws could be made more and more drastic". (p. 293).

In practice, Nickerson's suggestion was adopted effectively by abdication by New Deal legislatures. It was materially aided by the practices of Congress. Thus the gag rule limiting Congressmen's speeches on the floor of the House to one minute and barring publication of "extensions of remarks" in the Congressional Record unless unanimous consent is obtained, has served to muzzle the people's elected representatives.

Nickerson's blueprint was materially improved on by the New Deal practice of grafting on to it the Rockefeller-sponsored Communist program for attaining their goal by pseudo-philanthropy and by a mechanism that was so well expressed by their agent, Harry Hopkins:

"Tax! Tax!! Tax!!! Spend! Spend!! Spend!!!
Elect! Elect!! Elect!!!"

Under the New Deal the budgets presented by Roosevelt to Congress were so huge that no member of Congress dared add to them; so voluminous and complex that Congress did not have the time to consider them; and so fraught with self-interest for special groups and with "pork barrel" that few Congressmen cared to attack them for fear of losing their "cut". Congress abdicated its constitutional power of initiating budgetary legislation year after year, until, as the advocates of the plan expected, it has become the accepted practice that the budget bill shall be initiated by the President.

When that goal has been attained, Nickerson's blueprint then proceeds to the next step that reduces Congress to a mere advisory or consulting body, that is compatible with a feudal monarchy. He writes:

"When financial initiative had thus been fully secured to the monarch, the same principle might be extended to all legislation. The monarch is already charged with the duty of presenting at the opening of each legislative session a message as to legislative changes he thinks desirable. Constitutional amendments might enlarge this traditional function so as to make it his duty to draw up a formal 'budget' of legislation, and might compel the legislature to say Aye or Nay to each item of this program before embarking on any new proposals of its own. In normal cases public opinon could then be counted upon to compel the legislature to adjourn and leave the community in peace until the beginning of the next session. There would remain the right of the legislative body to *discuss public affairs* (ed. 'debating society') to *criticize* the elective monarch, and to veto such new departure of his as they might think unwise". (pp. 293-294).

This phase of the plan has been materially improved upon in New Deal practice even though it has not arrived at the point where they dare propose a Constitutional amendment to rob Congress of all right to legislate, and leave them merely the power of talk and veto. During Roosevelt's regime the conspirators used the *"national emergency"* device to prevent Congress from enacting any legislation introduced by individual Congressmen. The device was very simple and completely effective. Repeated situations were engineered by the conspirators that were declared *"national emergencies"*. Manipulation of national finance and the money system enabled the engineering and continuance of the depression. Disrupting the commerce and industry of the nation with an N. R. A. or an O. P. A. served to disrupt production and stimulate inflation. The very measures that were presented to fight inflation were designed to stimulate it for the purpose of creating a *"national emergency"*. Robbing workers of the right to work implicit in the Constitution, and farming it out to their agents, so-called "labor-leaders", in return for a share of tribute levied by them for the privilege of working, provided not only a source of revenue but also a dictatorial control of the rank and file of the nation. It permitted creating *"national emergencies"* at will by blackmailing industry and by strikes. And when all else failed the conspirators deliberately precipitated a real but tragic national emergency, Pearl Harbor and World War II, to further their commercial and political schemes.

All of these deliberately engineered *"national emergencies"* were used as the means of dragooning Congress into accepting the dictates of the conspirators. They utilized the too familiar device of innumerable messages to Congress on the state of the nation. The Constitution calls on the President to send to Congress at the time it convenes a message on the state of the nation. It was in no wise intended as a dictatorial device to force the will of the Executive on Congress. It was intended to be, and had been, an informative device.

The New Deal with its tremendous propaganda machine that was built up in the executive branch of the government with public funds for perverting and manipulating public opinion, used these messages as a device to force Congress into submission, abdication, and renunciation of the role assigned it by the Constitution. The function of initiating any legislation was thus fraudulently usurped by the President, in complete violation of the Constitution. There is no need for the renunciatory amendment to the Constitution demanded by Nickerson's blueprint. For this flaunting of the Constitution has become accepted practice in the conspiracy to destroy democracy and establish an open American monarchy.

With regard to the form that will be given American monarchy, whether elective or hereditary, Nickerson advised caution:

"Changes like the executive budget deriving most of their force from moral sources rather than from statute law, may creep in gradually . . . But even to give the President a longer term or to disregard the very strong tradition handed down from Washington himself against a third term for any individual President would be a sharp and noticeable change not to be masked by any form of words. Hence, though most elective monarchies of the past have been for life, all such questions must be left to the future".

Nickerson obviously reckoned not on the effectiveness of the General Education Fund and the Rockefeller Foundation in their control of education, of the press, radio, films, the government propaganda machine and every other avenue of exchange of information, in perverting and warping the minds of a nation. He reckoned without the *savoir faire* of the Rockefeller-Standard Oil regime, and the experience of its ally, the Roosevelt-Delano Dynasty. So thoroughly had their task been performed that a little over a decade after Nickerson wrote, the third and fourth Presidential terms and the numerous other violations of the letter and spirit of the Constitution, that he could not conceive as being accepted by the nation, were accomplished facts.

Nickerson points out a technique whereby the people could be painlessly robbed of their franchise, by which "all pretense of an election dependent on popular will would have vanished". (p. 295). It is a technique with which the Roosevelt-Delano Dynasty have had extensive experience—the third party movement. The idea is to split the electoral vote so that no candidate gets a majority, thus throwing the election into the lap of Congress.

It is significant that the salary of Henry Wallace as editor of the New Republic was reported to be $75,-000 a year. The New Republic has not made that many pennies profit in its entire existence. It has been subsidized by Anglophile Willard Straight of J. P. Morgan & Company and his son, Michael Straight. Undenied reports state that Henry Wallace's salary, travelling and campaign expenses are being paid by Michael Straight, Jock Whitney and *Nelson Rockefeller.*

After pointing out the great strength of the case for hereditary monarchy, Nickerson concludes:

"Come what may, monarchy in its elective form is firmly established as the chief American organ of government. It is the instrument through which, when the time is ripe, we may hope for a solution of our problems, for an honorable but separate status for the negro and jew, permitting us to utilize their distinctive gifts while preserving us from too much racial contact with the first and from the alien soul of the second . . . " (p. 302).

He points, in support of the first idea, to the proposal of the Town Board of Sudbury, Massachusetts in 1927, that Coolidge be made President for life; and to the fact that the Presidency "within a few generations has been clothed with awe and reverence which shone on the kings of old". His judgment has been fully confirmed by the obeisance and veneration of Franklin Delano Roosevelt, engendered by adroit propaganda in a large section of the populace.

"Already" he writes, "we are not far from 'divine Caesar' . . . " Indeed. no. Sadly enough, we are far beyond it.

As for his concept on alien minorities, Nickerson's ideas have been closely followed by the conspirators. They are being "utilized" or used to attain a destruction of democracy and the establishment of the American monarchy. They are being put in the forefront, in the firing line to take all the blame and punishment. But in a properly regulated feudal monarchy, there is no room for any minority. Their elimination is planned when the goal of feudalism has been attained.

There is an amusing phase to Hoffman Nickerson's "omniscient" prattling. He holds the "jews" in such abysmal contempt that he will not even capitalize their name; and he regards as one of the functions of his program, the elimination of the Jews. But he supports much of his blueprint, and justifies other sections with the Federalist writings of "the great Alexander Hamilton" (p. 246) whom he acclaims as the outstanding American patriot and the greatest mind among the founders of our country.

If he is as wise, well-informed and omniscient as he poses, he would know that his hero Alexander Hamilton was born Levine, the son of a Danish Jewish West Indies planter John Michael Levine. Alexander was the son of a Jewish father and a mulatto mother. Alexander's mother Rachael was unfaithful and left his father to live with James Hamilton. When her husband divorced her, she was forbidden to remarry but continued to live with Hamilton and changed her son's name from Levine to Hamilton. ("Money Changers", Gertrude M. Coogan, Sound Money Press, 1935, p. 188).

Posthumously his descendants undertook to attribute fatherhood to James Hamilton. They preferred to stigmatize their ancestor as a bastard, to acknowledging his Jewish and Negro ancestry. The absurdity of the effort is attested to by the fact that they place Alexander in charge of one of the largest mercantile businesses of St. Croix at the age of twelve years. Precocity they call it! But they place the date of his birth two years before that of his mother's divorce in 1759, and within a few months after her marriage to Levine.

CHAPTER VIII

FRANKLIN DELANO ROOSEVELT

Franklin Delano Roosevelt was the pathetic puppet of the conspirators scheming the destruction of democracy and the establishment of an American monarchy. For the role for which he was picked, he had every qualification.

F.D.R. was a direct scion of both the Roosevelt and Delano clans. On the Roosevelt side, he was descended from Claas Martenszen van Rosenvelt (or Rosenfeld) descendants of proselytized Sephardic Jews who had settled in Holland and later migrated to New Amsterdam in 1649. Claas, his son, was father of Johannes, the direct ancestor of Theodore Roosevelt, and of Jacobus, the direct ancestor of F. D. R.

Jacobus Roosevelt married one of the most affluent and picturesque woman of the time, Catherina Hardenbroeck. According to tradition, she was the hardest drinking, hardest cussing, hardest fighting woman who ever sailed before her own mast as skipper in the rum, molasses, slave and smuggling trade. Isaac, her son, was the man whose invitation to attend a wife's funeral, was rejected by George Washington because of a question of propriety .

The intervening ancestors were German, Swedish, and principally English, so that the original Dutch strain is thoroughly diluted. Col. Theodore Roosevelt, 26th president was a fifth cousin. F. D. R.'s half-niece,

Helen Rebecca Roosevelt married Theodore Douglas Robinson, son of Theodore Roosevelt's sister Corinne, the grandmother of Joseph and Stewart Alsop, the columnists.

By direct line of descent from Thomas Shepard and Anne Tyng, John Adams, second president, and John Quincy Adams, sixth, were sixth and seventh cousins. But the relationship of the two branches of the family have ben maintained in closer degree by intermarriage. The marriage of Fred B. Adams to Ellen W. Delano, a first cousin of F.D.R. has been mentioned.

Less directly, through intermarriage of the Van Deursens and the Van Burens, F.D.R.'s great grandfather was a third cousin of Martin Van Buren, eighth president.

On the Delano side F. D. R. was more or less remotely related to George Washington, James Madison, 4th president, General William Henry Harrison, 9th president, General Zachary Taylor, 12th president, Andrew Johnson, 17th president, General Ulysses S. Grant, 18th president, General Benjamin Harrison, 23rd president and William Howard Taft, 27th president. As has been stated, President Grant was F.D.R.'s closest relative among the presidents. It has been noted also that on the Delano side, F. D. R. proudly traces his ancestry to the King of England, Henry II, and through the Astors, by marriage, to George VI. The numerous intermarriages with European nobility have been mentioned. The royal background and ancestry were calculated to engender ambitions and fire the aspirations of a Pretender to an American throne; and the Dynasty's influence has made it a possibility.

Franklin Delano Roosevelt was the son of fifty-two year old James Roosevelt, vice-president of the Delaware and Hudson Railroad, director of several other corporations and retired country squire, and Sara Delano, twenty-six year old daughter of Warren Delano, merchant and clipper ship operator in the China trade, who made a sizeable fortune in opium smuggling. The Kean gang also entered the picture.

By the first marriage F. D. R. had a half-brother, James Roosevelt Roosevelt, a banker and appointee to the diplomatic corps by Grover Cleveland, a kinsman of his father. It is amusing to note that this brother has been kept a dark secret by the New Dealers because it would not be compatible with the picture of F. D. R. "throwing the money lenders out of the temple". James Roosevelt Roosevelt's first wife was Helen Schermerhorn Astor, daughter of the society leader, Mrs. William B. Astor and aunt of Vincent Astor.

Sara Delano Roosevelt, dominating mother, did not send her boy to school to mix with schoolmates but kept him home under the tutelage first of French and German governesses, and then of tutors until he was fourteen .Almost every year he was taken to Europe for several months. He attended public school at Nauheim two years, studying map reading and military topography. At an early age he conceived a great admiration for things German and became thoroughly imbued with Prussian militarism, and their lust for war on land, and especially, on sea. Summers were spent at Campobello.

Under the influence of his mother, who was derived from a sea-faring family and whose cousin, according to Daniel W. Delano (Pic, July 8, 1941), had designed and built the first armor-clad, screw-driven warship, F. D. R.'s keenest interest, at the age of twelve, was warships and navies.

At fourteen he was sent to school at Groton, which tries to be ever so British and mimics Eton. At eighteen he entered Harvard. He did little studying but managed to get by .His social life was more successful; and he attained an editorship on the Crimson. His guiding star was his distant cousin, Theodore Roosevelt. In his conversation he talked so much about his birth, social position and aspirations that he was twitted by his classmates about his "Royal Family". In 1904 he left Harvard and went to Columbia Law School.

Shortly after he had entered Harvard, F. D. R.'s father died. In his will he intimated that he did not trust Franklin's competence and left him nothing outright but merely $100,000 in trust. His mother inherited the estate, held the purse strings and "managed" him. She took up residence near Harvard to superintend his education.

Against his mother's will, F. D. R. proposed to Eleanor Roosevelt, niece of President Theodore Roosevelt. It is apparent that F.D.R. was dazzled by his distant cousin in the White House and that Eleanor's close relationship to him gave added lure. When the point for opposition had passed, Sara Delano acquiesced.

Teddy gave his niece, and godchild, away on March 17, 1905 at the homes of Eleanor's cousin, Mrs Henry Parish, Jr. and of her mother, Mrs. E. Livingston Ludlow, 6 and 8 East Seventy-sixth Street, New York City.

F.D.R. had no resources of his own. He was completely dependent on his mother's gifts, and she bossed the newlyweds thoroughly. She provided them a house at Hyde Park, a summer home at Campobello, and built for him a house adjoining her own on East Sixty-fifth Street. The bride reports she had no voice in the furnishing of her own homes. But marriage to Eleanor had its rewards for F. D. R. He was now especially welcome and became a frequent guest at the White House or at the home of Theodore Roosevelt's brother-in-law, Rear Admiral William Sheffield Cowles and he came in closer contact with his hero, the ruling Dynast. He had an opportunity to become thoroughly imbued with tradition and methods, and was able to make contacts which served him well later. He learned at first hand from the Master the use of showmanship and opportunism as political tools.

Mrs. Henry Parrish, on her death, left $250,000 to "my beloved niece Eleanor Roosevelt", and an equal amount "to my nephew, Sumner Welles". It is in the person of Sumner Welles, former Assistant Secretary of State during the Roosevelt regime, that certain family failings of the clan have come to light most notoriously. "CONFIDENTIAL" magazine, in its issue of May, 1956 (vol. 4, No. 2) openly accused Sumner Welles of homosexuality, quoting from public records. No mention is made of a predilection for colored minors.

In this connection, it might be noted that FDR's cousin, Ellen Roosevelt, reported that Eleanor Roosevelt's mother was a woman of some degree of color, who was indiscreetly attached to Theodore Roosevelt. Teddy's ne'er-do-well, dissolute brother, Elliott, appears on the family tree as Eleanor's father. But her mother is curiously glossed over in it

F. D. R. was uninterested in his law studies and was never able to graduate in law. He had no patience with rules or laws. As a spoiled brat he had always changed the rules of games to suit his whims. As a Dynastic heir, he planned to make his own laws, in the fashion of a Pasha. He gloried in the idea of laying down the law. Whenever he signed a new bill, even on his dying day, he would say to his secretary: "Here is where *I* make a new law." (Time, April 23, 1945, p. 18). But the influence of the Dynasty was great. The Bar Association made a rare exception in his case and admitted him to the Bar without a law degree; and, it is reported, without a rigid examination. He was given a job by his cousin's (Sara Delano, daughter of Warren Delano III) husband Roland L. Redmond, senior partner of Carter, Ledyard and Milburn.

His chief interest during this period, as previously, was military and naval history. He spent a large part of his time at Hyde Park in the role of country squire, and in summer at Campobello. His mother was still his main source of income for the support of his family. Indicative of his breadth of mind was the clause that appeared regularly in his advertisements for help for Hyde Park: "No Catholic need apply." This anti-Catholicism in later political activities was thinly disguised, but repeatedly emerged, and James Farley need not have been surprised at the treatment he received.

F. D. R.'s start in politics he owed to the power of the Dynasty and the popularity of the Roosevelt name. The members of the Dynasty then in control of the local political machine provided the opportunity. Chief Theodore Roosevelt was then engaged in vengefully wrecking the Republican Party and defeating Taft in the interest of Morgan. F. D. R. was dilly-dallying with law and other avocations at the time but was not making a living and had to be provided for. And he could not be provided for better than to place him on the public payroll where he could serve the Dynasty. They gave him the nomination for State Senator for Dutchess County and Putnam County, the old stamping ground of Martin Van Buren who had built up the political machine in that district almost a century earlier. His running mate for the Assembly was a distant relative, Louis Stuyvesant Chanler, great-great grandson of John Jacob Astor. The Senate district had always been Republican and it was not expected that there was any chance that the Democratic candidate would win. The Poughkeepsie Eagle commented on the situation:

"Presumably his (F. D. R.'s) contribution to the campaign funds goes well above four figures but the Republican nominee will not be disturbed by Mr. Roosevelt's candidacy."

But Theodore Roosevelt had disrupted the Republican Party in New York, characteristically following the pattern of disgruntled ex-officeholders of the ever treacherous and disloyal Dynasty, and had assured a victory to the opposition, the Democratic Party. F.D.R. was carried in by the landslide.

In the campaign he showed that he had learned from his paragon, Theodore Roosevelt, the device of catch-penny demagoguery which later proved a favorite device throughout his career. In the campaign there were elements of Ku Klux Klanism; and F. D. R. shone in the light of champion of the Protestant White Americans. Though his nomination had been given him by the local Dynastic bosses who controlled both parties, he made a sham fight on "Bossism" and a pretense of deserting his social class, for demagogic appeal. F.D.R. proved an apt pawn.

In the New York State Senate, the upstate Dynasty political machine once again made good use of the Roosevelt name and built up the repute of their man, F.D.R. The occasion was the unpopular plan for nomination of William Sheehan, candidate of Tammany's boss, Charley Murphy, to succeed United States Senator Chauncey Depew. Six district leaders, as well as J. Sergeant Cram, chairman of the New York Democratic County Committee, worked actively for his defeat.

The "fight" took the form of "passive resistance", refusal to attend the Democratic caucus, so that the majority would not be present. In all, seventeen Democrats under the leadership of the Osbornes led the "fight". Most of the upstate Democratic leaders who traditionally opposed Tammany, sought Sheehan's defeat. The influence of the Dynasty plus the news value of the Roosevelt name combined to credit the "fight" on Sheehan to F. D. R. and rob the Osbornes of credit for their leadership. The New York Times was particularly helpful in thus building up F. D. R. Inasmuch as the Times, belying its early-day virility and the public spirit that marked its fight on Tweed, has made obsequiousness to the powers that be its consistent policy, there can be seen the hand of Theodore Roosevelt and the Dynasty in the "build-up" of cousin F. D. R.

Word got around that there was an important element of anti-Catholicism in Roosevelt's opposition to Sheehan. In view of his previous exhibitions of anti- Catholicism and the Klu Klux Klanism, this was not surprising. With the objective of allaying resentment thus aroused, the "insurgents", after a prolonged holdout, voted for a Tammany candidate of Murphy's, Justice James A. O'Gorman.

Once he had gained the limelight, F. D. R. had no difficulty in holding it. In whatever he did he had the backing of the Dynasty and he played to the gallery with all the studied effort that he had learned from his cousin "Teddy". The Dynasty had prepared some new raw material for the White House to carry on its line of succession.

Roosevelt's campaign for reelection to the State Senate brought on the scene Louis McHenry Howe. He largely accounts for any element of political talent that Roosevelt is supposed to have possessed. Howe took over at the point that the Dynastic bosses left off. He was a one man "brain trust" who cooperated with a full time staff of reliable workers, including Margaret LeHand, in creating the Roosevelt known to the public, about whom there centered the Roosevelt myth. Before F. D. R. had reached the point where Rockefeller subsidized professional staffs did his thinking for him, Louis Howe did the job single-handed. Much of what the public has been led to believe is the personality of Franklin Delano Roosevelt, is merely a reflection of his ghost personality, his ghost thinker and ghost writer, Louis Howe.

Howe, who was the Albany correspondent of the New York Herald and Telegram, took complete control of Roosevelt's 1912 renomination campaign. Roosevelt was stricken with typhoid fever at the time. An uncannily shrewd politician who had studied the game from a point of vantage in Albany for many years, Howe drew up a platform for cooperative distributing and shipping societies and farmer's banks, with licensing of commission merchants by the State Department of Agriculture, which he knew the farmers had sought and would acclaim. On this platform of which Roosevelt had never conceived and had not the slightest knowledge, Howe secured his boss's reelection. From then until his death, Louis Howe was F. D. R.'s alter and wiser ego.

CHAPTER IX

THE DYNASTY'S NAVAL INTERESTS
F. D. R.—HEREDITARY NAVAL SECRETARY

President Wilson was a quite synthetic creation of the Wall Street interests. The principal figure in building him up and imposing him on the nation was his intimate friend and life-long associate Cleveland H. Dodge, a Princeton classmate of Wilson's and an in-law of the Rockefellers who together with Cyrus Hall McCormick, gave him the Princeton professorship, privately supplemented his salary in conjunction with Percy R. Pyne (National City Bank), promoted him to Princeton's president, and through George Harvey, the Morgan-Ryan-Rockefeller agent and president of Harper's Publishing Company, secured him the governorship of New Jersey from Democratic boss, Senator James Smith, Jr. on payment to him of $75,000 by Dodge. (McCombs' "Making Wilson President", p. 20) In 1908, Harvey predicted in Harper's Weekly, on behalf of the Wall Street crowd, that Wilson would be elected Governor of New Jersey in 1910, and President in 1912. And the clique carried out their scheme on time and without a hitch, while making it appear to the public that Wilson actually opposed the political bosses who put through the deal that made him President.

Dodge was not engaged in politics for his health. He was director of the National City Bank, a principal of the Phelps Dodge Copper Company, and heavily interested in the munition industry—including Remington Arms Company, Winchester Arms Company and Union Metallic Cartridge Company. With such heavy interests at stake it was necessary that he be assured that his pal, Woodrow Wilson, would take orders without question and that Wilson assure his associates of it. This Wilson did in dinners arranged with representatives of the Rockefeller-Morgan crowd. Among them was a dinner for Wilson held at Beechwood, home of Frank A. Vanderlip, President of the National City Bank, which was attended by James Stillman and William Rockefeller. (John Winkler, The First Billion.

p. 210). Wilson agreed to permit Vanderlip to write the monetary views for his speeches. But Wilson would not take these views directly from Vanderlip because he did not want the public to realize that his pretended opposition to the financial interests and the trusts was a fraud. William G. McAdoo served as go-between. (Frank A. Vanderlip and Boyden Sparks, From Farm-Boy to Financier, pp. 225-226).

At the time of Wilson's inauguration, Dodge was under indictment in the Territory of New Mexico and Arizona for a land deal fraud. Following Wilson's inauguration, the case was promptly dismissed.

Peace is not conducive to great profits in the munitions industries. Dodge was more than a little interested in a good sized war. Franklin Delano Roosevelt had campaigned for Wilson with the support of Dodge and his Rockefeller-Morgan allies. The hold that the Roosevelt-Delano Dynasty had on Wilson is illustrated by his appointment of Frederic A. Delano, F. D. R.'s uncle, as vice-governor of the Federal Reserve Bank, a key position in national finance.

On Wilson's election, nothing could have been more readily taken for granted than the appointment of Senator Franklin Delano Roosevelt, thirty-one years old, to the post of Assistant Secretary of the Navy, just as previously Theodore Roosevelt had been appointed to the post by McKinley. For naval armor, armaments and shipbuilding is one of the principal interests of the Roosevelt-Delano Dynasty. As Daniel W. Delano relates in "My Cousin In The White House" (Pic, July 8, 1941) it was a Delano, a cousin of F. D. R.'s who built the first armor-clad, screw-driven warship and for generations the family engaged in shipbuilding and seafaring. Under the influence of his mother, F. D. R. had passionately devoted himself to seafaring and specialized in a study of naval vessels and naval warfare to prepare him to carry on a family tradition.

For in the past half century the job of Naval Secretary has become a hereditary prerogative of the Roosevelt-Delano Dynasty. In every administration which has not been headed by one of its members as President, it has been represented by one or more Secretaryships in the Navy Department, to take care of their naval interests. A list of these is impressive.

HEREDITARY NAVAL SECRETARIES OF
ROOSEVELT-DELANO DYNASTY

President	Secretary	Asst. Sec'y.
McKinley		T. Roosevelt
T. Roosevelt		
Taft		
Wilson		F. D. Roosevelt
Harding		T. Roosevelt Jr.
Coolidge		T. Roosevelt Jr.
		T. D. Douglas
		(*T. R.'s nephew*)
Hoover	Chas. Francis Adams	
F. D. Roosevelt		Henry L. Roosevelt
		Nicholas Roosevelt
		Delano
		Delano
		Delano

Arrived in Washington, Franklin was still under Teddy Roosevelt's tutelage, as his Dynastic heir-in-the-making. He took residence in the home of Teddy's sister, Anna Cowles. To provide the brains, press relations and ghost writing, Louis Howe went along and was placed on the Navy Department payroll.

One of the most important shipyards in naval construction is the Newport News Shipbuilding & Dry Dock. It was built and privately owned by Collis P. Huntington, builder of the Southern Pacific Railroad. Miss Helen D. Huntington was the first wife of Vincent Astor, nephew and cousin of Franklin Delano Roosevelt. E. A. Adams was Secretary-treasurer of the Company and Charles Frances Adams, Hoover's Secretary of the Navy, became a director in 1940 when the stock was first sold to the public.

It is interesting to note how the business of the Newport News Shipbuilding soared whenever the Roosevelts were on the job. The Company received its first naval construction contracts—three gunboats—in 1897 when Teddy Roosevelt was on the job as Assistant Secretary. It received no new contracts until T. R. became President—two battleships in 1900, a third in 1901, a monitor in 1902, a fourth battleship in 1903, three cruisers in 1905, a fifth and sixth battleship in 1906, a seventh battleship in 1907, a fourth and fifth cruiser in 1908. Under Taft, Newport News did not do

THE NAVY JOB

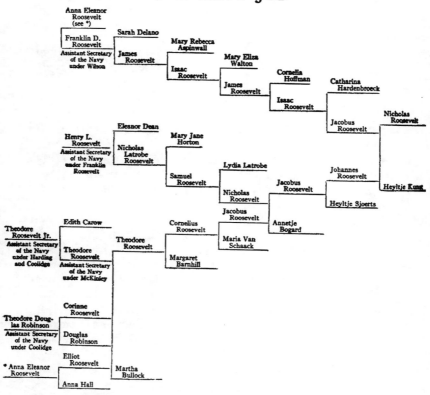

HEREDITARY TRANSMISSION OF NAVAL SECRETARYSHIPS
In Roosevelt-Delano Dynasty on the Roosevelt side is partly illustrated in this Genealogic Table.

so well; merely two destroyers and one battleship in 1910, one destroyer in 1911, and a destroyer and ammunition lighter in 1912. The drop in tonnage was even more significant. During Teddy Roosevelt's presidency Newport News had built 134,243 tons and under Taft a mere 23,652.

With a Roosevelt back on the job, this time F. D. R., Newport News business began to pick up again; in 1913, two colliers, 38,000 tons, more than the whole Taft administration; in 1914, one battleship and two oil barges, total 28,670; in 1916, one battleship, 31,-400 tons; in 1917, one battleship, 32,000 tons. The total tonage built by the shipyard *prior to our entry into the war* was 130,000, right back to the old standard.

F. D. R. was ready to realize his childhood dream, a real naval war with real battleships! The benevolent, philanthropic Rockefeller-Standard Oil interests provided him with not one, but with two wars.

In Mexico, the Rockefeller controlled Pierce-Waters Oil Company demanded of Diaz that he permit the importation of Standard Oil products from the United States tax free. Diaz refused. The Rockefeller interests financed Madero to stage a revolution. (They told Barron, p. 141). The British oil interests and Lord Cowdray backed Victoriano Huerta who in February 1913, ousted Madero and executed him. Wilson's angel Dodge and his Rockefeller-Morgan allies then financed and furnished with munitions Venustiano Carranza and Pancho Villa despite an embargo. When a German ship attempted to land arms at Vera Cruz, in April 1914, American warships shelled the town. On July 15, 1914, Huerta was forced out and Carranza took over for the Morgan-Rockefeller interests. Villa then turned on Carranza, resulting in American intervention. There was little naval action in the Mexican incident to delight the heart of F. D. R. and his munitions industry associates.

World War I, provided by the Rockefeller-Standard-Oil-British-Royal Dutch feud, made up with action aplenty. When the British capitulated to the Rockefeller-Standard Oil interests in Saudi Arabia and the Near East, we were doomed to enter the war. But the conspirators delayed the declaration until after they had engineered Wilson's reelection on a "keep us out of the war" platform. But they had made sure that their plans would not fail, by putting up an opposition candidate, Charles Evans Hughes, who was equally their agent. In the meantime F. D. R. had strained at the leash, he was so anxious to have his nice little war to play with. He reported, according to the New York Times (April 7, 1937, 20:6) that the Navy had begun extensive purchases of war supplies in 1916.

Franklin D. Roosevelt was 35 years of age and in good physical condition at the outbreak of World War I. But through the same family influence that enabled him to manage to evade the Bar examination requirement for the practise of law, he was able to evade the draft and active military service, by appointment to a swivel chair job as Assistant Secretary of the Navy. In that job he was in a position to help his kin profit enormously from naval construction

The support that F. D. R. had from the behind-the-scene bosses of the Wilson administration is clear from the fact that though he was merely Assistant Secretary, he exercised full and absolute authority and deliberately violated all laws and regulations with perfect assurance and absolute freedom of any checks or restraints. His rampant militarism and wild, unrestrained and profligate spending on munitions must have delighted the hearts of the Dodges and other munitions and armament interests among his backers and the Dynasty.

After the armistice, when plans of naval disarmament and of junking vessels in the service and scrapping many under construction, were under consideration, Franklin Delano Roosevelt continued to demand a greater Navy, more men and more ships "to put the Navy in fighting trim". He demanded a supplemental appropriation of over eighteen million dollars.

Investigation by the House Appropriations Committee subsequently revealed that under Franklin Delano Roosevelt's direction the keels of ninety-six destroyers costing $181,000,000 had been laid after the armistice; and that ten cruisers costing, on a "cost plus" basis, a total of $100,000,000 had been rushed ahead to completion after the armistice. When completed they proved defective or worthless. They were scrapped. The performance was little short of criminal and should have barred F. D. Roosevelt forever from holding public office in the opinion of the investigators.

Newport News Shipbuilding & Drydock Company delivered twenty small destroyers in 1919 and 1920. Business was good.

The next big spurt in Newport News Shipbuilding's naval construction business came in the mid-thirties when Congress authorized President Franklin Delano Roosevelt to spend a small fraction of P.W.A. appropriations on national defense. What money was spared from hoeing leaves was spent on naval construction. Newport News delivered between 1937 and 1939, two aircraft carriers, two light cruisers, and two destroyers, a total of 73,885 tons. During World War II Newport News fared splendidly.

In later days the "Big Three", Newport News, Bethlehem and New York Shipbuilding shared fairly evenly in the contracts so that all the interests got a break. The smaller shipbuilding companies did not fare so well. A representative of the Bath Iron Works testified before a Senate investigating committee that when he sought a Naval contract he was advised to "see" Eleanor Roosevelt's secretary.

John T. Flynn reports in his "Country Squire In The White House" (p. 23) that Franklin Delano Roosevelt boasted before an audience at the Brooklyn Academy of Music about wasting money during the war.

He did not hesitate to undertake huge expenditures even before Congress had made any appropriations. He even then had the contempt of Junker Bismarck for legislatures. "Roosevelt was a devotee to the use of commandeering orders", writes Ernest Lindley, his campaign biographer (Franklin D. Roosevelt, p. 143).

"It is perfectly true that I took the chance of authorizing certain large expenditures before Congress had actually appropriated the money," F. D. R. was forced to confess at a Congressional committee hearing in 1920.

He acknowledged that he had violated enough laws to send him to jail for 999 years. But Dynastic lawbreakers do not go to jail. They become presidents, dictators and kings.

When the Navy adopted oil-burning Diesel engines, and required oil for fuel, the interests of the Dynasty naturally turned to oil. The outcome was the Teapot

Dome scandal—a conspiracy to divert, by corruption of government officials, a large tract of Naval oil reserve land involving the Sinclair and Doheny oil companies, and in the background, the Standard Oil of Indiana, the Midwest Oil Company and others.

Theodore Roosevelt Jr. resigned from his position of director of the Sinclair Refinery Company to become Assistant Secretary of the Navy. At his request Harry F. Sinclair in 1919 gave the position of vice-president to his brother Archibald Roosevelt. Theodore Roosevelt Jr. then arranged to secure the release of oil lands by the Navy to Secretary of the Interior Albert B. Fall for disposal to Sinclair. Roosevelt then arranged to have President Harding sign an executive order drawn up by Secretary Fall giving the land to the Sinclair and Doheny interests.

Subsequent investigation and prosecution revealed that the deal was characterized by bribery and corruption on a large scale. Archibald Roosevelt was assigned the task of carrying a little black bag containing $100,000 in cash to Fall. Secretary Fall received a total bribe of nearly $500,000 of which $100,000 was paid by Doheny, and $230,000 in Liberty bonds and $106,000 in cash, including $35,000 for a trip to Russia to negotiate oil leases by Sinclair. Fall was found guilty of criminal malfeasance and sent to jail in 1931. The Standard Oil of Indiana, through its subsidiary Midwest Oil Company was paid $1,000,000 to relinquish claims to the field.

Rockefeller stood by Col. Stewart, President of the Standard Oil of Indiana in spite of exposure of this corruption. But when investigation revealed in 1928 that Stewart, like the other participants in Continental Trading Company had failed to turn over to their companies a 25¢ commission per barrel on over 33 million barrels of oil purchased for them, Rockefeller was compelled to display indignation on behalf of stockholders. He retired Col. Stewart on a mere $75,000 a year pension. But his sons Robert G. and James Stewart were well cared for in the role of Standard Oil executives. The investigation revealed that Harry Sinclair had boasted that the entire deal was "protected" by the Rockefeller-Standard Oil interests.

The Roosevelts involved in the Teapot Dome deal were shielded and immune from prosecution, as is usual with members of the Dynasty. The incident did make it very clear, however, that they are not in politics for their health. The Dynasty and its Navy interests are distinctly of commercial character. The Dynasty's interests in Rockefeller's Saudi Arabia oil, in the pretended interest of the Navy, will be related later. It was on so far grander a scale that it makes the graft in Teapot Dome look like peanuts.

CHAPTER X

FOLLOWING IN COUSIN TEDDY'S FOOTSTEPS

VICE PRESIDENTIAL CANDIDATE

From the day he had entered the political arena at thirty-one as State Senator, F. D. R. had been invested with the Dynastic leadership of the Hudson Valley Democrats handed down from cousin Martin Van Buren and with the full support of their political, commercial and industrial allies. He was pushed forward on every occasion.

In 1914 the Dynasty placed F. D. R. in the primaries for United States Senator against Murphy's candidate, Wilson's Ambassador to Germany, James W. Gerard. As usual, it was a case of an upstate political machine against a down state political machine.

In June 1918, Charles F. Murphy a henchman of Wilson's and F. D. R.'s sponsors, the Morgan-Ryan-Rockefeller crowd, offered the New York Democratic Gubernatorial nomination to Roosevelt. But the Acting Naval Secretary Roosevelt was enjoying himself too much with his bright new war. He condescendingly replied, according to Lindley, that in his opinion in time of war "when all questions of religion and party association were sunk" Alfred E. Smith would do as a candidate. (Franklin D. Roosevelt, p. 165).

In 1920, however, instead of being imprisoned for the 999 laws which he frankly acknowledged he had broken, for exceeding his authority as Acting Naval Secretary, and for other malfeasance of which he was guilty, Franklin Delano Roosevelt continued to follow in Teddy's footsteps. The Roosevelt-Delano Dynasty thumbed their nose at law, Congress and the nation, and nominated their agent, F. D. R., Democratic vice presidential candidate. The Dynasty had made its peace and merged with the Rockefeller-Standard Oil crowd and the nomination went off without a hitch.

James Cox, the presidential candidate, like Taft and Harding, were all Ohio henchmen of the Rockefeller-Standard Oil Ohio political machine. They selected Cox from the Democratic side of their machine to oppose Harding from its Republican side, in a framed fight. Cox published a chain of newspapers and was an associate of Charles G. Dawes, Comptroller of the Treasury under McKinley, in the Pure Oil Company.

Cox and Roosevelt were both reliable pawns of the bipartisan Rockefeller Empire. But the sanctimonious corruption of Wilson had so far lost popular favor, that it was decided to let the Republican pawns win. This was signalized by an apparent defection of Harvey, the agent of Ryan and the Rockefeller-Morgan group, from the original Wilson backers who were now supporting Cox and Roosevelt. Harvey predicted Harding's victory with his usual precision that derived from the dominant role that he played for the Wall Street crowd in manipulating elections.

In the course of the campaign some newspapers pointed out that the scandalous corruption in Franklin Delano Roosevelt's conduct as Assistant Secretary of the Navy that had been exposed by the Congressional investigating committee and the contemptuous disregard of the law to which he had confessed, should bar him forever from holding public office. Roosevelt bluffed and threatened to bring suit for libel. But he never did sue.

Following his defeat, Roosevelt was given, in January 1921, the job of Vice President in charge of the New York office of the Fidelity and Deposit Company of Maryland by an admirer, Van Lear Black, President of the Company and owner of the Baltimore Sun. He received a salary of $25,000 a year. This was the first salary that he had earned that was in anywise commensurate with his needs for supporting his family and maintaining a scale of living that had been much beyond his income.

Roosevelt devoted only one or two hours, when he was in town, to the Fidelity job. This left him free to exploit his name in many different directions. He was eager for "easy money" and had no scruples whether he worked for it or not, or how he got it. He became a partner in the firm, Emmett, Marvin and Roosevelt in 1921, and in 1924, he formed a law firm with Basil O'Connor as partner. He devoted a little time in the afternoon to his law clients. He took the job of President of the American Construction Council, formed to whitewash the corruption in the building trades that had been exposed recently by a legislative investigation. But the ugliest of his money-making activties were the malodorous stock deals to which he gave his name and in which he participated; and his Georgia Warm Springs business.

However, there were some reports of "irregularities" in his accounts. The money is supposed to have been paid up by subscription among his friends before he was inaugurated as Governor.

CHAPTER XI

INFANTILE PARALYSIS
"MY GEORGIA WARM SPRINGS BUSINESS"

In August 1921, Franklin Delano Roosevelt yachted to his summer home at Campobello, New Brunswick, with his employer Van Lear Black. There he succumbed to a paralyzing illness which had only recently begun to appear on an extensive scale in this country. The disease was called poliomyelitis or infantile paralysis by an orthopedic specialist who was not a specialist on acute infectious diseases.

Many rumors have circulated about the true character of Franklin Delano Roosevelt's illness. The rumors relate that he was delirious for an extended period in the acute stage of the illness. They point out that it left him with mental stigmata that are not characteristic of true poliomyelitis; that his judgement became impaired and he became so highly suggestible that he would agree with everyone and act on the counsel of the last person who advised him; and that he suffered from prolonged and uncontrollable attacks, or fits, of excitement and laughing alternating with depression and crying, that often were brought on by displeasure and stress at being thwarted, and sometimes by pleasure; and were publicly witnessed on a number of occasions.

So persistent were these rumors that Dr. Lindley Rudd Williams, son-in-law of Kidder of the Morgan affiliate, Kidder, Peabody and Company, and director of the Rockefeller subsidized New York Academy of Medicine, was called upon, just prior to the Presidential nomination, in 1932, to write for Collier's Magazine an article vouching for the state of Roosevelt's *physical* and *mental* health.

Roosevelt's condition can be very simply explained. There are two types of "infantile paralysis". There is the type that involves the spinal cord and only the lower, respiratory areas of the brain. That is known as poliomyelitis. This condition had become fairly well-known to the American medical profession after the severe epidemic of 1916.

There is a second type of "infantile paralysis" that was very little known and rarely recognized in 1921. Prior to that time it had begun to appear extensively among animals, especially horses; and to the veterinarians it was known as *equine encephalomyelitis*. In 1932, the first extensive human epidemic of the disease occurred in St. Louis.

The encephalomyelitic form of "infantile paralysis" also causes paralysis involving the spine and the lower centers of the brain. But in addition it involves the upper centers of the brain and generally damages them severely. Sometimes the disease assumes the form of "sleeping sickness". But almost always it leaves mental stigmata in addition to paralysis.

It is reasonably certain that Franklin Delano Roosevelt suffered from an attack of encephalomyelitis that was unrecognized because his was among the earliest group of human cases in this country. The diagnosis serves to explain the stigmata above mentioned. Eleanor Roosevelt and shrewd and loyal Louis Howe, carefully withheld the facts regarding F. D. R.'s true condition for fear that it would interfere with his career, if he recovered.

On his recovery, and his return to business, Franklin Delano Roosevelt became involved in a series of malodorous, messy stock flotations that the S. E. C. would now label highly fraudulent. There was absolutely no need for him to become entangled in such deals because of the many friends, relatives and business associates indebted to him anent war activities. It is obvious that his judgement was far from what it might be and that it was so seriously impaired that he was excessively suggestible and too easily talked into things.

George Foster Peabody, New York confederate of Rockefeller, approached F.D.R. during his recovery, in 1924, with a story of a Georgian, helpless victim of infantile paralysis who had recovered from the paralysis sufficiently to walk, by swimming in a pool at Warm Springs, Georgia. Peabody had bought the Springs and wanted to turn them over to him. Roosevelt visited the Springs and Louis Howe was on the job to see that he got a good press. A syndicated article entitled "Swimming Back to Health" brought Warm Springs into the limelight and kept the spot on F. D. R. The article brought a number of victims of infantile paralysis to the Springs. Roosevelt accepted Warm Springs from Peabody, attracted the attention of the Orthopedic Society, at its convention in Atlanta in 1926, by the device of asking for an investigation; and organized it as a hydrotherapeutic institute under the supervision of Dr. Le Roy W. Hubbard of the New York State Department of Health. In July 1926, at about the time that he invited investigation by the Orthopedic Society, F. D. R. organized in Delaware a business corporation that has been carefully shielded from the public eye, the Georgia Warm Springs Foundation Inc. of Delaware. Title to the property was placed in this holding company. Not even Lindley, Roosevelt's biographer knew about it.

According to Ernest K. Lindley, in his "Franklin D. Roosevelt, A Career in Progressive Democracy," Georgia Warm Springs Foundation was incorporated in the State of New York in January, 1927, to be given title to the Warm Springs property obtained from George Foster Peabody. Lindley does not relate the accurate data contained in the following letter, which has entirely escaped his notice:

Walter Dent Smith
Secretary of State

Dover, Del.
March 6, 1936

Dr. Emanuel M. Josephson
108 East 81st Street
New York City
"Dear Sir:

"Replying to your communication of February 1, kindly be advised the Georgia Warm Springs Foundation, Inc., incorporated under the laws of this State June 29, 1926, changed its name to Meriwether Reserve Inc. by Amendment filed in this Department August 1, 1927.

The annual report filed for the year 1934 shows office at 120 Broadway, New York City, together with the following named officers and directors:

President, Hon. Franklin D. Roosevelt, The White House, Washington, D. C.

Vice President and Assistant Secretary, Raymond H. Taylor, 120 Broadway, New York City.

Secretary-Treasurer, Basil O'Connor, 120 Broadway, New York City.

Assistant Treasurer, Arthur Carpenter, Warm Springs, Ga.

Directors, Hon. Franklin D. Roosevelt, Basil O'Connor, Raymond H. Taylor.

"Delaware corporations are not required to file a list of stockholders in this Department; therefore, we regret to be unable to furnish you with same."

"Yours truly,
"(Signed) Walter Dent Smith,
Secretary of State."

The existence of a holding company, obscure and hidden from public gaze, in the President's widely publicized philanthropy, strikes one with justifiable surprise. For President Roosevelt fought holding corporations of this type with the utmost venom and vigor. If Georgia Warm Springs is a private commercial activity of the President, one would have expected his own pronouncements in the case of Mayor James Walker to impel him to take the public into the secret, rather than to hide it in an obscure Delaware corporation. The generous gifts of the nation, amounting to millions of dollars in the past two decades,

Office of Secretary of State

DOVER, DEL.

March 6, 1936

WALTER DENT SMITH
Secretary of State

Dear Sir:

        Replying to your communication of
February 1, kindly be advised the Georgia Warm Springs
Foundation, Inc., incorporated under the laws of this
State June 29, 1926, changed its name to Meriwether
Reserve, Inc. by Amendment filed in this Department
August 1, 1927.

        The annual report filed for the
year 1934 shows offices at 120 Broadway, New York
City, together with the following named officers
and directors:

President	Hon. Franklin D. Roosevelt	The White House Washington, D. C.
Vice-Pres.) Asst. Secy)	Raymond H. Taylor	120 Broadway, N.Y.
Secretary)	Basil O'Connor	•
Treasurer)		
Asst. Treas.	Arthur Carpenter	Warm Springs, Ga.
Directors	Hon. Franklin D. Roosevelt Basil O'Connor Raymond H. Taylor	

        Delaware corporations are not required
to file a list of stockholders in this Department; therefore,
we regret to be unable to furnish you with same.

        Yours truly,

        Secretary of State

SW

THE STORY OF MERIWETHER RESERVE, INC. (DELAWARE)

Mr. Walter Dent Smith, Secretary of State of Delaware, gives facts regarding Meriwether Reserve, Inc. listed with his office. The "representative citizens", later classed as "malefactors of great wealth", whose names are found on the board of Georgia Warm Springs Foundation, Inc. and who contributed heavily to its support, are strangely missing in Meriwether Reserve, Inc.

should have compelled a frank publication of the accounts of this "holding company." But an inquiry directed to the Treasurer of the Foundation, Basil O'Connor, law partner of the President, elicited the following reply:

GEORGIA WARM SPRINGS FOUNDATION, INC.
120 Broadway
New York

President
Hon. Franklin D. Roosevelt
Treasurer
Basil O'Connor

July 1st, 1935

Dear Sir:
No annual reports have been issued by Georgia Warm Springs Foundation, Inc.
MERIWETHER RESERVE, INC., (DELAWARE) HOLDS TITLE TO THE PROPERTY.

Very truly yours,
(Signed) Basil O'Connor
Treasurer

The source of the half million dollars required for purchasing the surrounding property and the initial development of the Springs was kept a secret even from Lindley. He stated that "where this money came from has always been a mystery." (ibid p. 211). The names of only two of the donors were released, because they had no political implications. Henry Pope of Chicago gave twenty thousand dollars, and Frank C. Root of Greenwich, Connecticut. an unspecified sum. It may be reasonably inferred that the Rockefeller-Morgan-Ryan-Dodge group were as generous in their donations to Roosevelt's venture as they were to his campaign funds. They had spent considerable time and funds in grooming the heir-apparent of the Dynasty as their tool. His illness made him potentially even more valuable for the role for which he was being groomed. But his identification with their interests by publishing their names and contributions would be politically bad.

Mr. and Mrs. Edsel Ford, Lindley relates, contributed the money to build a glass-enclosed pool; and other gifts were received for specific purposes. The literature of the Foundation states vaguely:

"The funds required by the initial capital investments were subscribed by the Governor and a group of his friends"*.

July 1st, 1936.

Dear Sir:

No annual reports have been issued by Georgia

Warm Springs Foundation, Inc.

Meriwether Reserve, Inc., (Delaware) holds

title to the property.

Very truly yours,

Basil O'Connor

Treasurer.

**MERIWETHER RESERVE, INC. (DELAWARE) HOLDS TITLE TO GEORGIA
WARM SPRINGS FOUNDATION, INC. (N. Y.)**

This letter from the treasurer of the Foundation, Mr. Basil O'Connor, President Roosevelt's law partner, leaves no doubt as to the ownership of Georgia Warm Springs.

By 1927 Roosevelt and the Dynasty felt that his build-up had been sufficient to insure victory at the polls; and the Rockefeller-Morgan crowd felt that their plans would soon call for a change in political party on the national scene, just as had been done in 1920 to appease popular clamor, and decided to take their synthetic "statesman" out of mothballs. That he was directed no longer to refuse political office is indicated by the sudden change of name of the Georgia Warm Springs Foundation, Inc. of Delaware, the business corporation, on August 1, 1927, to Meriwether Reserve Inc.

To be sure, in the following year, Smith, Lehman, Raskob, and others at Albany, made a great show of extending the nomination to F. D. R. across the country at Georgia Warm Springs. Roosevelt made the grand-stand Caesarian play of thrice rejecting it with truly royal disdain. Louis Howe saw to it that the press was at hand and ate it up. The entire country was being held in suspense.

" . . . he put it by thrice, every time gentler than the other; and at every putting-by mine honest neighbors shouted." (Julius Caesar, Act 1, Sc. II.)

Julius Caesar and his "falling sickness" were child's play as compared with this scene for rousing public sympathy. Far indeed has the art of perverting public opinion progressed.

Finally Roosevelt who never missed a chance to turn an easy penny, interposed what he pretended was his main "objection" to accepting the nomination:

" . . . my Georgia Warm Springs business."

Raskob is reported to have shouted impatiently, "Damn Georgia Warm Springs, we'll take care of it."

Undeniably this enterprise was well taken care of. Franklin Delano Roosevelt was magnificently bribed to run for office. By the end of 1930 some seven hundred thousand dollars had been poured into the coffers of the Foundation. It is reported that Raskob contributed a quarter of a million dollars with a proviso regarding the nomination of Al Smith in 1932. A Board of Trustees was set up which read much like the board of directors of the enterprises identified with the Morgan, Rockefeller, Chase National and National City Bank groups. They were:

James A. Moffett, Vice President of the Standard Oil of New Jersey. He was rewarded among others

with an oppointment as housing czar under the New
Deal; and was able to secure for his Rockefeller-
Standard Oil employers from the Government, a thirty
million dollar appropriation of American taxpayers'
money to be paid by the British Government to the
King of Saudi Arabia to avoid the cancellation of the
concession, in Saudi Arabia, of the Standard Oil of
California and Texas Companies, and hundreds of millions more to maintain the Rockefeller-Standard Oil
crowd in the good graces of the King, Ibn Saud. Recently Moffett sued the companies for $8,000,000, the
price he alleges they agreed to pay him for his influence with Roosevelt and the New Deal in the successful raid on the U. S. Treasury. If he collects the eight
million dollars he will be amply repaid for his dona-
tion to Georgia Warm Springs. He was also instrumen-
tol, on behalf of the Rockefeller-Standard Oil interests, in bringing Roosevelt's innate duplicity into play
in promising Palestine to both the Jews and the Arabs,
to hold the loyalty and cooperation of both.

Jeremiah Milbank, Director of the Rockefeller- controlled Chase National Bank and Metropolitan Life
Insurance Company. His family are heavily interested
in the Borden Company and operate it for the controlling Chase National Bank-Rockefeller interests.
A. G. Milbank is President and Chairman of the Board
of Borden. His $55,000 gift, or bribe, to Roosevelt
through Georgia Warm Springs-Meriwether Reserve
brought magnificent returns. Shortly after its receipt,
Governor Roosevelt secured the passage by the New
York State Legislation of favorable milk laws that increased the price of milk from 5¢ to a minimum of
twenty-two cents a quart and put billions of dollars
into the coffers of the Rockefeller-controlled Milk Trust.

But that was only the beginning of the story of
what Jeremiah Milbank got for his $55,000 "contribu-
tion". He is the familiar brand of "philanthropist"
who insists upon having his odds very long. For example in 1928 he contributed $10,000 to the Republi-
can Campaign fund, Vice President Garner revealed
that this was followed by the following tax refunds:

"Jeremiah Milbank, New York, Director Chase
National Bank, refunded $41,239 in 1928; Direc-
tor Metropolitan Life Insurance Company, $32,-
102 in 1929, and $77,848 in 1930; son of Joseph
Milbank whose estate was granted a refund of
$46,344 in 1929."

Eugene F. Wilson, Vice President of the Rockefeller-Morgan controlled American Telephone and Telegraph Company. His company was munificently rewarded by the New Deal. Despite the attack on utilities and holding companies by Roosevelt and the New Deal, the A. T. & T., the greatest utility monopoly was never molested. The sham investigation, launched against it to quiet public outcry against its outrageous staggering of rates even during the depression, was conducted by the Telephone Company's own loyal employees. And when unfavorable evidence got into the records, they were destroyed by a mysterious fire and the investigation was hurriedly dropped. Under the New Deal the monopoly of the A.T. & T., instead of being broken down, had been greatly intensified. Even the use of radio-telephone that served so well in the war, is, by absurd licensing requirements, barred to the public except through payment of exorbitant tribute to the Telephone Company.

William H. Woodin, President of the American Car and Foundry Company; Director of General Motors; Member of the Executive Committee and Director of the American Ship and Commerce Company; and Director of Remington Arms Company. He was a J. P. Morgan and Co. henchman who stood high on their preferred list. He received the appointment of Secretary of the Treasury.

Leighton McCarthy, President of Canadian Life Insurance Company, Vice President and Director of Union Carbide Co. and of the Bank of Nova Scotia; and Director of Aluminum Ltd.

George Foster Peabody, President of Broadway Realty Co. and close associate of John D. Rockefeller, who participated with them in the foundation of the General Education Fund and other purposeful "philanthropies", of which this is a sample.

Frank C. Root.

There can be no question that Roosevelt paid his debts handsomely, — *with the taxpayers' money and when required, with their lives and the security of the nation.* This makes it hard to draw the line as in so many other similar situations involving the Roosevelt-Delano Dynasty, between "contribution" and plain bribery and corruption.

It is interesting to note that none of these generous trustees are to be found on the Board of Directors of Meriwether Reserve Inc. So far as has been determined, Meriwether Reserve is owned outright by FDR and his family. The land adjacent to the Springs, which normally sold at ten to twenty dollars an acre, was sold to families of the victims who wished to live near them at $500 a lot, in the name of Sara Delano Roosevelt, the supposed owner and mortgagor.

In 1931 and 1932 Governor Roosevelt engineered important changes in the milk industry, that were highly profitable to Milbank's Borden Company. The sale of synthetic milk, labelled "homogenized" and sold at higher prices, previously had been barred, as adulterated and inferior. It was now permitted. Likewise adulteration of milk with alkalinizers, in violation of the Pure Food and Drug Act, and the misrepresentation of pasteurized milk, as absolutely safe, was given the official stamp of approval.

By curious coincidence, in the self-same year which witnessed the momentous changes in the milk industry which added billions of dollars to the milk bill of the public and by the same amount enlarged the take of what Wallace termed the "Milk Trust", Governor Roosevelt's Warm Springs Foundation, received an additional grant of $5,000 from the Milbank Memorial Fund, the income of which is derived from the stock of one of the components of the "Milk Trust", Milbank's Borden Company.

To collect funds for President Roosevelt's "philanthropy", there were organized the "President's Birthday Balls". The moving spirit behind their origin was the notorious Cities Service utility magnate, Henry L. Doherty, whose dishonest manipulations cost the investing public hundreds of millions of dollars. He shuddered at the fate of Insull and the rest of the utility crowd who were not in Roosevelt's favor. Shying at attempting direct bribery, he turned for advice to his publicity man, Carl Byoir, who enjoyed the strategic position of also representing Roosevelt's Georgia Warm Springs. The outcome was the Birthday Balls which netted Roosevelt's "philanthropy" millions. Doherty calculated well. He was never harassed or prosecuted by Roosevelt's New Deal in spite of the flagrant character of his activities. The Birthday Balls had worked as a "pay-off".

For years, physicians throughout the nation bombarded the Foundation with applications to secure free admission of poor victims of infantile paralysis to Georgia Warm Springs. Though millions of dollars had been contributed by the nation for this purpose, applications for free services were made without success, except in rare cases. In the years 1933 to 1935, the physicians were flatly told by the Foundation that it did not welcome charity patients, except under very special circumstances.

Such special circumstanes appear to have been primarily publicity value. A paralyzed newspaperman sponsored by the Hearst newspaper chain closely identified at the time with the President was one such case accepted gratis. Poor patients for whom communities gathered funds and paid the charges were accepted. To be sure, amid clicking cameras and nation-wide publicity, Mrs. Eleanor Roosevelt, with great ostentation, turned over to a poor victim of the disease the thousand dollar prize awarded her by Gimbel & Company *for the specific purpose that it be spent at Georgia Warm Springs.* It looked much like taking money out of one pocket and putting it into another.

When favorable publicity was not involved, however, the physician was informed that the basic rate for stay at Warm Springs was about forty-five dollars a week, with various charges for extras. This charge is made in a section of the country where the cost of living is so low that the average Relief allowance a week for a family of six was two to three dollars. If the physician made so bold as to inquire what was being done with the millions gathered for the treatment of poor folks at the Springs, he was belatedly informed that in very special cases the basic charge would be reduced fifty percent.

With election in sight, and with an eye to an undercurrent of unfavorable comment on the activities of the Foundation and due to quiet but persistent investigation by interested parties, the tactics of the Foundation were changed. After the "Birthday Balls," a pretense of an accounting was made in the press. It related that part of the fund gathered from the parties was left with the local committee to pay expenses and to provide for local infantile paralysis work; and that a small fraction of the sum turned over to the President's Foundation had been paid out to specific institutions and investigators for research work on the disease.

A written request was made by me to the Foundation in April 1936, asking that two poor patients, who could manage to raise only enough money to pay their train fares to the Springs, be admitted for treatment of paralysis. It elicited the following reply:

THE GEORGIA WARM SPRINGS FOUNDATION
50 East 42nd Street
New York City

Franklin D. Roosevelt,
President

Keith Morgan,
Vice-President

Basil O'Connor, Treasurer

April 29, 1936

Emanuel M. Josephson, M. D.
108 East 81st Street
New York, N. Y.

My dear Dr. Josephson:

Your letter of April 28th has been received during the absence of Doctor LeRoy W. Hubbard, who is Director of Extension. Immediately upon his return, in about ten days, it shall be brought to his attention."

Very truly yours,
(Signed) Katherine Woods

On the specified date Dr. Hubbard communicated with me by telephone and explained that the capacity of Warm Springs is limited, and that only a few charity patients are taken. He offered the suggestion that the Springs therapy is not recommended for all victims of the disease. After inquiring the age of the patients, he definitely eliminated the school child, because he said the Springs were not advisable for younger children unless accompanied by nurse and governess.

He suggested that they might consider the admission of the adolescent victim, provided that after an examination by himself he felt that the patient might be benefited by the Springs. There was a change of tone and attitude as compared with previous communications; straightforward rejection of the charity patient was replaced by qualified evasion, which offers less startling contrast with the objects for which the public have been led to contribute to the institution.

My curiosity in the matter was aroused by my experience and information. I addressed the following letter to President Roosevelt:

May 27, 1936.

Hon. Franklin D. Roosevelt, President
Meriwether Reserve, Inc.,
White House,
Washington, D. D.

Dear Sir:

In the course of a study of various types of social

service and philanthropic organizations, and of their financial structure, for a volume which I am writing on the subject, I have come across the data relating to Georgia Warm Springs Foundation of New York and the Meriwether Reserve Inc. of Delaware, concerning which I ask your help and explanation.

In reply to an inquiry, Mr. Basil O'Connor, Treasurer of the Foundation, has informed me that the Foundation has issued no financial reports, and that its property is held by the Meriwether Reserve Inc. of Delaware, a business corporation.

The Secretary of State of Delaware informs me, on the other hand, that the Meriwether Reserve Inc. files no financial reports or list of stockholders.

1. Where may I secure financial statements, lists of contributions, and stockholders' lists of the Meriwether Reserve, Inc. for the years since 1926, when it was organized as the Georgia Warm Springs Inc., Delaware, until the end of the last fiscal year?

2. What is the exact relation between the Meriwether Reserve Inc and Georgia Warm Springs Foundation of New York, and what is the objective and function of the two different organizations incorporated in different states?

3. As a business organization so incorporated, does the Meriwether Reserve Inc. pay dividends on its stock?

4. If so, what have the dividend rates been since the date of organization?

5. In what manner does this dual structure affect the handling of charitable cases, and what percentage of the cases are free and charitable, part pay, and full pay?

I would highly appreciate an early reply to these questions, for the survey must go to press in the near future.

Very truly yours,
(Signed) Emanuel M. Josephson

This letter elicited several telephone inquiries from agents of the Meriwether Reserve Inc. about the source of my information. The inquiring agent assured me that I would receive a prompt reply. No reply has ever been received before or since the publication of the study.

Before the Birthday Balls of January 1938, there was announced a "reorganization of the philanthropy."

There was formed a new foundation, the National Foundation for Infantile Paralysis. The public was high-pressured by such a foundation propagandist as the avowed left-winger, Paul de Kruif, into contributing to this new Foundation. Keith Morgan, vice-president of the Foundation, took over the publicity and management of the campaign, and even larger sums of money were mulcted from the public. Dr. Joseph S. Wall, professor of diseases of children of Georgetown University Medical School, stated before the Subcommittee on Public Health, Hospitals and Charities of D. C. on January 7, 1938, that the money for the Foundation derived from the Birthday Balls would be devoted to animal research. "Not a penny of that fund will go to buying a crutch for a crippled child. The majority of the dollars in that fund will go for the purchase of monkeys," he testified.

About one month after the January 1938 Birthday Balls of the reorganized Foundation, a naive, pathetic letter by Mrs. Martha Hickok appeared in the Miami *Daily News*. She related the experience of her mother in her persistent attempts for six years to gain free admission of her child, a victim of infantile paralysis, to Georgia Warm Springs.

The application was repeatedly rejected by the "board of advisers" though Dr. Hoke considerately assured the mother that the child's dependence on crutches could be eliminated in two years at the Foundation. He offered as an explanation for the child's rejection the information that the Foundation limited its charity cases to a ratio of ten charity cases for every ninety full pay cases, the writer stated.

Mrs. Hickok related that not even the intercession of her postmaster or of Postmaster General Farley helped. She stated that she had a large collection of correspondence from the Foundation extending over a period of six years which showed she believed, that unless one had loads of money Georgia Warm Springs is just a crippled child's dream of paradise. She stated that her motive in writing was to correct the false impression that the Warm Springs Foundation is open and available to any infantile paralysis sufferer who admittedly might be helped.

A million or more dollars was raised by the 1938 Birthday Ball and by subscriptions for the National Foundation for Infantile Paralysis. The active principals of that Foundation nevertheless participated in introducing legislation at Albany in March 1938 which provided free medical care by the State or City of New York for the victims of infantile paralysis.

Accounts of some of the money collected for the Foundation were published in December 1939. But they were very loose and failed to account for much of the money that has been taken in. They showed, however, that at least some of the money collected for the relief of infantile paralysis victims may be used for that purpose.

There is much additional evidence on hand that Roosevelt cared as little for the victims of infantile paralysis as he cared for the interests of the nation at large, except where political and financial advantages accrued. Most flagrant was the death of scores of humans resulting from the administration of the so-called "immune serum" in the treatment of the cases suspected of having infantile paralysis during the epidemic of 1931. This was a case of deliberate risk and sacrifice of human life by experimentation, engaged in by a Committee of the New York Academy of Medicine which was headed by the late Dr. Linsley R. Williams, whose position interlocked Organized Medicine and Social Service. Dr. Williams also was mentioned as the prospective incumbent of the post of Secretary of Health which it was reported was to be created for him on the Cabinet of President Roosevelt, after he had written an article, published in *Collier's* magazine, certifying that Governor Franklin D. Roosevelt was physically and mentally fit for the Presidency of the United States.

The sale of the fake cure and the attendant publicity were designed to build up Dr. Linsley Williams as a national figure and to publicize the Medical-Social-Service Trust which he dominated, as a prelude to his expected political advancement and as a prelude to turning over the control of medicine, under national legislation, to the Trust. The infantile paralysis epidemic was used also as a pretext for raising the price of milk to the poor of New York City in the midst of the depression to a higher figure than prevailed in time of prosperity, by the elimination of loose milk. The Milbank Memorial Fund and the Rockefeller Institute played dominant roles in both campaigns.

In this exploit, the Medical-Social-Service Trust, under Dr. Williams, was up to one of its old tricks—stealing the stale thunder of medical experimenters as a pretext for a wild burst of quackish publicity. The "immune serum" was known to be worthless and dangerous long before the human experiment was started. Within two weeks before the date when it was advertised and publicized as a "cure" for infantile paralysis, the National Health Institute of the United States Health Public Service reported on a series of cautious experiments and studies made with it on monkeys over a period of three years. The Institute reported that the serum was both worthless and dangerous when used in many of the manners suggested.

The serum goes back to the days of the French investigator, Levaditi, who discovered in 1911 that the virus contained in nasal drippings of victims of the disease, which would cause infantile paralysis when injected into the nervous system of monkeys, could be neutralized and made harmless by the blood of adults or of persons who had had infantile paralysis, when the two were mixed in a test tube. In the New York City epidemic of 1916, Dr. Herman Schwartz had tried out such a serum on a group of his patients. He reported that he found it not only worthless but actually injurious and deadly when used in certain manners.

The best informed authorities on the subject including Dr. Josephine Neal and Dr. William Parks of the New York City Health Department Research Laboratories, both of whom were members of the Committee, constituting a minority, had unequivocally condemned the serum on the basis of accumulated data. They pronounced it to be of questionable value and actually injurious when used in certain manners. As early as 1929, Dr. Josephine Neal had pointed out in her publications the danger of the use of the serum in poliomyelitis, and had condemned it in no uncertain terms. All the cumulative evidence pointed to the fact that this supposed "cure" exploited by the Academy was both worthless and injurious.

Dr. Williams, himself, characterized the use of this serum at a hearing, of the Board of Censors of the New York County Medical Society of March 11, 1932, as a "clinical study," or experiment on humans, undertaken by the Committee to prove or disprove the value, or lack of value of the serum. Dr Williams stated at the hearing,

"This study was made, really, upon the recommendation of Dr. Simon Flexner and Dr. George Draper.

Dr. Flexner and Dr. Draper were particularly interested and also was Dr. Amoss and Dr. Aycock. Dr. Neal did a great deal of work on this subject some eight or nine years ago in the 1918 epidemic, and I think she has always had the feeling that this serum was of very doubtful value."

In other words, Dr. Williams placed the responsibility for this disastrous experiment squarely on the Rockefeller Institute, of which he was a director, and on its staff.

At a discussion before the Society of Medical Jurisprudence on October 12, 1931, Dr. Josephine Neal said:

"I have always opposed the use of serum intraspinally on account of the consequent meningeal irritation that so *often* follows . . . *sometimes with disastrous results.*"

Dr. Sobel, an eminent pediatrician, confirmed Dr. Neal's statement in the following words:

"If the truth were told about the use of the serum intraspinally I am afraid that some sad stories would come out. I have some good reason to believe that several deaths have occurred as a result of its use in this way, and while names such as status thymolymphaticus have been used for the cause of death, it has been more directly attributable to meningeal irritation than anything else."

The concurring statement of Dr. Neal and Sobel make it clear that it is widely known in the medical profession that it is a common expedient of the Medical-Service Trust in its exploitation of public health to falsify records to make them show results desired by them. In this manner they often hide from the public the sacrifice of human life that results from their activities.

In spite of its worthlessness and its known danger, the Committee on Poliomyelitis of the New York Academy of Medicine undertook to experiment on humans with this "cure" in manners that were known to be most dangerous, including injection into the spine. It solicited the serum from former victims of the disease among the public, most of whom contributed their blood free of charge. Governor Roosevelt contributed 500 c.c. of serum. In the role of an "authority" on the subject, he wrongly informed the public that doctors who would not use the "cure" were ignorant and not to be trusted. This statement proved as true and reliable as have many of his other statements on the subject of health, medicine and other topics.

The Academy then sold this serum to the public through its agents, young and inexperienced physicians, for as much as the traffic would bear, usually twenty-five dollars a dose. In violation of the municipal law of New York City, even charity patients in municipal hospitals were compelled to pay a minimum price of twenty-five dollars for this supposed cure; and were led to believe that failure to use it meant death or worse.

The outcome of this experiment was exactly what might have been expected on the basis of accumulated data, highly disastrous. The published report of the Committee stated that the serum had been used only in cases which had developed no paralysis. This meant that many of those cases did not have infantile paralysis to begin with; for there is no positive method of diagnosis of the disease until paralysis develops. The death rate, however, among the group treated with the serum was considerably higher than among the proved victims of infantile paralysis. The incidence of paralysis among the former was also higher than among those not treated with the "cure."

The case of Marvin Zanger illustrates the danger of the serum. The story is best told in a letter which his mother wrote me.

November 28, 1931.

Dr. E. M. Josephson
Dear Sir:

Read your statement in the papers of a week ago pertaining to the serum which was used during the epidemic. May I state my case, please.

On August 19, my boy, nine and a half years old, became ill . . . We took him to the Morrisania Hospital at 168th Street and Walton Avenue, The Bronx. While admitting my child who was so, so very ill, I was told that it was necessary to use serum and it would cost twenty-five dollars. I'm an American woman, and had been reading the paper, but had never noticed a fee for serum mentioned. I spoke of this to one of the doctors and he informed me there was a charge for it at all times. Of course, being a mother and so frightened, I borrowed the twenty-five dollars to pay for it. I sat with my dear child for three hours before Dr. . . . [an agent of the New York Academy of Medicine] came . . .

My child died anyway. I have not been able to write you before this, as my heart is broken. But in order to help others who may not be able to borrow as I did, and to help you who are brave and big enough to come forward [I write].

Mrs. Diana Zanger
1925 Gerard Avenue

The circumstances and the records of the case left little room for doubt that the death was directly due to the irritation of the serum and its mode of administration.

Another equally tragic case was related by another mother who wrote to Mrs. Zanger:

"Several weeks ago, I read in the New York *American* about your suit against the New York Academy of Medicine for the loss of your child from infantile paralysis.

"Your sufferings find an echo in my heart, for I am also an unfortunate mother who lost a four-year-old son. I have a daughter aged twenty, in the hospital, who is a sufferer from the same dreadful scourge.

"My boy was running around well in the hospital until the serum was administered. He died within five days.

"My daughter was paralyzed following the serum. She is in the hospital for the past seven months. God, if I could only lose my memory completely!"

The suit brought by Mrs. Zanger for the death of her child was settled by the parties out of court.

To stop the sale of this quack cure, I filed charges with Governor F. D. Roosevelt against the Academy and its Committee, accusing them of sacrificing human lives in what they chose to call an "experiment." The Academy pleaded "charity" in defense and extenuation of its acts but stopped the sale of the serum. The fate of these charges reveals in its full extent the sincerity of Roosevelt's "humanitarianism."

My indictment of Dr. Williams, and of the Academy Committee and their serum was embarrassing to Governor Roosevelt for several reasons. First, Dr. Williams was a personal friend and an important political ally. Second, his Georgia Warm Springs enterprise had been widely publicized as supplying some of the serum used for the "cure." Third, Roosevelt and his campaign managers had used the serum as the basis of large number of "human interest" press releases, and his campaign had played up his "humanitarianism" thus manifested.

STATE OF NEW YORK
EXECUTIVE CHAMBER
ALBANY

FRANKLIN D. ROOSEVELT
GOVERNOR

February 15, 1932

Dr. E. M. Josephson,
993 Park Avenue,
New York City.

My dear Dr. Josephson:

I have read very carefully the
latest charges which you have submitted
to me under date of January 30, 1932. I
have also read the several previous communications you addressed to me and to the State
Health Commissioner, Dr. Thomas Parran, Jr.

I have been fully informed concerning the activities of the State Department of Health in its splendid efforts to
minimize the effects of the poliomyelitis
epidemic and to limit the spread of this
disease, for which I requested a special
appropriation from the Legislature and received their approval.

The charges you make are not
substantiated by facts, and are therefore
dismissed.

Very sincerely yours.

Franklin D. Roosevelt

This letter was received in reply to my protest against State Commissioner of Health
Dr. Thomas Parran's dismissal of my charges branding the infantile paralysis "curative"
serum a worthless and dangerous quack remedy, the use of which resulted in many deaths.
This letter constituted in substance an affirmation of the value of the serum. It is dated
months later than the report of the Poliomyelitis Committee which fully supported my
charges. Dr. Parran has risen to greater heights of authority and power since this incident,
on appointment by President Roosevelt. The use of the serum has been abandoned.

For obvious political reasons, the Governor failed to act on the charges himself. He passed the buck to New York State Commissioner of Health, Thomas Parran, later Surgeon General of U. S. Public Health Service. Dr. Parran owed his appointment as Commissioner to Dr. Linsley R. Williams and had himself actively advocated the use of this infantile paralysis "cure."

As might have been expected, Dr. Parran refused to hold hearings on the charges. Several months after they had been filed with him, Parran brushed aside my charges in a letter released to the press, in which he stated that he himself was involved in the charges, consequently they could not be true. Dr. Parran's denial of the truth of the charges followed closely upon the tacit acknowledgment of the Committee in its own report that my charges were absolutely true.

Commissioner Parran recommended, furthermore, that my zeal in protecting the health of the public and in preventing human sacrifice should be rebuked. He recommended that I be censured for my efforts.

I protested in vain to Governor Roosevelt against this formerly un-American procedure of permitting a man accused of a crime, and confessedly guilty, to be his own judge. The Governor replied affirming, in substance, the value of the "cure," directly contradicting the report already rendered by the Committee.

The trail of deaths arising from human experiments with infantile paralysis did not terminate with the tragedies of the "curative" serum. On the contrary, the protection offered to human experimenters by government authorities and the powers of State Medicine, constituted by the Health Departments and their Commissioners, seconded by the great influence of the interested social service rackets, encouraged further human experimentation.

Financed in part by a small grant from the moneys collected through the "President's Birthday Balls," Dr. John A. Kolmer of Temple University, Philadelphia, undertook to infect a group of children with infantile paralysis virus that was supposedly attenuated by treatment with sodium ricinoleate, a soap made from castor oil. On October 8, 1935, Dr . T. M. Rivers of the Rockefeller Institute, reported the results at a meeting of the American Public Health Association. Dr. Rivers' announcement read as follows:

"Only *eight* out of twelve thousand children who

were injected (with the infective material) developed the disease."

In defense of this situation, Dr. Rivers offered the
"In the case of the eight children, *it is probable* that they had incurred the malady before they had been injected."

It is also possible, nay probable, that the infections and deaths were caused by the injected virus.

These deaths illustrate the menace of authoritarian, irresponsible State Medicine to the health and life of the public. They should be a warning to repudiate the various compulsory health insurance schemes which the self-same group as were responsible for these killings are now seeking to foist upon the public.

In 1943, in response to the pressure of an aroused public opinion which demanded a truthful statement of the uses made of the moneys raised for Georgia Warm Springs, a report was issued by the Foundation. No mention was made in the report of the huge individual donations that had been subscribed initially by the Moffetts, the Milbanks and others; or of Meriwether Reserve Inc. of Delaware, its resources or its connection with the Foundation or the uses that it made of the moneys that had been diverted to it; or of how much of the funds raised by the public goes to help the 63% of the victims which it classes as "aid", in contrast to the fully and exorbitantly charged "pay" victims; or if any of the victims are really full charity cases or if a large income is required to supplement the help given the "aid" cases; or if discrimination against colored victims despite acceptance of contributions from colored folks, will ever be eliminated in the institution controlled by a family who have given so much lip service to the colored cause.

There is no record that any colored victim of infantile paralysis has ever been admitted to Georgia Warm Springs. It is a case of "Do as I say, not as I do."

Dr. Haven Emerson, Emeritus Professor of Public Health Administration at Columbia University condemned the racket that has been built up about Georgia Warm Springs in no uncertain terms, in giving the annual Cutter Lecture at the Harvard University Medical School November 28, 1947. He stated:

"There is no more pitiful picture of the importance and ineptitude of popular enthusiasm about widely publicized disease than the *fantastic promotion of un-*

profitable measures financed with reckless extravagance for the control of poliomyelitis.

"These manifestations of newspaper or public relations experts *concerned with dime collections on a percentage basis* makes monkeys of honest health officers while hysterical warnings and inflated news items inflame local fears of a disease *which no health officer has yet said with honesty that he has modified as to prevalence or fatality.*"

The last statement is of exceptional interest because Dr. Emerson was himself a member of the New York Academy of Medicine Poliomyelitis Committee that sold the phony serum "cure" in 1931. He confirms the charges which I made against the Committee to Governor F. D. Roosevelt and which quack "Dr." Roosevelt denied, in company with his distinguished Commissioner of Health, later Surgeon General of the U. S. Public Health Service, and Trustee of the Rockefeller Foundation, *Dr.* Thomas Parran.

"Voluntary agencies", Dr. Emerson continued, "rising high on the emotional appeal of the dramatic deformities and sudden deaths from infantile paralysis so mask the truth and exploit the seasonally recurrent prevalence of this disease that rational education of the public *as to the state of our ignorance of effective measures* is almost unheard amid the din of personalities.

"The health officer is humiliated and his prestige is lowered before the public when daily bulletins come to the press from the hirelings of philanthropy instead of from the responsible officers of the United States Public Health Services, which is (Ed. this unfortunately is not true because of the calibre and allegiance of some of its Surgeon Generals) the only trustworthy source of reliable information of any of such epidemic disease and its national aspect."

Though there appears an element of professional jealousy in Dr. Emerson's statements, there emerges a picture of the enormous commercial and political pressure that was brought to bear on him, and other honest health officers, to have compelled him before his retirement to support such frauds as the New York Academy of Medicine's "immune serum", Georgia Warm Springs, and other equally creditable "philanthropies" that have been wrought by Bismarck's imitators as political devices.

The use of foundations and other pseudo-philanthropies for commercial and political purposes is quite commonplace. The "non-profit" corporation is the only type that can be readily chartered in New York State for medical and social service purposes, and have the advantage of being tax exempt. Many of them have proved extraordinarily profitable to their operators. No clear statements have ever been issued by Georgia Warm Springs Foundation, and no statements have been issued by Meriwether Reserve to indicate what profit, if any accrued to Franklin Delano Roosevelt or his family from them, in addition to the publicity and political advantage. But the Dynasty members are far too practical to go into any venture solely for their health or for principle.

The picture presented by Roosevelt's infantile paralysis activities does not bespeak integrity or even humanitarianism. It confirms the picture presented by so many of his activities, cupidity, corruption, low cunning and duplicity.

CHAPTER XII

FRANKLIN DELANO ROOSEVELT
HIGH FINANCIER

Franklin Delano Roosevelt, as poor relation of some of the wealthiest clans in the world, could have become identified through them with some of the leading enterprises in the country. But the mental aberration and lack of judgement, that made it impossible for him to attain a passing grade in his law studies and to graduate, was aggravated by the after-effects of the attack of encephalomyelitis that intensified his high suggestibility. This led to his being used in a number of off-color stock jobbing deals that rooked the investing public. It is questionable whether any one man was more consistently identified during the prosperous 1920's with enterprises that trimmed the investors than "high financier" Franklin Delano Roosevelt. His record was consistently putrid.

It is more or less consistent with his admiration of things German, with which he was imbued in his childhood, that three of the four stock flotations with which he was identified related to Germany. The fourth re-

NEW ISSUE

600,000,000 German Marks

Divided into 60,000 Common Shares, par value 10,000 Marks each
Application will be made to increase the Common Share Capital of this company.

UNITED EUROPEAN INVESTORS, LIMITED

(Incorporated under Charter of the Dominion of Canada)

PRESIDENT
Hon. Franklin D. Roosevelt
Vice-President, Fidelity & Deposit Co. of Maryland

VICE-PRESIDENT & CHAIRMAN EXECUTIVE COMMITTEE
William Schall
William Schall & Co., Bankers, New York

TREASURER August Scherer 45 William St., New York	**SECRETARY** A. R. Roberts 7 Pine Street, New York

DIRECTORS

William Schall	Hon. Franklin D. Roosevelt Almet F. Jenks, New York	Andrew Haydon, Ottawa, Canada

ADVISORY BOARD IN GERMANY
Senator August Lattmann
Former partner, G. Amsinck & Co., New York

Senator John von Berenberg Gossler Partner, John von Berenberg Gossler & Co., Hamburg	Alfred Arnthal Hamburg

BANKERS AND DEPOSITORS
William Schall & Co., New York

Deutsche Bank, Hamburg	Norddeutsche Bank, Hamburg

TRANSFER AGENTS
The Bank of America, New York

The purpose of this company is to exchange its shares for German marks held by American investors, and to invest these marks in actual values in Germany. Carefully selected investments will be made in real estate, mortgages, securities and participation in Industrial and Commercial enterprises.

The company's facilities and connections enable it to secure attractive and sound investments; the directors will take advantage of the present money stringency in Germany and of the purchasing power of the mark, which is far greater than is reflected by exchange quotations.

Mr. William Schall, Chairman of the Executive Committee, was sent to Germany by the company on a special mission to make a careful survey of German economic conditions. Mr. Schall conferred with the leading German financial authorities, and with their assistance selected the German Advisory Committee.

We summarize as follows the correspondence received recently from Mr. Schall:

> "Since arriving in Germany on July 13, 1922, I have been in frequent conference with leaders in Banking, Industrial and Commercial circles.
>
> I find that the purposes of your Company meet with general approval here and are deemed financially and economically sound. . . . .
>
> There is a great stringency of money and credit in Germany at present; and sound and attractive investments can be secured for marks at prices which should ensure profitable returns coupled with safety of principal.
>
> We are fortunate in having secured the services of men composing our German Advisory Committee. Their standing and record in business and financial circles in Germany and their intimate knowledge of German conditions and opportunities ensure adequate supervision of the company's investments.
>
> I have also arranged that the Deutsche Bank and the Norddeutsche Bank at Hamburg shall be the Company's depositories."

The shares being of Mark denomination enable all owners to acquire them in exchange for their holdings of German Marks.

PRICE Par: 10,000 Marks per share

Applications for subscriptions to the Common Shares of the United European Investors, Ltd., at 10,000 German Marks per share, will be received by the undersigned, if, as and when issued. Subscriptions will be entered in the order in which they are received. The right is reserved by the Company to reject any application, to make allotments on subscriptions, or close the subscription books at any time without notice.

This company does not in any case advocate the further purchase with American dollars of German marks. Its purpose is solely the placing of actual values behind marks already owned in America.

The legality of this issue has been approved by counsel for the Company: Jenks & Rogers, New York, and McGiverin, Haydon and Ebbs, Ottawa, Canada.

Application will be made in due course to list these shares on the N. Y. Curb Market.
Application for these shares may be filed with any recognized broker or financial institution or with:

William Schall & Company
45 William Street
New York

(The statements contained herein, while not guaranteed, have been obtained from authoritative sources, and we believe them to be correct.)

Hon. Franklin D. Roosevelt was President of the UNITED EUROPEAN INVESTORS, LTD. a Canadian corporation. Its object was "to take advantage of the money stringency in Germany". The SEC would be sure to reject its offer of *"profitable returns and safety of principal"*. As might have been expected under the circumstances, the German government adopted regulations which trapped money invested by foreigners and eventually wiped out the principal.

lated to the elimination of labor from merchandizing. As in the case of Cousin Ulysses S. Grant the glamour of the family name was peddled to none too scrupulous manipulators to assist them in unloading questionable stocks on the sucker public.

The first of these dubious ventures, launched in 1922, was the United European Investors Ltd., that was incorporated under the charter of the Dominion of Canada. Its president was listed as Hon. Franklin D. Roosevelt, then vice president of the Fidelity & Deposit Company of Maryland. His associates in the enterprise included August Scherer, William Schall, Senator John von Berenberg Gossler, partner of the Hamburg banking firm of the same name and Alfred Arnthal of Hamburg. Its stock was payable in German marks and was sold to the public in denominations of 10,000 marks a share, with a total capitalization of 600,000,000 marks. Its purpose as stated in its advertisements was "to take advantage of the present money stringency in Germany". The advertisements represented that "sound and attractive investments can be secured for marks at prices *which should ensure profitable returns coupled with safety of principal*". At a time when many colossal fortunes were piled up in Germany by shrewd, able manipulators such as Stinnes, Thyssen, Cagliostro and others by taking advantage of the manipulation of currency, FDR's enterprise came to an ignominious end.

In 1927 Franklin Delano Roosevelt was identified with another stock jobbing scheme for the benefit of Germany that cost the American investment public heavily—the International Germanic Trust Company. Its purpose was to further trade with Germany and to deal in German acceptances. The enterprise showed losses from the very start. The stock which was sold to the American public for $170 a share was eventually liquidated for $19 a share.

The following year found Franklin Delano Roosevelt used as "sucker bait" on the board of directors of the Consolidated Automatic Merchandising Company abbreviated to "Camco." The purpose of the enterprise was to eliminate labor from the sale of an ever increasing array of merchandise, and to sell by means of automatic vending machines. Eleven million dollars were extracted from the public purse for stock in units of one common and one preferred share at $55 a unit, in July 1928. At about this time Roosevelt secured the gubernatorial nomination.

FRANKLIN D. ROOSEVELT, Vice President, Fidelity and Deposit Co. of Maryland,
was window trimming for 'CAMCO'' that rooked investors to the tune of $11,000,000.
It lost money from the very start and failed in one of the periods of highest prosperity
in the nation's history. But the American investor has been swindled just as ruthlessly
by all of the New Deal measures supposedly designed for their protection.

It is a curious fact that in this instance, as in others that involve Roosevelt and the Dynasty, the radicals and so-called "liberals" made no outcry of "Wall Street candidate" against Roosevelt. In publications that attacked the wealthy, no mention was ever made of the Roosevelt-Delano clan except in the most favorable light. Thus left-winger Ferdinand Lundberg in his "America's 60 Families" advertised as a "sensational exposé" of "malefactors of great wealth", makes no mention of the Roosevelt family or of the Delanos except to mention Fred Delano's position with the Federal Reserve Bank. This appears to make it clear who inspired these attacks.

The advertising and literature which was used in the sale of "Camco" stock was so laden with deception and misrepresentation as to be notorious even in those days. The advertising dilated in glowing terms on the prospects of the industry, quoting numerous authorities, including Babson, on automatic sales machines, in a manner as to lead the prospective buyers to believe that they commended Camco.

But they mentioned nothing about the assets. To cover up the question of assets, the publicity matter expounded on "good-will industries" in which it classed Camco with the William Wrigley Jr. Company and the Coca Cola Company. It stated that the Company had a five year plan, of the type that is so familiar in the world of crackpots; and it represented that by the third year the dividends would be 18%.

Despite the prosperity which prevailed in the nation at the time it was started. "Camco" lost money from the beginning. A little more than a year after the stock was unloaded on the public, it was selling for fewer pennies than it had had originally sold for dollars. Virtually the entire sum was a dead loss to the American public. It is difficult to understand why those involved were not prosecuted for using the mails. Their political influence was probably what accounted for their immunity.

By 1935, President Franklin Delano Roosevelt, ex-Wall Street buccaneer, had "got religion" and assumed the appearance of virtue. Pontifically he pronounced in one of his fireside broadcasts, in December of that year,

> "One of the greatest curses of American life has been speculation".

At the very time he was making this broadcast, he was

The "Camco" prospectus might well be a model for the New Deal SEC, so far as concerns any protection that it offers to investors. But it would be sure to reject this prospectus subscribed to by its conceiver—with its offer of dividends, with its effort to mislead the investor to infer that Babson recommended the issue, with its omission of reference to assets and its substitution of a comparison with "good-will industries", whatever that might mean, and its insinuation that the issue was of the quality of the fabulous "Coca Cola", or of the "William Wrigley Jr." issues. One wonders why the mail authorities failed to act. The stock became worthless in a short time after issue. Few prospectuses of the time can match this one in its lurid misrepresentation. One wonders whether FDR had this product of his in mind when he sanctimoniously pronounced: "One of the greatest curses of American life has been speculation."

engaged in making life easier, and making plucking the public safer, for the nation's grand-scale swindlers by advocacy, support and administration of his Agricultural Allotment Plan, his SEC, the I.C.C. which he had packed in favor of Dynastic plunderers of the railroads, and his utility death sentence.

The American investor has been swindled out of more money under the New Deal in a decade, by measures that it pretended were designed to protect the public, than it had been by all the prior frauds in a century of Wall Street's history. The New Deal made swindling ultra-safe, ultra-legal and enormously profitable for the Dynasty and its allies, by arranging to have the frauds perpetrated for them by government agencies, with the full sanction of the law; and has given them a virtual monopoly of all important industries.

From the viewpoint of the Dynasty, the business and stock market policies of their agent, President Franklin Delano Roosevelt, were a "New Deal" indeed. From the viewpoint of the public, they were the same, swindling "Old Deal" intensified to the *nth* degree, with all possibilities of legal redress against the swindlers wiped out, and their swindling legalized and perpetrated for them through government agencies which they control.

CHAPTER XIII

SYNTHETIC "LIBERAL"
NEW YORK'S DYNASTIC GOVERNOR

Georgia Warm Springs, Meriwether Reserve Inc. and their principals were munificently provided for by the interests that wanted to use the Roosevelt name for their own political and financial advantage. F. D. R. was groomed to be advanced along the path followed by two of his Dynastic predecessors—Martin Van Buren and Theodore Roosevelt—to the post of Governor of New York State, as a stepping stone to the White House.

For almost half a century the Dynasty, with its allies in politics, commerce, industry and the press, had devoted all its efforts and spared no energies in making the name "Roosevelt" a magic word by which to conjure mobs. First Teddy and then Franklin had been made to espouse every rabble-rousing cause and device by the ghost-writers who thought their thoughts and wrote their speeches for them. Great care was exercised, however, so that their thoughts and acts in the fields that immediately concerned their bosses such as finance, commerce, industry, and raids on the public treasury would be all that they should. The lack of public interests in those vital topics simplified the situation. This made it possible for President Theodore Roosevelt with absolute impunity to further the cause and advocate the views and objectives of Morgan bankers who constituted his cabinet; and even to have ghosted such statements of policy as his third annual message by James Stillman, President of the National City Bank.

Especial efforts were made by the Dynasty to identify the Roosevelt name with so-called "Liberalism". By "Liberalism" is meant following the pattern of Marxism disseminated by Bismarck, that pretended an interest in the "lower" or working classes and supported warfare by them on the community and the "upper classes". Anyone who questioned the wisdom of such class warfare or the consequences of the adopted measures, in disrupting the unity of community life, was labelled "reactionary".

The powers-that-be and the shrewder elements among the banking and commercial fraternity including the Rockefellers and the banker-masters of the Roosevelt-Delano Dynasty, were quick to recognize, as had Bismarck, that the mechanism of Marxist or Communazi totalitarianism could serve their dictatorships and monopolies excellently, if properly framed and manipulated. Thus while the monopoly of industry and commerce was forbidden by law and was railed against by the demagogues and by the "Liberals", a monopoly of labor, through labor unionism, was fully approved by them. And a monopoly of labor is even more effective in attaining a monopoly of industry than monopolist control of industry itself and far more completely enslaves of the worker.

Consequently the politicians formed alliances with the labor "leaders" or barons, extended to them privileges which put them above the law, rendered them completely immune from liability for any of the consequences of their monopoly, and extended them the privilege of levying a private tax on workers for the right to work. The politicians in effect preyed on labor through the agency of the Labor Barons, and collected their share of the extra-legal tax levied on the workers, in return for having robbed them of their Constitutional rights and sold them out. To the befuddled workers these malefactions were misrepresented as championing labor's "rights". When industry provides jobs that pay the workers salaries, the "take" runs into the hundreds of millions and possibly billions of dollars; and when business depression deprives workers of jobs and incomes, the politicians can still dip their hands into the pockets of the public, worker and non-worker, through the Treasury and taxes.

At the back of the politician, taking the bulk of the spoils, are the real overlords of Labor, the banking element. With their remote control of Labor through Labor Barons, they are in a position to call strikes and manipulate wages to suit their purposes, whether they be crushing a competitor, slowing production so that surplus can be dissipated by industry freed of the need of paying wages, or numerous other malevolent purposes. The ultimate disruption and disintegration of national economy and security which this program implies is exactly the effect that, like Bismarck, the Rockefeller-Standard Oil and the Roosevelt-Delano Dynasty allies seek in their plan to attain an American dictatorship and monarchy.

Over a period of fifteen years, the Dynasty had thrown its energies and influence into building up its heir apparent and puppet "leader", Franklin Delano Roosevelt. Theodore Roosevelt, himself, had chosen the husband of his favorite niece as his heir, to carry on in the opposition party when his own would have been voted out. Teddy had not only groomed F. D. R. but had used his presidential patronage to further the latter's career in the Democratic Party. Then he assured the success of that Party by splitting the Republicans with his Bull Moose, third party movement.

The Dynasty's "brain trusters", who served in lieu of F. D. R.'s brains, modified the activities, speeches and platforms on which they ran ran him for office to match the temper of the times and the audience. Thus in his first Dutchess County campaign, Franklin Delano Roosevelt's platform was highly satisfactory to the Ku Klux Klan element that preponderated in the community; and it truly represented F. D. R.'s own inherent anti-Catholic sentiments that were as deeply rooted as his Sephardic Jewish, Huguenot and Episcopalian ancestors. One must appreciate this to understand fully F. D. R.'s treatment of Sheehan and James Farley.

The same opportunism that dictated Klanism and anti-Catholicism in Dutchess County politics, forbade it on the wider, state and national scenes. There F.D.R. was built up as an eager friend of the Catholic, the Jew, the Negro, and all other minorities and fragments. For they still have votes! Al Smith was F. D. R.'s Catholic foil. Roosevelt rejected the New York gubernatorial nomination in Smith's favor, in 1918, condescendingly suggesting that the issue of religion made no difference to the electorate *in wartime* (Lindley, p. 165.) F. D. R., of the Roosevelt name, was volunteered to put Al Smith in nomination at Madison Square Garden in 1924, and again in Houston, in 1928, in order to give him and his newly developed and politically motivated tolerance of the Catholic, a national build-up.

So successful was this maneuver that even the supporters of Smith who had rallied to him and financed him as a champion of Catholicism, supported F. D. R. with alacrity. Raskob agreed to support Georgia Warm Springs Foundation to bribe F. D. R. to accept the Democratic nomination for governor, and contributed to that enterprise a quarter of a million dollars on condition that Roosevelt would not oppose Smith in 1932, if defeated in 1928. As might be expected of a Dynast F. D. R. accepted the money and double-crossed Raskob and Smith. The total "inducement" that Roosevelt received by way of Meriwether Reserve Inc. and Georgia Warm Springs Foundation is reported to have been more than three quarters of a million dollars. Al Smith's presidential backers furnished ample funds for F. D. R.'s campaign.

It is noteworthy that never once in a period of over two decades did the Dynasty fail to secure for F.D.R. the offer of some top nomination in each election. Though each time it was rejected, except the 1914 nomination for U. S. Senator, this device served to keep F. D. R.'s name before the public and build him up as a great white hope.

Roosevelt's "infantile paralysis" was an unfortunate accident that might have completely upset the Dynasty's plans. But fortunately for them, F. D. R. became more amenable than ever because of the very stigmata of his ailment. His high suggestibility was especially valuable in this direction, when the right party was at hand to do the suggesting.

The designation of the suggesters as "Brain Trusters" is inappropriate. They are more appropriately termed "Brains", for they served in lieu of them. The first of these, Louis Howe was put on the job in 1907. Those men thought F. D. R.'s thoughts, wrote his speeches and often spoke his mind for him. They did arrange, however, to have his speech and radio voice trained for him and stylized, so that he would better serve as a mouthpiece for their ideas. His tongue was so glib it took a veritable host of ghostwriters to keep up with it—and they were all "Liberal" a euphemism for what we now recognize as Communist. Never has Charlie McCarthy had a better counterpart in real life.

Some amusing stories of ghost-writing for FDR and his ventriloquism have emerged. The ghost-writers of Roosevelt's speeches were a legion. Many of them had diametrically opposed views. The ghosts included Louis Howe, Raymond Moley, Hugh Johnson, Adolph Berle, Ernest Lindley, Tom Corcoran, Cordell Hull, Sam Rosenman, Robert Sherwood and numerous others. Some of them were written by several ghosts and expressed diametrically opposite views within a single speech.

Moley tells the story of the Chicago acceptance speech. A speech was written for Roosevelt by him and several paragraphs were added by Rosenman. But the orders from above were that it was not to be delivered unless it met with the approval of Louis Howe. In Chicago Howe had written another acceptance speech himself, the contents of which were unknown to Roosevelt. As FDR was being introduced to the convention, Howe handed him, to read, the speech he had prepared. Roosevelt arose with both Moley's and Howe's speeches in his hands. He started reading the Howe speech expressing Howe's views, which he had never seen before, and then went on with Moley's speech expressing the views of Moley and Rosenman, which in no wise agreed.

Roosevelt's tariff speech came into being in the same fashion. Moley asked Cordell Hull to write a speech on the tariff. Hull's production called for free trade or at least a 10% cut in all tariffs. Feeling that this was extreme, Moley called on Hugh Johnson, an advocate of protective tariffs and reciprocal trade treaties, to write another. The two were diametrically opposite.

Shown to Roosevelt, he glanced through them and then asked Moley to "weave the two together". ("After Seven Years," by Raymond Moley).

Roosevelt had practically nothing to do with the writing of his first inaugural address. FDR merely "Charley McCarthyed" expedient ideas prepared for him by the Dynasty's ghosts. Roosevelt had the faculty of mouthing the ideas of others with perfect ventriloquist effects.

The chief contributors to F. D. R.'s gubernatorial campaign funds were: Edward S. Harkness, of the Standard Oil Company; Vincent Astor of the Roosevelt-Delano Dynasty; Bernard Baruch of the Ryan-Morgan-Rockefeller group; Owen D. Young of the General Electric Company, a Morgan henchman, Jesse H. Jones and Percy S. Strauss.

One of the first acts of the Roosevelt Administration as might be expected was the organization of a personal "publicity", or "news", bureau, at the expense of the taxpayers. F.D.R. and his financial backers never lost sight of the importance of a constant perversion of public opinion by a stream of "slanted" and poisoned propaganda labelled "publicity".

The Tammany elected and supported Governor of New York, Franklin Delano Roosevelt, paid off well the Rockefeller-Morgan interests that had "taken care" of Meriwether Reserve Inc. and Georgia Warm Springs Foundation, as has been related. He engineered a tighter monopoly for the Milk Trust and a tremendously higher price for milk; at the same time there was provided a special tax on milk compelling the public to pay for false advertising on the value of milk as a food, to encourage the public to drink more of the expensive milk; and an inferior grade of synthetic milk was approved for sale at a higher price than that of natural milk.

The Dynasty and its agent, F. D. R., rewarded the traditional enemy, Tammany Hall, with a sly double-cross that is characteristic of their treatment of everyone except their inner clique and their financial allies. The Rockefeller interests required a change of party in New York City because Tammany opposed the plan of the Rockefeller interests to have the City bail them out of their New York elevated railroad and subway bonds, which they had purchased at a large discount. They wished to force New York City to exchange them for City stock on an equal basis at full face value.

Tammany also traditionally supported the five cent fare and opposed any increase. The transit systems could earn ample with a five cent fare to pay a good return on money actually invested and to provide amply for replacements and new construction, if honestly managed. But the Rockefeller and allied interests had milked them dry and grossly mismanaged them. The Rockefeller plan was to have the City take over the transit systems, rebuild and repair them, build needed additional lines, unify them into a single system, increase the fare to ten cents, and then return the renovated system to them to bleed again. Fiorello LaGuardia was the man whom the Rockefeller interests chose to accomplish their skullduggery, when they could break Tammany's back. The back-breaking job was assigned to F. D. R.

Franklin Delano Roosevelt, on the advice of his "Brain Trusters" refused to take any action on the corruption that Rockefeller controlled agencies and later Judge Seabury, by pre-arrangement, kept exposing to public gaze—until after he had secured the Democratic Presidential nomination at Chicago with the support of Tammany's votes. Two months after the nomination, in time to play a role in the pre-election campaign dramatics, it was arranged that Roosevelt should hear charges against Tammany's Mayor James Walker, with Martin Conboy as counsel. The strategy of letting Martin Conboy do the dirty work was that Conboy was a ranking Catholic and action taken on his counsel would not alienate the needed Catholic vote. By this action Roosevelt prepared the way for Rockefeller's LaGuardia and the Fusion ticket. He turned on Tammany only after having enjoyed the benefit of its support at the Chicago convention, when it was too late for that organization to withdraw support. To the voters he presented a pretense of virtue.

Roosevelt's term as Governor was marked by the usual clap-trap "social" measures, such as Workman's Compensation that protected the employers against lawsuits but fail to give adequate compensation to the injured; old age pensions that are totally inadequate for the aged to live on but bar the way to more adequate provision; labor laws that bolster and confirm the unConstitutional and dictatorial powers that had been given to the Labor Barons to levy private taxes on workers, to regiment them and to deprive them of freedom of employment. These gains for Labor Barons, and their goon, thug and ex-convict henchmen, are sardonically referred to as "Labor's gains". Roosevelt manifested his financial incompetence by leaving the State a ninety million dollars deficit.

Roosevelt's suggestibility, evasiveness, and shiftiness became proverbial during his stay at Albany. He promised everything to everyone and courted the favor of all; but served only his Dynasty and its financial supporters while pretending to champion the "underprivileged" and Labor. As his circle of advisers, manipulators and Brain Trusters grew larger, his pronouncements grew even more contradictory. But they developed the technique of having F. D. R. say one thing and do the very opposite. The behind-the-scene rulers of the Dynasty discovered that with proper publicity the public paid attention only to what was said and forgot or failed to understand what was done. F. D. R. anticipated Goebbels and led the way in the technique of brazen lying that is so loud and insistent that the moronic mobs come to believe the lies more firmly than they ever believed the truth.

The Morgans and the banking fraternity identified with the Dynasty were served to good advantage by the wiping out of the Bank of the United States. In this crime Franklin Delano Roosevelt played a determining role through the New York State Banking Department. The Bank of the United States was then more solvent than the majority of its competitors. This was proved by its paying almost 100 cents on the dollar to its creditors even after it was mercilessly rooked in liquidation proceedings. The reason for it was that Morgan and others of the Dynasty's financial backers objected to the competition and multiplication of Jewish bankers. Roosevelt served them by eliminating the Bank of the United States and by forcing Jonas and his associates to turn over to the Morgan-Rockefeller gang the control of Manufacturers Trust Co.

Chapter XIV

HEARST, DUPONT AND ROCKEFELLER ELECT F. D. R.

It is questionable whether in all history a nation has been more completely flim-flammed than in the matter of the supporters and objectives of President Franklin Delano Roosevelt. By the crudest type of deception, that depends for its effectiveness solely upon the uncritical gullibility, the defective memory and pathetic dullness of the average citizen, the public have been led to believe that Roosevelt was an enemy of the very people whose creature he was, who financed his campaigns and controlled him in office. Some of the ablest perverters of public opinion, otherwise known as publicity men, headed by Louis Howe and Charles Michelson engineered this deception.

The public have been led to believe that William Randolph Hearst, the Du Ponts and the Rockefellers were F. D. R.'s worst enemies. But it was they who aided the Dynasty and made him President to serve their purposes and do their bidding. Some of the facts can be gained from an examination of campaign contributions. Contributions to clean up the debt of the Democratic National Committee including $345,250 owed to John Raskob, a Du Pont associate were: $39,-500 by Pierre S. Du Pont in 1931 and 1932; $125,000 by Raskob in 1932.

To F. D. R.'s 1932 election campaign there was contributed by : *William Randolph Hearst*, $30,000; Edward S. Harkness, of Standard Oil Company, $12,-000; John J. Raskob, $23,000; Bernard M. Baruch, of the Ryan-Rockefeller-Morgan group, $45,000; Francis P. Garvan, representing the Brady interests, $15,000; and indirectly the Association Against the Prohibition Amendment supported Roosevelt with sums up to $100,-000 contributed by Lammot Du Pont; Pierre S. Du Pont, Vincent Astor and William H. Woodin, $35,000 each; Cyrus and Harold F. McCormick contributed $5,000 and Eleanor Patterson, $2,000.

William Randolph Hearst's motive in supporting Roosevelt was a matter of urgent personal necessity. Hearst had repeatedly earned the enmity of Rockefeller. In the late 1920's Hearst and Brisbane had expanded their real estate holdings tremendously, financing them through S. W. Straus and Company which they are reputed to have controlled. When the American Bond and Mortgage Company, a competing real estate mortgage house affiliated with the Rockefeller-interests, collapsed directly after the 1929 panic, Hearst and Brisbane saw an opportunity to boost S. W. Straus and Company and their bonds. They ran a running campaign which on one day demanded criminal prosecution of the crude frauds perpetrated by the American Bond and Mortgage Company, and on the following day called on the public to buy, as the safest type of investment, S. W. Straus and Company bonds. "Never A Loss In Fifty Years" was the slogan of the Straus Company that they hammered away in their columns.

Intensive publicity of the type that Hearst and Brisbane hurled against the American Bond and Mortgage crowd easily might have led to criminal prosecution. To avert that eventuality, the interests involved had to do something to smash Hearst and Brisbane. The readiest way to accomplish the destruction, in view of their extended and highly mortgaged realty holdings, was to smash the real estate market throughout the country. And the quickest way was to force foreclosure of the highest quality real estate, business property in New York City. That was an important function of the Rockefeller Center.

Rockefeller's Radio City differs in its legal status from any real estate in the country. By Bill No. 296, the 72nd Congress, rushed through in the last hour of the session by Rockefeller's principal agent in Congress, Senator Robert F. Wagner, Rockefeller Center was made a free-port, the only free-port in the United States. This means that merchants on the west side of Fifth Avenue and Fiftieth Street, in Rockefeller Center, could import merchandise from abroad and display it for sale without paying duty.

This law implies discrimination against every other port in the country, which is prohibited by the Constitution. It also implies discrimination against all other property holders. For it enabled Rockefeller Center to lure tenants from other buildings with the inducement that it would require less capital to engage in the import business because the property was a free-port. To make matters worse, the ground on which the Center is built is tax-exempt because it belongs to Columbia University, and its rentals can be correspondingly lower.

The vacancies resulting from the wholesale exodus of tenants into Radio City from other properties in New York City was equivalent in its effect to "short selling" real estate, and it sharply depressed the property values in New York City. Interested parties were able to grab up property thus depreciated at bankrupt prices. The tactics employed in this process were the basis of at least one lawsuit against the Rockefeller interests that has come to public attention, brought by August Heckscher. Its disposition has been kept secret. This sharp and highly lucrative business deal has been represented to the public as a philanthropic enterprise to combat depression by the Rockefeller publicity men.

Millions of people throughout the country lost their properties, their homes, their farms and their businesses as a consequence of this characteristic Rockefeller "philanthrophy". Like all of the Rockefeller fake "philanthropies", this one also bore the feature of virtually tax-exempting the Rockefellers; and shifted the burden of their taxes on to the shoulders of the rest of the nation, on us whom the power-drunk conspirators delight in calling "peasants".

The terrific smash in real estate values thus stimulated, drove S. W. Straus and Company into bankruptcy and spread ruin among its mortgage bondholders including numerous widows and orphans. But Hearst and Brisbane were wiped out at the same time. The Hearst publications and the Hearst properties were taken over by the Rockefellers through their Chase National Bank.

In the meantime Rockefeller's money had put Dewey in the District Attorney's office in New York. Dewey was put to work on an investigation of the white slave and numbers rackets, which were backed by identical financial interests, in order to fill the headlines of the newspapers and divert public attention from the quiet dismissal of the American Bond and Mortgage fraud cases in Brooklyn. The service thus rendered marked this scion of the Dynasty for advancement to the top.

The only possibility open to Hearst of rescuing his cherished estates, San Simeon and Wynkoop, lay in a revaluation of gold. Hearst, through his ownership of a controlling block of stock in Homestake Mining Company as well as investments in other gold mining property, is one of the largest, or perhaps the largest, individual gold producer in the world. If he could increase the earnings of these companies, Hearst would be able to salvage his estates. That required a revaluation, a rise in the Treasury price, of gold.

For the purpose of obtaining a revaluation of gold, Hearst made a deal with Ex-Senator William Gibbs McAdoo, Wilson's son-in-law, who had control of the

California delegates to the 1932 Chicago Democratic Convention, with John Nance Garner of the Texas delegation, and with Mayor Anton Cermak of the Illinois delegation, thus insuring control of the Convention. McAdoo or Garner, who agreed to a revaluation of gold, were to be the candidates. But neither of them could get enough votes to capture the presidential nomination.

Hearst would not release the delegation except to a candidate who would agree to revalue gold. Roosevelt agreed to do so as the first act of his Administration as well as to take Garner as a running mate. Hearst made Roosevelt President by releasing the three delegations to him, even though he did not particularly trust him. Had Roosevelt been assassinated at Miami, Hearst's original choice of President would have prevailed.

However systematically F. D. R. violated his promise to the nation's voters, he rarely was permitted by the Dynasty to fail to live up to the letter of his pledges to his financial backers and bosses. He revalued gold as the first act of his Administration, after closing the banks.

Aside from Hearst and his financial predicament, the revaluation of gold was entirely uncalled for. Under the circumstances of the depression and the New Deal controlled economy, it did *not* serve to bring about inflation and a rise in wages and prices, though that was the principal excuse offered for the act. In recent years, when there has been good reason to fight price rises, it has served as a tremendous stimulus to inflation.

The revaluation of gold meant eventually that persons or groups permitted to retain ownership of gold, and producers of new gold, received an increased price of $15.00, or 75%, per ounce. But the rank and file of the citizenry, every man, woman and child who owned gold which was surrendered, bonds, savings, insurance or liquid cash, were robbed to the same extent. It meant that the purchasing power of the American dollar in foreign markets was reduced by the same amount, and that each American living at home or travelling abroad was robbed by his government of that amount. Revaluation of gold was not merely uncalled for. It was downright dishonest as well as injurious to the country and served the nation no good purpose.

For the banking groups, who retained gold or who exported it to foreign countries in advance of the gold order, the revaluation meant huge profits. Such banks as Rockefeller's Chase National Bank exported billions of dollars worth of gold bullion successively to France and England, beginning in October 1929. They profited when they increased the price of gold in France, when they manipulated the rise in the pound sterling in England from $3.05 to $4.86; and when they returned the gold to the United States they gave themselves $15.00 an ounce more for their gold, as a reward for helping to bring on the 1929 crash and the depression by exporting the gold.

Aside from its basic dishonesty, the gold order originally issued by Roosevelt was unconstitutional as I pointed out in letters published in the New York Times and other publications at the time. For the order called for surrender of the gold to the Federal Reserve Bank, a private, quasi-public stock company. Though the Constitution permits of confiscation for eminent domain, it bars confiscation for private interest.

F. D. R. called upon Congress to pass a bill in the following year compelling surrender of gold to the Treasury, supposedly to correct the illegality of his first gold order. But this law was treated with their customary contempt by F. D. R. and his New Dealers. After two years of investigation, I forced an admission from Secretary Morganthau that $10,000 gold notes were being issued by the Treasury Department solely to member banks of the Federal Reserve System for the gold that had been surrendered. In other words, the gold hoard that is being protected by the United States Army at Fort Knox belongs to the member bankers of the Federal Reserve Bank and not to the United States Treasury. This is a violation of both law and Constitution.

Revaluation of gold saved Hearst a part of his fortune. Profits of Homestake Mining Company and other gold mines rose enormously. The price of gold stocks rose accordingly, and Homestake Mining Company stock rose from $50 to over $500 within a short period after the gold order.

Republicans and honest Democrats alike condemned the gold order and fought it, in one case to the Supreme Court where it was speciously upheld. They threatened to reverse the order when it would be in their power to do so.

Hearst was in abject terror over the threats to reverse gold revaluation. He had to get the higher price for gold over a long period of time to retrieve part of his fortune. It was imperative for him that Roosevelt should be repeatedly reelected. But he knew that his continuous championship of Roosevelt would drive his numerous enemies into the opposition.

The task of making Hearst a real asset to Roosevelt's re-election campaigns instead of a potential liability and of perverting public opinion, was placed before a group of outstanding publicity men. They advised that Nazism and Fascism was becoming extremely unpopular in the United States and F. D. R. was following public opinion in opposing them. They suggested that William Randolph Hearst and his publications launch a sham fight on Roosevelt, and at the same time pretend to support Nazism and Fascism, thus throwing the Anti-Nazis and Anti-Fascists into the Roosevelt camp.

The plan was a bitter pill for Hearst to swallow. He hated both Nazis and Fascists, if for no other reason —because they interfered with his news services. Nevertheless Hearst accepted the plan. With great ostentation and publicity he announced a visit to both Hitler and Mussolini, the outcome of which was the appearance in Hearst's publications, under control of the Rockefeller interests, of articles by Goebbels, Goering, Gayda and others. As the perverters of public opinion expected, the gullible public raged at Hearst and flocked to the standards of Roosevelt, blind to the fact that he was giving them another of the same brand of dictatorship.

The antagonism between Hearst and Roosevelt was utterly sham and an absurd hoax, as can be discerned from the things that Hearst was doing simultaneously for the Roosevelt family. Immediately after the inauguration, and after a threat made by F. D. R. to prosecute airmail overcharges, or "frauds", Elliott Roosevelt at the age of 21 and with no experience in aviation was given, with suspicious eagerness, the job of manager of the Gilpin Airlines with a total retainer of $15,000 a year. The airmail "frauds" were never prosecuted.

The pattern of this situation, which became familiar and oft-repeated in the Roosevelt family during

F. D. R.'s administration, bore so many of the earmarks of a "payoff" that it started tongues wagging. The financial interests behind the Administration were frankly as worried about it as they were about the BeVier toilet kit scandal that involved New Dealer Harry L. Hopkins. In the midst of this concern, Hearst stepped into the breach and offered Elliott, whose major experience with aircraft was to watch them fly, the job of aviation editor of his newspapers at a higher straight salary than he received from Gilpin Airlines.

Thereafter Hearst provided munificently for the son of his "enemy", Elliott Roosevelt. Elliott's talents were turned to radio, working for Southwest Broadcasting Company which later turned over four of its stations to the open ownership of Hearst. His position was vice-president. Elliot Roosevelt handled for Hearst the radio presidential election campaign against his father in 1936. It hardly can be conceived that Elliott Roosevelt would have done anything really intended to harm his father. The trail of Hearst's benefactions anent Elliott goes further.

But Hearst did not stop with Elliott in his benefactions to the family of his "enemy", F.D.R. Anna Roosevelt Dall Boettiger, F.D.R.'s daughter, and her husband were both given highly paid jobs on the unsuccessful Hearst paper, The Seattle Post Intelligencer. Anna was made columnist with a reputed salary of $12,000 a year and her husband, publisher at a salary running into six figures. May the Lord give us more "enemies" of that calibre.

The story of the enmity that the Du Ponts displayed against Roosevelt in public is much the same type of flim-flam staged for political, vote-getting purposes. The Du Ponts heavily financed the Democratic as well as the Republican Party. They carefully avoided financing Roosevelt's campaigns openly, but indirectly contributed heavily through the Association Against the Prohibition Amendment and other channels.

Shortly after Roosevelt's nomination, the two families got together and in true monarchic fashion the Du Ponts arranged an alliance with the Royal Family by sealing the engagement of young Ethel Du Pont and Franklin Delano Roosevelt Jr. It was a natural alliance because of the identity of interests. Both the Du Ponts and the Roosevelt-Delano Dynasty are heavily interested in munitions and armaments, in war.

It was decided, however, that it would never do to

let the public know of this alliance, because its war-like character would be so obvious. Any stories that leaked out regarding the alliance and the engagement were promptly denied. It was kept a dark secret until exactly one week after F.D.R.'s second election.

The same policy was followed in making the Du Ponts an asset to Roosevelt, to help assure his reelection. As in the case of Hearst, the Du Ponts appeared to be enemies of their prospective in-law, Roosevelt. The Du Ponts were intensively publicized as war-loving, war-thriving munition kings. On the other hand fire was added to the pacifist movement that had been planted in the land by its designing enemies. The Liberty League was then set up for the ostensible purpose of attacking Roosevelt and fighting his reelection. This served to throw the entire pacifist vote into Roosevelt's camp and helped assure his reelection.

How fully deliberate was this malign purpose can be seen from the publicity about the Liberty League on which the Du Ponts spent millions of dollars. This publicity, as is instanced by the "Hate Roosevelt" dinner given in Washington, served to present the Du Ponts to the nation as a laughing stock. Ordinarily business men do not regard ridicule as good publicity and invariably discharge the publicists who make the mistake of heaping it on them. But the Du Ponts continued to pay publicist Jouett Shouse $50,000 a year and an unlimited expense account, repeatedly to hold them up to ridicule. Apparently they were willing to go far to insure Roosevelt's re-election.

And curiously enough, Franklin Delano Roosevelt, who was viciously vindictive and invariably sought to "purge" his enemies, did not resent the sham attacks of Hearst and the Du Ponts, in the slightest degree.

The Rockefeller-Standard Oil group carefully stayed in the background and made no open and direct contribution, other than those of Harkness, to Roosevelt's election campaign. But their hand in effecting Roosevelt's election is evinced by a number of facts. The majority of the members of the Roosevelt Cabinet were drawn from their crowd. These included: Harold Ickes, Standard Oil attorney for the Chicago area, Secretary of the Interior; Frances Perkins, Rockefeller almoner, Secretary of Labor; Henry A. Wallace, Rockefeller protege, Secretary of Agriculture; oil man, Jesse Jones; and Harry L. Hopkins, Rockefeller almoner and their key New Deal agent in controlling Roosevelt's policies. A staggering number of appointive positions in policy-making agencies of the government were drawn from their subordinates. And for the first time in history an American President dared openly appoint a Rockefeller to office—Nelson Rockefeller in the ultra-strategic post of Coordinator of Hemispheric Defense.

Under Roosevelt the United States Government became totally subservient to the Rockefeller Empire and made possible its conquest of the world. The appointment of J. P. Morgan's nephew, Joseph Grew, as Ambassador to Japan prepared the way for Pearl Harbor, the rescue of Rockefeller-Standard Oil property in China, and the complete conquest of Japan by the Rockefeller Empire. At the same time it gave them, at the expense of tens of thousands of American lives and a huge proportion of the national wealth, the control of the enormously rich Saudi Arabian and other Near East oil fields.

CHAPTER XV

F. D. R. LAUNCHES "NEW DEAL"
BUILDS PROPAGANDA MACHINE AND
BANKING MONOPOLY

From the very start Franklin D. Roosevelt's Administration began carrying out the blueprint of the New Deal drawn up by Hoffman Nickerson. Some aspects of the plan were improved upon with the objective of better furthering the original purpose of serving the Dynasty and its rich allies, while pretending to guard the interests of the common man. Changes in the blueprint were made necessary by the fact that the Dynasty had completely merged with the Rockefeller Empire and the Empire's program called not merely for dictatorial domination of the United States, but of the rest of the world as well; for the Rockefeller Empire seeks a conquest of the world and a dictatorship dominating all lands.

The first move was building up a propaganda system that was so vast that it could distort in the desired manner any intelligence that reached the public. Roosevelt made two of his fellow members of the official propaganda agency of World War I, the Naval Information Committee, his White House assistant secretaries: Marvin Hunter McIntyre, he placed in charge of appointments and political affairs; and Stephen Early, former Editor of Stars and Stripes, the A. E. F. propaganda agency, in charge of the press and public relations.

In every other direction Roosevelt, in 1933, rebuilt the war machine of World War I. From the start of his Administration it was quite apparent that its objective was another war to further the interests of the Rockefeller Empire and the Dynasty. The same "patriotic dollar-a-year men" were back on the job taking care of their interests. This was relatively simple because with the aid of the Rockefeller "philanthropies" and the General Education Fund the whole World War I machine, had been put in storage by the plotters in schools, colleges, universities and businesses, in the interim between the Wilson and Roosevelt Administrations. It was brought out of the storage and set to work as soon as Roosevelt entered the White House. They were ready for the bright new war in the making. In the meantime, they hatched up and played with other less amusing New Deal "emergencies".

Numerous censors and propagandists of World War I were assigned to perform the same job in the New Deal departments. Hundreds of editors and reporters, and many publishers were placed on the payroll of the various government departments and bureaus for purpose of suppressing or distorting the truth and of propagandizing the nation into acceptance of the "New Deal".

Through the Federal Radio Commission's power of life and death over radio stations, the radio was brought under censorship. The Motion Picture Industry later was forced, to serve the New Deal propaganda by the ambiguous but stringent Motion Pictures Code Authority, NRA, and by the planting of Roosevelt's son-in-law, John Boettiger in a high salaried position in the Will Hays organization. A similar code was imposed on the press, with a tongue-in-cheek proviso of freedom of the press, and pressure from the Post Office Department supplemented the frank bribery of newspaper men with offers of higher salaried government positions.

Pay was no object and some of the propagandists did very well for themselves. Thus J. Franklin Carter, Washington representative of the McFadden publications, who wrote "free lance" articles on politics for Liberty Magazine especially on the subject of agriculture under the name of Jay Franklin, at the same time drew a salary of $5200 a year under the name of John Carter on the payroll of the Department of Agriculture. Previously he had been in the employ of the State Department until it was discovered that its secrets were leaking into the press in articles signed by "Jay Franklin" (Michael Handout, p. 182).

Books were ghosted by government employees on taxpayers' time and published in the names of Professor Rexford Tugwell, Henry Wallace, F.D.R., Eleanor Roosevelt, Anna Boettiger, Howe, McIntyre and Early, for their private profit.

One of the most important functions of this propaganda was to create the Roosevelt myth—to create the pretense that he was a deserter of the classes and a champion of the masses; to portray him as a saint who passed his days in the slaying of the demon Capitalism, who could do no wrong and was *indispensable*; to surround him with a royal aura, with a figurative crown, until a literal crown should come to hand; and finally to deify him. It was all done in the true tradition of the Caesars, even down to the New Deal largesse patterned after that of ancient Rome.

All who opposed the Administration or sought to expose its corruption were hounded, persecuted and bedevilled. They were made the victims of a persistent and unrelenting vendetta. Every government agency was brought into play in this, especially the Secret Service and the Income Tax Bureau. The author was trailed for three months and threatened by Allen Straight, head of the Secret Service in New York, on direct order from Roosevelt, because he published and distributed a biography of Harry Hopkins that he acknowledged to be truthful. The reason given was that Hopkins was regarded as the "brains" of the New Deal and found the truth with regard to his past activities embarassing. Distribution of the biography was continued on a larger scale.

That biography, the author acknowledges, did not do Harry Hopkins full justice, as a Rockefeller-Soviet conspirator, in view of data which subsequently came to hand. In later years, Murray Garsson, the munitions manufacturer who was convicted for bribery and irregularities in connection with war contracts, reported that Harry

Hopkins had been very helpful to him in securing and handling those contracts. In return for his help, Hopkins had demanded and received liberal payment for his influence. Garsson regularly paid Hopkins's numerous losses on bets on the horse races. But one form of payment demanded by Hopkins, stood out as most odd, Garsson said.

Garsson maintained quarters at the Wardman Park Hotel in Washington, in connection with his war contracts. But he spent his weekends in New York with his family. Harry Hopkins demanded of Garsson that he permit him and his friends to use the quarters during the weekends, and that he defray the cost of refreshments and entertainment. Garsson permitted Hopkins and his guests to charge their expenses to his account.

In looking over his bills, Garsson noted the names of the persons who had signed the tabs charged to him. Among Harry Hopkins's associates who had signed tabs were Carl Aldo Marzani and the whole array of the members of what was later proved to be the Hal Ware (Communist) cell that operated in the Government. Garsson stated that he did not become aware of the fact that he was acting as involuntary host to Hopkins's Communist cell, until after Marzani had been convicted and sent to jail for perjury in swearing in his State Department application that he was not, and never had been, a member of the Communist Party.

President Franklin Delano Roosevelt himself was subjected to Dynastic censorship. George Michael reports in his "Handout", (G. P. Putnam, 1935, pp. 26-30) that Roosevelt was blocked from answering, or did not dare answer, questions asked at the supposedly "open-and-above-board" and "uncensored" press conferences, unless they had been submitted in advance. Members of the family or the secretariat interposed and engaged F. D. R. in conversation to block answering, and the conference was quickly closed. F.D.R. was used as a mouthpiece by the "powers behind the throne". He was not trusted to answer without instruction and coaching by them. Michael stresses the frequent presence of Cousin Henry L. Roosevelt, Assistant Secretary of the Navy, at the press conferences. The same behind-the-scenes censorship of F.D.R. is revealed by his frequent overnight reversal of policies that he had freshly announced the day before.

The device of attacks by pretended enemies or on supposed enemies for the purpose of befuddling and bamboozling the public, as in the cases of Hearst and DuPont, was a technique that was systematically used by Roosevelt and his New Deal. Theodore Roosevelt had used it in successfully deceiving the public; but in the Administration of his cousin, Franklin, the technique was developed into a fine art. As a consequence, those who are well informed can usually feel sure that the reverse of any significant statements of policy emanating from New Deal Washington is the truth.

The adherence to the ultimate New Deal objective stated by Nickerson in his blueprint in "The American Rich", was clearly revealed in the trial balloon so characteristically released by the Administration through Vice President Garner and quoted by Michael (p 13):

"What this country needs to get out of the depression is a *dictator, a man like Roosevelt.*"

In the quest for dictatorship it was necessary to regiment the nation, through the device of a "managed economy". The Bismarxian program, originated by Karl Marx and propagated by Bismarck, or in other words Communazism, was accepted as the shortest road to dictatorship in the presence of the democratic spirit. The Rockefeller interests had prepared the way with their fostering of Communism for almost three decades through the General Education Fund and through the Rockefeller Foundation.

The first step in the regimentation of the nation has been long sought—the absolute monopolistic control of the nation's finances, banks and its Treasury Department by the Dynasty and its allies. From its inception Frederick A. Delano, Roosevelt's uncle, whose appointment was dictated to President Wilson, was Vice-Governor of the Federal Reserve Board. The Dynasty's hold on the finances of the nation was still further tightened by F. D. R.'s appointment of his cousin, Preston Delano to the key jobs of Comptroller of the Currency, and director of the Federal Deposit Insurance Corporation. The absolute monopolistic control of the nation's banking and finances was the principal purpose of F. D. R.'s closing of the banks.

No greater service could have been rendered the nation at the juncture, the complete demoralization of the private banking system, than recapture for the government of the right which those banks had usurped that gave them a throttle hold on the nation's economy.

Had Roosevelt been intent on serving the nation, instead of his banker relatives and their allies, he would have withheld any Treasury support from the banks until the bankers had agreed to turn over their institutions and their control of the nation's life blood, its credit and currency, for nationalization. Never was there a more opportune occasion to accomplish this vital reform, that is so essential for a prolonged national existence.

Instead, the private bankers gave themselves, through their stooge, President F. D. Roosevelt even more complete control of the Treasury. With or without pretext, the banks which competed with the monopoly were not allowed to open up again, no matter what their condition. But the banks controlled by the Dynasty were freely assisted by the United States Treasury with loans amounting to a total of more than two billion dollars. They were reopened no matter what was their condition.

But while Roosevelt babbled for public deception about "throwing the moneylenders out of the temple", the Dynastic bankers were saddling themselves on the nation more firmly than ever and were rendering themselves another life-saving service at the expense of the Treasury and the taxpayers. The numerous barter plans which had arisen throughout the nation during Hoover's Administration were terribly feared by the bankers because they were making the people conscious that they need not depend on the bankers and pay tribute to them, but could exchange commodities and services directly. Also they were becoming acutely conscious of the fact that real wealth is not gold or money, but the necessities required for existence.

Logically the next step would have been to widen the monetary base and rest it on a wide array of the staple necessities of life. That would mean an end to the idea that "money must be scarce to have a value". Since money should be, rightly, a medium of exchange, not the medium of monopoly and control that it is now, it should bear a relation to business like that of the hat-check. Any man who tried to run down a hat-checking business with the idea that there must be fewer hat-checks than hats to be checked instantly would be recognized as insane. But that insane idea applied to money is the life blood of the existence of the banker's profitable credit function and of speculator's profits. Money should expand as rapidly as does nation's wealth and should be as plentiful. Its value should be stabilized by recognizing that money must be, is, and should be based on the essentials that folks seek to purchase with money—staple necessities of life. No longer would it be necessary to manipulate scarcities and leave hosts of people in want to maintain prices. A sufficiency for everyone and the setting up of surpluses of commodities against the time of need would become possible. Money would be a mere medium of exchange and would cease to be a mechanism of manipulation. Business would be stabilized and the ownership of wealth would become secure for all mankind. The depression would have been relieved rapidly and automatically, and future depressions would have become impossible.

Franklin Delano Roosevelt averted the upset to the plans of the bankers and of the Dynasty by his edict abolishing all barter plans as soon as he took office. He exhorted the public to go back to their banks, to enshrine in their temples the moneylenders whom in the same breath he threatened to oust. But the public has been so completely befuddled on the question of money, that they had no intimation of the fact that Roosevelt was contemptuously thumbing his nose at them and dooming them perpetually to be fleeced by the Dynasty's bankers. Sardonically he called it a "New Deal".

As an additional lure to the sucker public, to induce them to abandon their barter plans and once again throw themselves on the (not so) tender mercies of the bankers and speculators, there was set up the private Federal Deposit Insurance Corporation. F. D. R. made his cousin, Preston Delano, director.

"Your banks are now safe and your deposits insured", he told the public. "Take your money back to the banks."

That "safety" and insurance will eventually prove to be a snare and delusion if present policies are continued.

The Roosevelts are well represented in the management of some of our leading banks: George Emlen Roosevelt, Secretary and Trustee of the Bank for Savings in New York, Director of Hanover Safe Deposit Company, Director of Guaranty Trust Company; Philip J. Roosevelt, Director and member of the Advisory Board of Chemical National Bank; W. Emlen Roosevelt, Trustee of Central Hanover Bank and Trust Company, Trustee of Chemical Bank and Trust Company. All of them are partners of Roosevelt and Sons. Nicholas Roosevelt, Trustee of the Dry Dock Savings Institution; Oliver W. Roosevelt, First Vice President and Trustee of the Dry Dock Savings Institution; Charles Frances Adams, Director of the Old Colony Trust Company, Trustee of Providence Institution for Savings, Director, Security Safe Deposit Company, Trustee, Union Safe Deposit Vaults, Trustee of the Bank of New York and Trust Company; Vincent Astor, Director of The Chase National Bank of the City of New York. The Roosevelt-Astor banking interests tie in closely with those of the Rockefellers. There is no evidence that any of them have been thrown out of their temples; indeed they are more safely ensconced than ever.

Franklin Delano Roosevelt was the best friend the "moneylenders" ever had. He saved their hides and their rackets—until the next time they become thoroughly enmeshed in our absurd and unworkable banking and monetary system. Some day there will be no F. D. R. to stooge for them and bail them out. They will then regret that they ever had F. D. R. block the sound and logical solution of the money and banking system to which the barter plans would have led, that would have made them safe and secure in their wealth. For an honest currency system would benefit everyone and harm no one. He who has, would be secure in all his wealth. And he who has not, would be free to carve out for himself as much wealth as he cared to work for.

Control of the banking system enabled regimentation of the nation and its wealth in a tight scarcity economy—euphemistically called a "managed economy"—as the means to attaining the ultimate goal, dictatorship, enslavement of the nation, and a complete monopoly of its industries, commerce and wealth. The prime value to the conspirators of banking control was that, for the purpose of monopoly and dictatorship, it made possible one of the most dastardly and brutal acts of the Dynasty, the deliberate prolongation and maintenance of the depression throughout the 1930's. For, depression psychologically favored the acceptance of dictatorship, and depression prices and bankruptcies favored monopolies. The gold revaluation, which has been detailed, did not materially alter the situation of depression.

When Roosevelt spoke of "throwing the moneylenders out of the temple" and of "soaking the rich" he meant only *certain* moneylenders and *certain* rich. It was really designed to let the Dynastic rich grow richer, but as far as possible, to deny others the opportunity to acquire even sufficiency. The man who works for a living is taxed as high as 90%, of his income in the higher brackets. The man who does not work but merely speculates and takes only capital gains, is taxed no more than 25%. But if he joins the Rockefeller- Standard Oil crowd in oil production, he pays taxes on only 25% of his income. And if he makes money producing oil overseas, as in Saudi Arabia, with the money of the U. S. taxpayers, he pays no income tax at all.

CHAPTER XVI

WHY WARRING U. S. STARVED FOR SUGAR JIMMY WRITES INSURANCE

The New Deal developed strictly along the lines of the spoils system. Since "Charity begins at home", it was a New Deal first of all for the Roosevelt family and second for the Roosevelt-Delano Dynasty. This is perfectly illustrated by the story of why the United States starved for sugar during the war.

The Adams branch of the Dynasty traditionally are heavily interested in the West Indies sugar industry. One of the cogent reasons for this patrician family throwing in its lot with the "rabble" during the Revolutionary War period was England's interference with the rum, molasses and slave trade with the West Indies.

When Franklin Delano Roosevelt entered office the Dynasty was well represented in its holdings in the sugar industry. "Cousin" Frederick B. Adams, in addition to his interests in the munition industry signalized by his position of Chairman of the Board of the Air Reduction Company and Director of the Remington Arms Company, held many key positions in the sugar industry including: Chairman of the Board of Directors of the Atlantic Fruit and Sugar Company, President of the Cuban Dominican Sugar Company, President of the Santa Ana Sugar Company, Director of the

Sugar Estates of Oriente, President of the Barhona Sugar Corporation, and President of the Tanamo Sugar Corporation; subsequently he became President of the West Indies Sugar Company. "Cousin" Charles Francis Adams, whose interests ran more to local utilities and to shipbuilding and naval construction, represented the Dynasty in only two sugar companies as Director of the American Sugar Refining Company and Director of the Central Aguirre Sugar Company. Robert C. Adams was Director of the Warner Sugar Company. In short the Dynasty was more than a little interested in sugar. Also interested in sugar were the Rockefeller-Morgan clique and the National City Bank.

The sugar industry at this time was in a state verging on bankruptcy and the condition of the West Indies companies was particularly bad. In a commercial Dynasty such as the Roosevelt-Delano, this called for prompt action. Roosevelt's action was particularly prompt. The New Dealers deliberately conspired to destroy the American sugar industry and to favor the West Indies sugar industry.

In the course of the 1932 campaign Hoover had accused Roosevelt of planning to injure the American farmer, among other things, by lowering tariffs. Roosevelt denied the charges. But a year later, his Secretary of Agriculture, Henry Wallace, began, on behalf of the Dynasty, the campaign to destroy the continental American sugar industry on special behalf of the West Indies and Latin American industry. On July 31, 1934, Wallace pronounced in a speech to farmers at the free Chatauqua held on the campus of the Louisiana Polytechnic Institute, Ruston, Louisiana, what Charles A. Farwell, executive of the American Sugar Cane League called "Wallace's death sentence on Louisiana's sugar industry." Wallace pronounced according to the report in the Times-Picayune published on that date and quoted, December 1938, by the journalistic genius, Meigs Frost, in a masterly series of articles in the New Orleans State,

"Sugar is an inefficient industry. I am willing to say that in Louisiana where sugar is produced . . . *I do not believe the Louisiana sugar or any other inefficient industry should be put out of business all at once.* That would be hard on human right. But it should be exposed gradually to the winds of world commerce."

That Wallace was assigned by his Dynastic masters

to accomplish some particularly vicious dirty work, is revealed by the testimony given previously by one of his subordinates, A. J. S. Weaver, before the House Committee on Agriculture, February 23, 1934 (quoted from the Government report):

"Hope: Well then in other words, the policy is . . . eliminating the (continental American) sugar industry before it gets any bigger. Am I correct in that assumption?

"Weaver: Yes, if you mean limiting the industry. I think that is a reasonable statement.

"Cummings: Is it a reasonable assumption that the object of the bill (Representative's Bill No. 7907: Includes Sugar and Sugar Cane as Basic Commodities) then is to give us a kind of shot in the arm and put us out of business while we are partly unconscious?

"Weaver: Yes.

"McCandless, of Hawaii: What is it, do you believe, will destroy our sugar production?

"Weaver: Reduction in price and reduction in tariff.

"McCandless: If it had not been for the protection and holding up of the sugar industry in the United States, would we not be at the mercy of foreign countries for our sugar?

"Weaver: Oh that is conceivable and there is some danger in that.

"McCandless: And has not the sugar industry employed thousands and thousands of men in the United States?

Weaver: Well a great amount of labor is employed, yes . . . But the total in terms of seasonal employment even is . . . I should say—not significant, but I hesitate to call its total important. Furthermore it is quite possible that by producing sugar we have robbed ourselves of the chances to employ men to produce goods which we might have traded for sugar, if we had not employed them.

"McCandless: We have now 8,000,000 or 9,000,000 unemployed men, is that not so?

"Weaver: That is right.

"McCandless: Would we not have more if we destroyed the sugar industry?

"Weaver: Well the sugar industry is not in *immediate* danger of being destroyed.

But the American Sugar Cane League officially presented convincing evidence that the danger of destruction of the American sugar industry was imminent and was deliberately planned and clearly indicated in Secretary Henry Wallace's acts affecting the Louisiana sugar industry. They stated:

"The federal wage-hour law specifically exempts agricultural labor from its provisions. But the complicated Sugar Act, passed September 1, 1937, supposed to be for the salvation of the American sugar industry gives the U. S. Secretary of Agriculture power to rule on cane field wages and hours; the only agricultural industry in which the United States government has power to dictate wages and hours. It provides that the Secretary of Agriculture can do so only after a public hearing. Secretary Wallace has adopted the policy of holding two such public hearings a year.

"In the midst of the sugar-cane harvest of 1937, when Louisiana sugar growers were fighting tooth and toe nail to get their crop harvested before freezes followed by warm weather could ruin it, when men were being cut off from W. P. A. pay rolls and rushed like armies into the cane fields, Secretary Wallace called a hearing on sugar cane harvest wages. Harried sugar planters had to stop work to prepare briefs, attend and testify. Then, when the harvest was virtually over, and some 1,000,000 tons of sugar cane had been ruined, caught by freeze and thaw in the fields, in December 1937, Secretary Wallace issued his rulings on cane field harvest wages for that same season—and made them retroactive clear back to September 1, 1937! Sugar cane planters stood under federal orders to look up men long since finished with their job, often scattered far and wide, and pay them additional back pay ordered by Secretary Wallace. There were penalties for violation of those orders. It was a situation said to be without precedent in American agriculture. Some $250,000 in back pay was involved, for thousands of workers in small amounts.

"Sugar cane planting starts each year in September and October. But in February, 1938, Secretary Wallace ordered a hearing on cane planting wages for the planting season finished long before the hearing was called. The hearing was held. Secretary Wallace's rulings didn't come out until June, 1938, the "lay-by" period in sugar growing, when cane field labor mostly has gone fishing, or is scattered anywhere. And again it was a retroactive ruling, causing the Louisiana planters as much trouble and expense as if that had been its purpose, which some of the League officials say they believe it was.

"Planting of the 1939 sugar cane harvest started as usual in September, 1938. So Secretary Wallace waited until September 27, 1938, when many of the planters had completed their planting, to call a hearing at Baton Rouge, La., to determine how many acres each sugar cane grower would be permitted to plant—on a crop that many of them already had finished planting! The Department of Agriculture men holding the hearing discovered that many planters had finished planting their crop by October 1, and that some for varied reasons had lagged behind. So a ruling was issued giving preferential status to the growers who had finished their planting by October 1, 1938. What was described as 'only a tentative quota ruling' was made by Secretary Wallace. He set a deadline of November 14, 1938, for sugar cane growers to file formal notice that they elected to keep the acreage they had planted by October 1, 1938. Department of Agriculture employes are compiling those notices yet. Secretary Wallace has indicated in a public announcement that a quota cut of up to 25 per cent is possible. No man knows just when the official ax may fall.

"The result, officials of the American Sugar Cane League point out, is that thousands of Louisiana sugar growers, after every effort to comply with the Federal law, don't know to this day whether the acreage they have planted is legal or not."

(Editor's note: It was the object of the Dynasty through the New Deal to place all business except their own in a status of illegality through a constantly changing flow of arbitrary edicts by bureaucratic agencies. With all business forced to resort to bootlegging, "Black Markets" and other activities that were made illegal, blackmailing of industry and crushing competition became simple.)

" 'If it is not, Secretary Wallace has a stick to hit you on the head with,' says Mr. Farwell. 'All he needs to say is: "You're going to lose your benefit payments if you don't plough under every furrow of sugar cane you've planted in excess of this quota I'm giving you after the planting season is over." Under present conditions in this government-bedevilled industry, if you lose your benefit payments, your've got to quit. And nobody in Louisiana knows when Secretary Wallace's official ax is likely to swing.' "

In the Harvard Business Review of Autumn 1938, John E. Dalton, former high Federal official with wide authority in sugar affairs, in an article entitled "Federal Sugar Control", wrote:

"The outstanding feature of this enormous American sugar machine is that it is under the immediate direction of the Federal government. No other industry in the United States, excepting perhaps public utilities, experiences such a high degree of government control, a control extending to output, prices, agricultural practices, and labor conditions."

"'And all this power,' points out Mr. Farwell, 'is in the hands of one man, Secretary of Agriculture Henry A. Wallace, open and avowed enemy, by the printed, uncontradicted record, of continental American sugar as an industry.'"

However, Wallace's harassment of the Louisiana sugar growers and his employment on them of the New Deal "lettres de cachet", confiscatory retroactive wage and acreage ruling, that were as dishonest as they were doubly un-Constitutional and un-American—for they confiscated property without the due process and made a man retroactively guilty of violating a law which did not exist at the time of the act—do not fill the whole picture of the conspiracy.

The Department of Agriculture through education of the sugar growers and development of new strains, had brought about a ten-fold increase in production of sugar in Louisiana, from 45,000 to 450,000 tons per year; and the per acre yield had been more than doubled. The Resettlement Division of the Department of Agriculture had brought back thousands of acres into production. A pretentious sugar experimental station had been built by the Department at Houma. The Government had engineered the building and putting into operation of seven new co-operative mills in which five million dollars had been invested, 60% by the government and 40% by the sugar growers. Employment was increased and wages rose. All this was done for the purpose of increasing employment in the sugar industry.

While these developments were under way Roosevelt proceeded to lower the price of sugar, by lowering the tariff on Cuban sugar produced with cheap labor, from $2.10 to 90¢ per hundred pounds. Pawn Wallace, in the meantime, had forced the 40% reduction in acreage planted under a pretendedly "voluntry" plan. It was laden with coercion and intimidation by "marketing licenses" which made the sale of "non-assented" cane impossible. He also threatened an additional retroactive 25% cut in acreage, or ploughing under of the cane after the crop had been planted and the expenses incurred; and imposed retroactive wage increases. Simultaneously, the Dynasty's and their Wall Street allies' agent, Cuban dictator, Col. Fulgencia Batista, visited Washington at their behest, and on leaving announced that he had made a deal, on the basis of which he predicted that Congress would reduce the tariff on Cuban sugar from 90¢ to 75¢ per hundred pounds and increase the quota admitted. Shortly thereafter Wallace issued a false statement of the type that are so dear to New Deal commodity speculators of the Barney Baruch type, which forced the price of sugar down 25 points to the lowest reached in the depression.

No move was overlooked in the effort to depress the price of sugar or to bankrupt the Louisiana and other continental American producers. Peru was permitted to ship 50,000 tons of sugar to the United States on a deal that involved the Grace interests. Peru was so completely a newcomer in the field of sugar that she had not the machinery to grind the cane. It could not be pretended even that this deal stimulated the United States heavy industries. For with funds supplied by the U. S. taxpayer, Peru bought the grinding machinery from the Krupps in Nazi Germany in order to be able to ship the sugar into the American market and further depress it.

The pattern of the Dynasty's plotting in sugar makes its objective obvious. They were utilizing every device to expand and bankrupt the American sugar growers so that they could take over their holdings and build up a complete monopoly. In the meantime their enormous profits in the West Indies industry, which were gained in the process of bankrupting the American industry, would help to pay for the purchase of the latter at a forced sale.

The outcome of these maneuvers was increased unemployment and a reduction of the continental American sugar production to less than 25% of our depression needs. At a time when war was theatening, the United States was made completely dependent for its sugar on overseas sources. The seriousness of the situation and the threats that it offered were clearly and prophetically portrayed by Clarence J. Bourg, President of the American Sugar Cane League in an address before the New Orleans Association of Commerce, December 1, 1938, quoted from Meigs Frost's report in the New Orleans States of the following day:

"Let us consider another national program. In the past several weeks we have read from day to day dispatches speaking about war. Preparedness is the watchword of the Administration. I am no alarmist and have no intention of stirring people to the fear of war, but the Federal Government is using every element of its propaganda machine to justify the expenditure of billions of dollars for the purpose of building armaments in the cause of preparedness. We subscribe to and support this program of national defense but we point out that armaments and guns and battleships are not the only sinews of war. People must eat whether they be soldiers or civilians back home. What has that got to do with sugar? Almost every day we read where the Japs have told the American government in so many words to jump in the ocean and that suggests there might be a war with Japan. If there is a war with Japan, of what possible good will the Philippine Islands be as a source of supply of sugar? Do you think that a cargo of Philippine sugar will ever reach the United States when they are as far away as the Japanese themselves. And then there is Hawaii in the middle of the Pacific Ocean where they can be easily surrounded by submarines and airplanes. The possibility of our receiving sugar from Hawaii in times of war could not be relied upon. Now there are two million tons of sugar from Hawaii and the Philippines that we depend upon as our source of supply. But suppose the Japanese are content to confine themselves to Chinese invasion. On the Atlantic side we have Hitler to contend with. I do not want to arouse alarm about Hitlerism, but the American government is sufficiently concerned to send its Secretary of State down to Peru to have an international conference, the purpose of which is to build up a united defense in the Western Hemisphere. Suppose Hitler does make war on the Atlantic side. Of what good will Puerto Rico be as a source of supply? Yes, of what good will Cuba be with the submarines and the airplanes doing their diabolical work? We depend on those two islands for three million tons of sugar. Two million tons on one side, three million tons on the other side, and only two million tons allowed to be produced in the United States. And supposing the Germans and Japs get together and make war on both sides. What is the answer?"

It is to the everlasting credit of the Louisiana cane growers that they spoke up and fought despite very real fears of reprisals. But it availed them little.

During all this time that the continental American sugar growers were being forced to the wall by a treacherous and traitorous conspiracy by Government officials acting on behalf of American controlled foreign interests, the West Indies sugar industry had enjoyed a subsidy paid by the U. S. taxpayers of $119,000,000 and had flourished and profited enormously. This is made clear by "Cousin" Fred B. Adam's report of the West Indies Sugar Corporation November 16, 1937:

"The statistics set forth above (year's gross income, $9,270,094.18; year's final net profit, $909,714.16, and others, including 'your corporation has no current indebtness save that contracted in the usual routine of business') present such a marked contrast to the conditions existing in the industry five years ago (1932, when a Republican administration sat in Washington) that it is fitting at this time to make some acknowledgement of the part played by the Administration at Washington in effecting this change. It was the example of the United States in bringing about more satisfactory conditions through the establishment of production and import quotas of sugars . . . The role played by the government, therefore . . . has become one of great importance. So much so that government policies today do more than any other single factor to preserve or upset the balance between the varied interests of the industry . . ."

"Cousin" Fred's tribute to "Cousin" Franklin's help and cooperation is patent. It is notable that the West Indies Sugar Corporation alone was permitted to send into the United States more sugar (319,425 bags) than all the growers of the State of Florida were permitted to produce under the quota allowed them; also that in 1938, Wallace listed Cuba for a quota of 1,954,303 tons and Louisiana for 429,553 tons.

The consequences for the nation of this traitorous conspiracy were inevitable. Clarence Bourg's prediction were completely fulfilled. On the eve of the war, the U.S. had been deprived by a treasonous conspiracy of even her barest needs of sugar, a vital food and chemical raw material, just as by similar conspiracies she had been deprived of rubber, tin, oil, scrap iron and other vital war materials, exactly as is being done today once again in the face of another war. Fortunately for the nation, Wallace had not succeeded in carrying out his Dynastic bosses' orders to completely destroy the "inefficient" American sugar industry, or we certainly would have starved literally and lost the war.

The Dynasty is quite loyal in dealing with its own, and invariably there is a "pay-off", direct or indirect. While thousands of workers in the American sugar industry were thrown out of work, and the American people were being doomed to starve for sugar, when war had come, James Roosevelt was collecting fat dividends on the service that his father's Administration had rendered the West Indies sugar industry. In an interview which he gave Walker Davenport of Collier's Magazine, that was published in the August 27, 1938 issue under a facsimile of the "crown prince's" signature, captioned "I'm Glad You Asked Me", James Roosevelt stated:

"We got the contract with the West Indies Sugar Company because its president, F. B. Adams is my cousin. And we did a good job too."

Though "Prince" James was immodest in claiming full credit for the job, it must be acknowledged that it was "a good job", in the sense of thoroughness, that was done in ruining the continental American sugar industry and in sugar-starving and endangering the security of the nation. It must have been a great comfort to Americans hungering for sugar to know that Jimmy was collecting commissions on Cuban sugar company insurance policies.

Florida alone could supply the sugar needs of the United States. But the New Deal had blocked the development of Florida's sugar industry to an even greater extent than it has throttled Louisiana's. With war once again on hand, national safety demands that continental United States shall be made independent of any off-shore sources.

An investigation of each and every phase of the New Deal Agricultural Allotment plan, represented as Roosevelt's boon to farmers, would reveal exactly the same type of devious subsidy of speculators and financial interests, allied with the Dynasty. And in each case there could be found a similar "pay-of".

Anent the club which Jimmy wielded in building up his insurance business, Hamilton Fish relates an illuminating story. He relates that, though he himself is in the insurance business, he took Jimmy to the office of President Gifford of the American Telephone and Telegraph Company and urged the wisdom of giving him some of the A. T. T. insurance business.

"You know who that is, don't you", Fish told Gifford.

"Yes", Gifford replied.

"Well, it is a good thing to have a friend in court", Fish advised.

Gifford refused to permit blackmailing his Company. Shortly thereafter an investigation of the A. T. T. was launched.

Even Jimmy's "liberalism" was bought and paid for according to Robert W. Kenny. He stated in an A.P. dispatch dated September 6, 1947,

"In 1946, Mr. Roosevelt was paid $25,000 to support progressive candidates, but he was too busy selling insurance to make more than a few perfunctory appearances."

However loyal F. D. R., and his New Deal, may have been to the Dynasty and its financial supporters in the matter of sugar, it is obvious that he was equally disloyal, or traitorous, to his "solid Democratic" Louisiana voters. But he felt, no doubt, that there was no need to court even with promise an electorate stupidly loyal to him, even while he was engaged in betraying them.

The same pattern was repeated ad infinitum and ad nauseam in all the various industries in which the Dynasty and its financial supports were interested. In the interest of kinsman William C. Clayton, of Anderson, Clayton and Company, and their foreign cotton monopolies (that had been built up with the aid of Roosevelt and the Dynasty during World War I) the cotton growers of the South were betrayed and bankrupted by the New Deal in even worse fashion than were the sugar growers. Indeed, it can be said without much fear of contradiction that in times of need President Franklin Delano Roosevelt was the worst enemy the South ever had.

Though the Democratic and Republican branches of the Dynasty make a great display of animosity to the public, behind the scenes they cooperate very amicably in raiding the Treasury. The Roosevelt Steamship Company, Inc. is an excellent example of such cooperation. Kermit Roosevelt, Republican son of Theodore Roosevelt was its President and Director; he also served as Director of the American Line Steamship Corporation, President and Director of the United States Lines Company, and Vice President and Director of the United States Lines Operations Inc. Vincent Astor, nephew and close intimate of President Franklin Delano Roosevelt and heavy contributor to his campaign funds, was also Director in the same companies. Until the Dynasty and Democratic Senators raised objections, in the early days of the New Deal, that the public might grow suspicious of the association and forbade it, F. D. R. spent most of his weekends on Vincent Astor's yacht, the Nourmahal. Archibald B. Roosevelt, partner of Roosevelt and Sons, was also Director of Roosevelt Steamship Company.

The dealings of the Roosevelt Steamship Company and the other lines controlled by the group with United States Shipping Board under the terms that were most amazingly generous to them, have cost the American taxpayers enormously. The City of Rayville, for instance had two Busch diesel engines replaced on one trip at a cost of over half a million dollars, at the expense of the taxpayers. The Shipping Board paid the bill, the Company collected the revenue. How many millions were drained out of the U. S. Treasury by the relative "enemies" of Roosevelt make interesting though disgusting reading. But they are an eloquent commentary on the sham enmity between the two branches of the Dynasty, faked to ensure that they will continue in power no matter which political party wins elections

Chapter XVII

THE ROOSEVELTS MAKE HAY

The most disgusting spectacle of the Roosevelt administration and of all American history, was the exploitation of the office of President by the members of the Roosevelt family. It became the accepted practice to resort to open bribery of the President or his entourage, or to subsidize a member of his immediate family, when seeking Presidential favor. Not even the dog Fala escaped. I cite a few instances.

Henry J. Kaiser, who borrowed hundreds of millions of dollars from the government agencies, much of which he seeks to avoid repaying, and who did an enormous government business, presented President Roosevelt in 1944 with a not so trifling Christmas gift —a $25,000 solid platinum ship model.

In appreciation of his efforts in engineering billions of "Lend Lease" and in securing our entry into the war in her behalf, England, through Lord Beaverbrook, presented Harry L. Hopkins and his wife with a $3,-000,000 emerald parure and other such trifling jewels. Exposure led to a weak and equivocal denial.

Anna Roosevelt Dall Boettiger and her husband's lucrative employments that derived from Presidential favors have been recounted. A more recent one that is very striking was publicized in an article in the December 2, 1947 issue of LOOK magazine entitled "The World's Most Generous Man". It recounts the case of Charlie Ward, President of Brown and Bigelow. Ward had been sentenced to ten years at Leavenworth in the early 20's, for the illegal possession of narcotics. The sentencing judge called him "a man beneath contempt". He was released in 1925. President Roosevelt gave Ward a full and unconditional pardon in 1935. LOOK reports that Ward "is believed to have partially subsidized" the *Arizona Times*, which Mr. and Mrs. Boettiger now publish as their latest "assisted" venture with $50,000 and Barney Baruch with $10,000. It is now reported that Boettiger has been applying to his former employer, Col. H. McCormack of the Chicago Tribune.

James, Elliott, and Franklin D. Jr. junketed at the expense of taxpayers and enjoyed a family picnic at Casablanca. They were on the job when overnight, President F. D. Roosevelt announced a hundred percent increase in the value of the franc, from 100 to 50 for a dollar. It is doubtful that the boys lost any money on the deal.

James Roosevelt, who had difficulty in getting a start prior to his father's presidential nomination, did very well in his insurance business. An article published in 1938 in the Saturday Evening Post entitled "Jimmy Has It", related how young and inexperienced Jimmy was able to take away from veteran brokers enormous policies of concerns that had matters to square with the Administration, or sought its favor, good will or business. For a time "Crown Prince" Jimmy sought to take over political control of the Massachusetts Democratic organization from the local bosses; but he lost out.

In the midst of an intense war between rival slot machine and juke box operators, featuring such notables as back-scenes Tammany boss, Frank Costello, Jimmy Roosevelt entered the motion picture-juke box business in association with the Mills Manufacturing Company. From there it was a short step to a well paid executive position in motion picture business in Hollywood. The industry faced Federal indictment which was subsequently squashed.

It is interesting to note the connection of the group with the Automatic Voting Machine Co. The machines were denied acceptance until they became associated with the enterprise and the machines were found satisfactory for special purposes. Though the machines are merely mechanical counters, they jam with surprising regularity in districts whose vote is not "dependable". "Shims" that serve to cause registration on counters other than those intended, load the pockets of "inspectors". Though it could be done simply, the voter is given no way of knowing for what candidate his vote is counted. Elections can be stolen easily.

For a while, wandering Jimmy was tucked under the wing of his father as Presidential secretary and assistant. During the war, he flew far and wide on lend-lease business—in advance of grants to various appreciative lands. He made an astonishing success of his army career. Overnight he became a Lieutenant Colonel in the Marines and in April 1944, no doubt for military genius manifested, he was promoted to rank of Colonel.

In March 1946, Jimmy was named national director of the political organization of the Communist front, the Independent Citizens' Committee of The Arts, Sciences and Professions. He announced the organization's program of political action which included extension of price control and the OPA, repeal of the poll tax, permanent Fair Employment Practices Act, support of the Taft-Ellender-Wagner Bill, and support of the United Nations. He sat on the platform with ranking members of the Communist Party and fronted for them.

The latest reports place James Roosevelt in the employ of one of the principals of the Barbary Coast, reaching for control of the Democratic machine in California and seeking a return to the public payroll. He has been suggested by Sen. Claude Pepper for the Secretary of the Navy job, that is hereditary in the family, and for nomination for offices ranging from Congressman to Governor and President. Shrewd politicians who would like to use the "magic" of the Roosevelt name for moronic voters, regard him a poison for the Catholic vote because of his divorce. They have no fear of an adverse public reaction to his many ambiguous activities. According to columnists, Jimmy Roosevelt contemplated a political deal with Henry Wallace of which nothing has come to light, unless the third party move is a part of it.

Franklin Delano Roosevelt Jr. married Ethel Du Pont in a prearranged alliance between the Dynasties, graduated from law school, entered the Navy as lieutenant and was rapidly promoted on the same day as his brother in April 1944, to the rank of Lieutenant Commander. He identified himself as veteran with various left wing and Communist front veterans' organizations and with the P.A.C. Though he undertook to berate landlords who seek some return on their investments, and other capitalists, he has not yet renounced the considerable dowry that came with his wife or turned over any of his inheritances to the proletariat.

When Communism became unpopular, he shifted to a stand a bit less to the left and engaged in the usual tactics of the Marxist dialectician, shadow-boxing with Communism. In February 1946 he was appointed chairman of a Committee of 1000 of the crimson Union for Democratic Action. In April 1947, he joined forces with Eleanor Roosevelt's favorite, the perpetual youth Joseph P. Lash, in the wholly Red Americans for Democratic Action, at its state convention in Albany.

He has joined the ranks of the Labor Barons. August 7, 1947, his appointment as counsel for the Upholsterers International Union of North America (AFL) was announced. Despite rumors of divorce, the F. D. R's Jrs. as recently as August 6, 1947 were picked up by the police for chasing one another in speeding cars along the Nassau Boulevard in the early hours of the morning. In May 1948, Louella Parsons reported that Mrs. F. D. Roosevelt Jr. made public appearances with some fresh "shiners" which she intimated were evidence of her husband's military prowess. She reports a divorce is once again in the offing.

Elliott Roosevelt's phenomenal rise in the business world, on the wings of Hearst's anxieties, has been related. He was not content at the age of twenty-eight with a mere $50,000 income with which Hearst provided him as Vice President of Hearst's radio chain. In 1938, with the support of Charles F. Roeser and Sid W. Richardson, Texas oil operators, who invested $500,-000, Elliott set up a chain of 23 radio stations in Texas. This provided him, according to the Washington Times-Herald of August 29, 1945, with an income of $76,000 a year, more than his father earned as President of the United States. The enterprise is reported to have lost $100,000 in the first three months. The Transcontinental Broadcasting Company was liquidated in 1941.

Elliott Roosevelt is possessed of all the financial genius of his father who was his mentor and aid. In 1939, to expand his radio properties, Elliott arranged a series of loans. Through Congressman William I. Sirovich and Caruthers E. Ewing, Elliott approached John Hartford, president of the Great Atlantic & Pacific Tea Company for a loan of $200,000. The Atlantic and Pacific Tea Company chain was then under fire of the New Deal. Hartford was originally reluctant to make the loan. Elliott phoned President Roosevelt at the White House and had him intercede with Hartford on his behalf. With a greeting of "Hello John," to Hartford, whom he had never met, the President urged him to make the loan as "a sound business proposition and a *fine thing*". (Ed. for whom?) After he had come to an understanding with F. D. R., Hartford made the loan.

In 1942, Jesse Jones, Secretary of Commerce, told John Hartford, according to Ewing, that the Roosevelt *family* wanted to compromise the indebtedness. John Hartford was "induced" to settle the loan at two cents on the dollar and surrender the stock, which was represented as worthless, to Jesse Jones.

"It was settled satisfactorily to all parties, so I took the note and the stock certificate to Jesse Jones in person." Ewing said, according to a U.P. report of June 12, 1945 from Danville, Illinois. "He gave me a check payable to John Hartford for $4,000, which was all he received on the loan, and the whole thing was closed."

Elliott was not even called upon by the Internal Revenue, to pay income tax on his net profit in this transaction, though John Hartford was permitted to deduct his losses from his income in an extraordinary tax ruling. It pays to be of the Dynasty even in income tax matters. Not even a Congressional investigation, largely perfunctory, altered the situation.

An anti-chain store bill had been introduced in Congress three months before this $200,000 "loan" of John Hartford's to Elliott. It would have crippled the A & P stores, but died in committee three months after the loan, due to opposition to it from the White House. The outspoken Deadwood Pioneer Times, in its issue of July 8, 1945 commented caustically:

"All this tends to leave a bad taste in the mouth of Mr. Average Citizen. The ease with which a man with ability to pay was able to settle a $200,000 account for $4000 and the evident willingness of Mr. Hartford to accept such a settlement—at a time, remember, when an anti-chain store measure was being presented to the House of Representatives—leads one to believe that the deal came right off the bottom of the deck. *We'd rather be the President's son than President.*"

It points out that Roosevelt had been instrumental in getting Congressman Patman to introduce the anti-chain store bill; and that Congressman Sirovich who had approached Hartford for the "touch" had pointed up the debate on the floor of the House by directly referring to the A & P in the debate. It intimates that this loan was one of the characteristic New Deal blackmails of industry and commerce in which FDR participated personally and directly. Congressman Sirovich died *suddenly,* shortly after the deal was consummated.

The further history of this loan and its stock collateral is notable. At the very time that this loan was settled, the stock that had been represented to Hartford as worthless, had already begun to rise in value. Jesse Jones turned over the recovered stock to President Roosevelt personally. F. D. R. held the stock until November 9, 1943. By this time the stock was so valuable that F. D. R. personally sent it to Elliott's divorced second wife, Mrs. Ruth Googin Roosevelt Fidson, in a settlement to provide for the childen of that marriage.

By 1945, the stock issue, according to a statement which Elliott Roosevelt made to a reporter of the theatrical sheet, Variety, was worth more than $1,500,000. Its value had been materially increased by another intercession by President Roosevelt on behalf of his ex-daughter-in-law, Mrs. Fidson in the affairs of the Alamo Broadcasting Company of San Antonio, as was related in a petition filed with the Federal Communication Commission, December 15, 1945, by Norman Baker of Laredo. Baker was President of the Cia Industrial Universal Mexico that had previously owned the powerful Mexican radio station XENT. In his petition, he stated that, while he was serving a term in Leavenworth, the Alamo Broadcasting Company had obtained by collusion an option to buy the equipment of station XENT through a fraudulent act of one of his employees.

Five months after President Roosevelt had turned over the stock to his ex-daughter-in-law, Mrs. Fidson, Baker stated, she had visited the President at the White House to seek his support for the application of the Alamo Broadcasting Company to the Federal Communications Commission for an increase in the power of its radio station. The FCC granted the application rapidly and without notice or hearing for interested parties, and a construction permit for the new station, in November 1944.

Baker was blackmailed with the threat that he would be sent back to Leavenworth if he did anything to interfere. He did however obtain a decree from the President of Mexico forbidding the exportation of the equipment of his station XENT. This decree was violated by the conspirators, and on a dark night in April 1945 the equipment was smuggled across the border in trucks.

The Hartford loan was but one of a series made by Elliott Roosevelt in connection with his radio venture. From David G. Baird, a New York insurance man, Elliott borrowed on his radio stock, $70,000, which was later settled for $29,800; and $50,000 from Maxwell M. Bilofsky, a radio equipment manufacturer looking for government business, settled for $20,000; and Charles Harwood, $25,000. (He was later appointed Governor of the Virgin Islands by Roosevelt).

Elliott Roosevelt did not limit his business genius to the field of radio. His early interest in aviation was never lost. It is reported that Elliott had a hand in the cancellation of the airmail contracts in 1935, with an eye to the delivering of the airmail contracts to one company as a monopoly. The fatal accidents to the army aviators who attempted to fly the mails in totally inadequate "crates" did much to block this deal through public indignation.

World War II found Elliott Roosevelt in the service,

not in the non-commissioned ranks like his fellow citizens of equal education and lack of experience, but as an officer, as befitted a member of the Royal Family, in charge of the War Department reconnaissance branch. While he was chief, General Arnold ordered the purchase of one hundred planes of the type designed by Howard Hughes, a protegé and intimate friend of Jesse Jones, and associate of Elliott Roosevelt, at a cost of $44,000,000, in spite of the opposition of Major General O. P. Echols. An investigation was made in June 1947 into the failure of Hughes to deliver any of the planes which the government had ordered from him and advanced money to construct. In the course of the investigation it was revealed that Col. Elliott Roosevelt had accepted the largess of Howard Hughes, directly, or indirectly through the latter's public relations agent, John E. Meyer.

The records and evidence submitted to the Senate War Investigating Committee indicated that Meyer catered to the whims and needs of government officials ranging from Secretary of the Interior Krug to mere Army officers with whom Hughes did business. He supplied them with everything from wining, dining and hotel accommodations to call girls. The girls were rewarded with gifts and money. A letter dated September 26, 1944 introduced in evidence disclosed a gift of a costly bag to the actress Faye Emerson. Several months later Meyers gave Faye Emerson in marriage (his third) to Elliott Roosevelt in a spectacular wedding at Grand Canyon; and threw a wedding party for him. Evidence indicated that this costly entertaining was charged to the Government account, but nothing has ever been done about it.

Elliott Roosevelt has been a staunch supporter and advocate in the U. S. of Soviet Russia and the Communists, as has his intimate Henry Wallace. As recently as April 19, 1947, the Associated Press reported that Elliott Roosevelt lauded Wallace "as a political messiah with a true vision of the World and of the American political situation". Late in 1946, Elliott went on a trip to Russia as a guest of the Soviet government, with the wife that Meyer gave away to him, to secure material for an article for Look magazine. At an entertainment at the United States Embassy in Moscow, Elliott Roosevelt is reported to have said:

" . . . the United States has no business concerning itself with what happens along the Danube . . . the

Russians should get the Dardanelles from Turkey . . . Russia has never broken her word whereas the United States and Britain have often welshed". Finally he said, "Can anyone here name one instance in which the United States acted to further the cause of peace? . . . You know as well as I do that the United States is supporting the U. N. for purely selfish and imperialistic reasons.."

An affidavit filed by Mrs. D. Sherover and reported in the press on March 19, 1947, in her N. Y. Supreme Court action for divorce revealed that her husband and fellow traveller Charlie Chaplin had joined Elliott Roosevelt in fostering Communist propaganda by exhibiting Russian films in the U. S.

Elliott has been a great help and comfort to a host of subversive agencies and organizations. He has never missed an opportunity to trade on his father's reputation, including a series of books which he has written or had ghosted for him.

Elliott Roosevelt and F. D. R. Jr. have presidential aspirations. This has led them to turn against presidential candidate Wallace in a statement denouncing him in favor of Eisenhower, who says he is not a candidate. This episode was amusingly cartooned in the New York World Telegram under the caption "Children's Hour". The Roosevelt children evidently think that if they can stir up enough dissension in the Democratic Party, one of them may be picked in 1948 or 1952, to carry on the royal line as called for in Nickerson's blueprint of the New Deal.

Reports in the press on April 8, 1948, indicate that Elliott's genius has found a new outlet. He and his mother are opening a tavern, the Val Kill Inn, at Hyde Park nearby the memorial which F. D. R. set up for himself, directly on the road on the same side, where it might do a better business than the competing inn which they are trying to induce Howard Johnson to set up one hundred feet off the opposite side of the road on land they are trying to sell. It is sincerely to be hoped that in the tavern enterprise they have at last attained a status satisfactory to their intellectual and social level, and the land will be no further annoyed.

His variegated activities have netted Elliott $1,175,-000 in twelve years, according to the Washington Times-Herald report of August 29, 1945.

John Roosevelt has enjoyed little publicity. It is

reported "he believed the war was unnecessary . . . was precipitated by lovers of war, refused to enlist or to serve in any military capacity whatsoever. Finally, under pressure from his mother he accepted a military post in the South Seas with the understanding that at no time would it be necessary for him to take a life or engage in combat."

His flair is ladies' dresses and he has recently purchased an interest in a California drygoods business. He is the only member of the family who has refrained from exploiting the Presidency.

Eleanor Roosevelt, generally referred to sarcastically as Queen Eleanor, was a bit less crude than the boys, but far more systematic in her exploitation of the President and the Roosevelt name. F. D. R. had never managed to make enough to enable the family to live in the manner born. Eleanor had helped support the family with various enterprises including the Todhunter School and the Val Kill furniture store. Fortune magazine, in its October 1932 issue expanding on the inadequacy of F. D. R's. income for the support of his family made the significant statement:

". . . he has always been able to live on a higher scale than most people of his means."

By the time that F. D. R. had reached the White House, most of the children were grown up, even though they had not managed to make a living for themselves. There was no real pressure to force Eleanor to cheapen the office of President by exploiting it so shabbily, other than desire for money.

The situation which the Roosevelts created by their exploitation of the Presidency emphasizes the need for provision of a munificent salary and life-long annuity for the Chief Executive of the land. There would then be no excuse for commercial exploitation of the office and it should be prohibited by law and by tradition.

In her commercial activities Eleanor Roosevelt did her share to further the drive for dictatorship. This was particularly true in her editorial work. At times her indiscretion gave the game away. This was particularly true of the article she wrote for the December 31, 1938 issue of Liberty Magazine on the Jewish question. She revealed how closely she and the New Dealers followed the Nickerson blueprint. The Jews, she stated, are a problem and to be feared by the Gentile world. She decried the treatment accorded the Jews by the Nazis, but not on ethical or moral grounds.

She decried it because "by doing it it seems we would arouse 'compatriots' living in other countries to defend their brethren". Note she wrote "compatriots", not "co-religionists", implying that the Jews are aliens. She proposed, as a solution, the restriction of the number of Jews and other minorities (including Negroes) who might occupy "high places" in politics and enter vocations, which is known as the "numerus clausus", and a government-fostered migration of them so as to minimize the influence of their vote.

The attitude of the Roosevelts can not be said to differ materially in these matters from those of Hitler, of the Ku Klux Klan and other of the more notorious purveyors of hate or the blueprint laid down by Hoffman Nickerson in his book. For them Negroes, Catholics and Jews are not Americans, but are inferior minorities that are merely to be tolerated and used by the Roosevelt clan and their allies, to whom they conceive America belongs by "Divine Right".

It was not unnatural that Eleanor who poses as an uplifter, should pretend that her activities supported charities. This pretense was sadly punctured by a number of events, especially the Burlington, Vermont incident, which was brought to the attention of Congress by Congressman Plumley. Eleanor R. (Roosevelt, not Regina) had been invited to address the Mary Fletcher Hospital Auxiliary to raise money for the hospital. She said her agent, W. Colston Leigh, insisted that she would not lecture for less than one thousand dollars, charity or no charity. The embarassed Auxiliary, with misgivings, agreed to pay the thousand.

"As a charitable venture to raise money for the hospital". Plumley reported to Congress "the affair was a minus quantity. As a revenue producer for the *First Lady* it was a success to the tune of the $1000, she charged the ladies auxiliary".

On this occasion, Eleanor R. was shamed by the report to Congress, into really contributing to charity, with the comment:

"Since they are evidently inexperienced in business affairs, I have asked Mr. Leigh to refund *my share of the money.*" Her *"charity"* extended only to giving back a part of what she had extracted, even when thus confronted.

Another such incident was that of Johnson City, Tennessee. When Eleanor arrived to lecture, she was sadly informed that they had raised only $500. She grimly replied that her contract forbade her opening her mouth for less than $1000, on the line and in advance. The Committee hurriedly borrowed the extra $500 from the local banker on personal notes. Then Eleanor opened her mouth, and charity and wisdom fairly drooled from it, a thousand dollars worth. To pay the note, the town raffled off a Chevrolet car, that is now known as "Eleanor's car".

When on another occasion she was given a prize by Gimbel Brothers, she ostentatiously gave it to "charity". She stipulated that the money should be used in F. D. R.'s business, Georgia Warm Springs. It looked much like taking it out of one pocket and putting it in another.

The only contributions of Eleanor Roosevelt's that ever have been authenticated were those to the Communist front and the fellow traveler organizations. To them, Eleanor gave unstintingly of her time, her energy, and her funds. They gave in return. She is no parlor pink, but has been an intimate associate of the founders of the Communist Party in the United States almost from the beginning. It was as much her influence as that of Rockefeller's agent, Harry L. Hopkins, that played upon F. D. R.'s suggestibility and constantly warped him to the left.

Though Eleanor Roosevelt persistently has denied membership in the Communist Party, her actions have spoken louder than her words. Her leftist attitudes, in view of her quest for wealth and her eagerness to serve capitalistic industry in her broadcasts and elsewhere was obviously an expedient pose that she regarded as politically advantageous. She undoubtedly is cognizant of the program to use Communism to destroy democracy and set up a dictatorship in the United States. She was the virtual head of the left-wing "Youth Movement" and her conduct with its active leader, the perpetual youth, Joseph Lash raised considerable scandal. The press reported with especial gusto the flight made by Eleanor Roosevelt in a Red Cross uniform and an Army bomber to the Solomon Islands. When she arrived there it was reported, she kissed Joe Lash squarely on the mouth and rubbed noses with the natives.

Her intervention eliminated the enemy whom the Communists most hated and feared, Robert Stripling, chief investigator of the Un-Americanism Committee, by having him drafted though he should have been exempted. She could be relied on to effect entry for the most dangerous and objectionable Communists. She was almost entirely responsible for the entry into the country of the Communist ringleaders, the Rockefeller subsidized Eislers who recently have been deported. Ringleaders of the subversive Red and fellow traveler organizations were always welcomed by her as guests in the White House.

Eleanor R.'s projected trip to Russia to join the subversives in doing homage to Stalin, however, was blocked by the powers-that-be, through the State Department and F. D. R.

Eleanor's domination of F. D. R. as President was not a matter of uxoriousness. For there were rumors of impending divorce in 1927 and various names were mentioned. Eleanor Roosevelt was seldom at the side of her husband, even in his most serious ailments. It has often been remarked that as a rule, except during election campaigns, wherever Franklin went, Eleanor went in the opposite direction. In 1933, Fraser Edwards commented in the syndicated column, Washington Sideshow on the extraordinarily friendly relations of Harry Hopkins and Eleanor Roosevelt as follows:

"Mrs. Eleanor Roosevelt through her intense interest in unemployments relief, is a frequent caller on Harry Hopkins, Federal Relief Administrator. To call, she must ride up nine floors in a far-from-modern elevator. When she gets to Hopkin's office, modestly Mrs. Roosevelt sends in her name. Hopkin's secretary announces 'Mrs. Roosevelt is waiting to see you.' In she goes.

* * * *

"Hopkins with old-fashioned courtesy escorts Mrs. Roosevelt down the elevator to the front door, and she walks back to the White House, two blocks away, unaccompanied and scarcely noticed."

The picture is so affecting that one wonders why Fraser Edwards was relieved shortly thereafter of his Washington Sideshow assignment and his by-line, on demand from on high.

In the November 1936 issue of Vogue, J. Franklin Carter, who was often called upon to do personal publicity work for the President, published an article justifying the relations of Harry L. Hopkins and Eleanor Roosevelt.

Following the death of Harry L. Hopkin's second

wife, Eleanor Roosevelt brought up in the White House his daughter Diana. As indicative of the moral tone of the New Deal, this marriage is noteworthy. When his first Jewish wife, né Ethel Gross, brought suit for divorce against Harry L. Hopkins, two of his former friends came into the court and testified before Judge Phillip McCook that Harry had invited them to spend the night at an apartment in which he was keeping a Barbara Duncan; they testified that on her person Harry Hopkins had extended to them the hospitality of a Bedouin in the desert, after which he himself spent the balance of the night in the bedroom. In the morning they had breakfast together. Following the divorce, Barbara Duncan became the second Mrs. Hopkins and the Second *Lady* of the Land. The story was reported, curiously enough, in only one edition of one American newspaper, the first edition of the Daily News, March 21, 1931, so effective was the censorship, even at this early date, of the press by the Dynasty.

Through her syndicated column, 'My Day," Eleanor earned a high income, appealed to the gossip-loving, had a forum for propagandizing Marxist New Dealism, insidiously waged a continuous campaign, and very transparently revealed her attachments. In those columns one reads of Esther Everitt Lape, of Harry Hopkins, of Earl Miller, of Marion Anderson, of Marys Chaney, of Rexford Tugwell, of Joseph Lash and of the amiability of the Africans. She press-agented leftist periodicals, books, plays and personages. A boost in her column was regarded as having a high commercial value.

It is in Eleanor Roosevelt's radio broadcasts that the commercial exploitation of the Presidency became most patent. Mrs. Ernest K. (Betty) Lindley "sold" her to the Pan-American Coffee Bureau. The Bureau sought favors of Washington in quotas and pricing of coffee that meant the ruination of the American coffee trade. She sold the prestige of the White House, and the desire to influence the Government Bureaus and secure their cooperation was undoubtedly a consideration. Eleanor's fees from the P-A Coffee Bureau are reported to have been more than $2000 a broadcast. These broadcasts were financed indirectly by the United States Government through subsidies granted Latin American countries. Thus Eleanor probably indirectly collected from the United States Government a greater salary than did the President.

This took place at the time that Nelson Rockefeller, who had evaded the draft and military service by ordering his appointment as Co-Ordinator of Hemispheric Defense, had obtained for himself a coffee empire in Brazil by cunning and unscrupulous use of the funds, totaling about six billion dollars, that he had induced Congress to entrust to him for "South American defenses". He thereby became one of the largest coffee producers in Brazil. And with the aid of more taxpayers' funds via the Import Export Bank, he cartelized coffee in Brazil and around the world, cornered the coffee market and jacked up the price of coffee from pennies to more than a dollar. This typical Rockefeller "philanthrophy" gouged the same taxpayers, whose money had made the corner possible, out of tens of millions of dollars. In that loot, Eleanor Roosevelt undoubtedly shared, because of her "cooperation".

Eleanor's services were sought and paid for at about the same rate by the candy manufacturers who feared that candy would be declared non-essential and banded together to form the Council on Candy as a Food in the War Effort. Among these paid broadcasts was her "report to the mothers of the nation" following her return from Europe.

There was a premonitory significance to the richly jewelled gold crown and other rich gifts which King Ibn Saud presented to Eleanor R. (Roosevelt not Regina) to show his appreciation for the many millions of American taxpayers' money that Roosevelt handed over to him on behalf of the Rockefeller-Standard Oil interests.

The Dynasty's New Deal charity-begins-at-home pattern did not stop with the immediate family. Our diplomatic corps was packed with cousins of all degrees. Colorful Sumner Welles, a remoter cousin, was made Assistant Secretary of State until Cordell Hull forced his resignation for dark and obscure reasons. With Nelson Rockefeller he instituted our "good neighbor" policy which was designed to place, with the taxpayers' money, control of the resources of Latin America in the hands of the Rockefeller Empire and the Dynasty. David Gray, another cousin, was made Ambassador to Ireland. Cousin Lincoln MacVeagh has been Ambassador to Greece, where $400,000,000 sent as part of the "Truman plan" to "stop Communism" in Greece resulted in establishing a Communist government in the northern half of the country. Cousin A. J. Drexel Biddle was Ambassador to Poland during its debacle and subsequently served in the same capacity in France. Cousin Francis Biddle was one of the most pro-Red Attorney Generals. Cousin James L. Houghteling, was pro-Red Commissioner of Immigration and was subsequently transferred to the position of Director of the National Organization Division of the Treasury where he worked side by side with Cousin Charles W. Adams, Assistant National Director of the Division. The list of the Dynastic relatives who are cared for out of the public payroll could be extended indefinitely; but it would merely serve to further illustrate the extent of nepotism and favoritism that taxpayers support.

Uncle Frederic A. Delano, in addition to his Federal Reserve Bank appointment, also holds the following: Chairman, Advisory Council, Bureau of Plain Industry, Soils, and Agricultural Engineering; Director, Columbia Institution For The Deaf; member, Commission for the Construction of Washington-Lincoln Memorial Gettysburg Boulevard; first vice president, Washington National Monument Society. He served also, for a time as chairman of the International Commission of the League of Nations On Inquiry Into The Production Of Opium In Persia. This appointment had an amusing aspect. Warren Delano, his father and FDR's grandfather founded his fortune on smuggling opium into China.

The most pathetic aspect of this corrupt and ruthless commercial exploitation of the Presidency is the apathy of the public and the depravity that has led to their acceptance of the cheap, sordid and revolting exploitation of the highest public office; and their acceptance of the idea that all public officers may be expected to be crudely dishonest and vilely corrupt.

CHAPTER XVIII

ROCKEFELLER EMPIRE AND DYNASTY MERGE

A "NEW DEAL" FOR MONOPOLIES

World wide monopoly of industry and commerce is the goal of the Rockefeller Empire and its allies and agents, the Roosevelt-Delano Dynasty. That is the planned purpose of "New Deal" for themselves.

The industrial monopolies which they control are fed from the Treasury and the public's purse. Their Milk Trust's monopoly was extended, and even in depression the price of milk was tripled. Their monopoly of food has been widened, with the cooperation of the truckmen's unions, to the point where they maintain a constantly high price even for produce, throughout the nation the entire year.

The seizure of industries which they did not control and the setting up of new monopolies assumed a fresh pattern under their New Deal. No longer was it necessary for them to resort *as individuals* to the racketeering of the South Side Improvement Company type and risk public indignation. Their agencies, the Government and the unions, do their dirty work, undermine the industries which they seek, smash them so as to force out the investing public and form them into monopolies to be taken over.

When these things are done by the "New Deal" they have the complete support of the very radical and labor elements which would rail at them if done by private enterprise for itself. By some curious quirk of mentality akin to faith, they are happy and content when these crimes are committed for the benefit of the same private cartels through public agencies by themselves as agents, at public expense. For the "liberal" or radical does not seek to remedy evil situations. He merely seeks to be master of them himself. He is motivated not by principle but by envy and unprincipled greed. That was the Machiavellian idea that lay behind the Rockefeller support of Communism and its incorporation in the New Deal mechanics for attaining monopoly and dictatorship.

The NRA (National Industrial Recovery Administration) and the Federal Securities Act with its provision barring holding companies and enhancing the Federal Reserve Board's power to regulate money, constituted the initial effort to accomplish a complete cartelization of all industries.

The NRA was openly a device for setting up monopolies or giving legality to existent monopolies, in their own interest, in every industry. It specifically suspended the Sherman-Clayton Anti-Trust Act and permitted each industry to organize itself under an absolute code authority.

The man who controlled the Code Authority wielded dictatorial powers over an absolute monopoly. The rules promulgated by the Code Authority had the force of law for both industry and the nation. It fixed prices, controlled production, licensed producers, admitted or barred newcomers from the industry, set conditions of competition, prescribed the amount of space and the machinery that could be used; and also possessed police and judicial powers and could put violators in jail. As a sop to Labor, a minimum wage of $12 to $15 per 40 hour week was provided and Section 7A recognized the *right* of collective bargaining. In other words the NRA created a syndicalist or corporate state in the U. S. at about the same time as had Mussolini and Hitler, whose sponsors were the same as those of the NRA.

The SEC established by the Federal Securities Act, is a device for tightening the monopoly of industries by control of financing. Its power to block new financing is absolute. Likewise its order to wipe out investments in railroad and utility securities is final. But it offers stockholders absolutely no protection. On the one hand numerous securities that have been passed on by the SEC and marketed, have been wiped out within a period of one or two years. On the other hand numerous worthwhile and essential enterprises have been barred from financing. Its effect on the mining industry for instance, has been devastating; and as a consequence the U. S. is becoming constantly less self-sufficient in strategic minerals and metals.

In short the SEC was never intended to serve the interests of the investor, but was planned to foster the purposes of the monopolies. This is quite manifest in its utility securities activities. In this group of securities alone, the SEC has wiped out, in a decade, more of the public's investments than all of Wall Street's swindles of a century past.

The Roosevelts, the Adamses, the Rockefellers and many other of the Dynasty and its allies are heavily interested in local utilities. They did not, however, join the ranks of the utility magnates who scrambled to attain in the twenties, with banking support, widespread utility empires in the wildly speculative market. It was not because the Dynasty did not realize the tremendous riches of the basic and essential power industry. On the contrary, in their plans a monopoly of all sources of power and energy, as comprehensive as their American Telephone and Telegraph Company in its field, that will extend from the Arctic to Tierra del Fuego, looms very large. It was because they control the currency and banking system as well as the government and have acquired even greater strength through the enhanced powers they have given themselves through the Federal Reserve Bank. They were confident that they were safe in permitting others to develop the power systems with moneys invested by the public. Then by manipulating a depression as well as by retroactive laws written for the purpose, they could rob their rivals of their work and the public of their investments. That is the purpose of the abolition of holding companies and the power over utilities incorporated in the Federal Exchange Act.

The SEC has directed a looting of the public of its investments in utilities that is fully comparable with those perpetrated by the Nazis and Communists. By dishonest and wholly illegal and un-Constitutional acts that have been supported by corrupted and packed courts, the conspirators that control the SEC deliberately depressed and manipulated the market for utility securities by its orders and rulings. The TVA was used for the malevolent purpose of smashing the market in utility securities. On the day that the ruinously low rates for TVA power were to be announced, the press and the nation were kept waiting for Commissioner David E. Lillienthal from 10:30 A. M. until after the markets had closed. In the meantime a terrific wave of short selling hit the utility bonds and stocks that depressed them terrifically. Washington phone calls to Wall Street were particularly heavy that day, especially from the Reconstruction Finance Corporation offices. There can be no question that the announcement of the TVA rates was a prearranged signal for a "killing" in the market by the conspirators. These maneuvers cost the investing public hundreds of millions of dollars. The market for utility securities was smashed, and they dropped steadily thereafter.

The Federal Reserve Board has ably aided and abetted the swindling of the public by manipulation of margin requirements. Repeatedly it has forced the public out of stock desired by the powers-that-be by raising margin requirements, at the bottom of the market, just before large upswings were planned.

The conspirators then bought up at their own price, or virtually stole, a particular class of security in each company. It has been a simple matter for them to dictate that the particular class of security which they had cornered shall be given complete control of the utility in question, all senior securities shall be retired and junior securities wiped out, without regard to earnings or values.

It is safe to predict that when the nation's utility companies will have been "simplified in structure" (a euphemism for "stolen") they will be, in due time, merged into a nation-and continent-wide Power Trust, under the domination of the Rockefeller Empire and its Dynastic allies. This they have accomplished through their agent, FDR.

The public has been looted, under the direction of the Interstate Commerce Commission, during the Roosevelt Administration of many more billions through another industry dominated by the Dynasty and its allies, through the railroads. The Roosevelts, the Delanos, the Rockefellers, the Harrimans and numerous others of America's rulers are heavily interested in railroads.

The Interstate Commerce Commission which they dominate, exercises absolute control over the minutest details of the operation of the railroads and their rate structure. It is a simple matter for them to boost the earnings of the railroads when they own their securities, and to wipe out the earnings and force them into receivership after they have unloaded the securities on the public. This is done periodically.

The I.C.C. dictates the terms for lifting of the receiverships, subject to court approval.

The Supreme Court decision in the Chicago, Milwaukee and St. Paul Railroad case has introduced several new "principles" into American jurisprudence, that contrast oddly with what has been regarded as honesty and sound law consonant with it.

The railroad had been in 77b receivership for several years following a period of earnings that were fixed by the I.C.C. so low that it could not meet its fixed charges. After the onset of hostilities in Europe, the earnings of the road rose rapidly to a point where all arrears on bonds could be paid off in full out of cash on hand and leave the company more than adequate capital for its future operations—in short the road became completely solvent and highly prosperous. If it were required, refinancing could have been arranged readily.

If this condition should arise in the affairs of a private individual in bankruptcy, he would be deemed guilty of fraud if he failed to pay off his indebtedness in full and thus secure discharge from bankruptcy. But in the case of the railroad, the Court ruled that the company **is not bound by the ethical** or legal principles that apply to individuals. Instead of ordering the corporation to pay off its indebtedness and secure its discharge from receivership, as it wished to do, the Supreme Court did the reverse. It ordered the railroad to do what would be ruled as fraudulent on the part of a private individual, i.e. to refuse to meet its obligations in full, to wipe out the major part of its debts, to defraud its creditors and stockholders, and to settle even mortgage and other protected claims at a fraction of their face value.

The legal support of fraudulent bankruptcies by the highest court of the land is a new "principle" in American jurisprudence.

But an even stranger departure is the reason assigned by the Court for its decision.

The Court acknowledged that the railroad was completely solvent at the time of the hearing. But it assumed the role of oracle and undertook to predict that after the war the earnings of the road would drop and it would no longer be solvent. For this reason it ordered a fraudulent settlement to be compounded by the Company. Subsequent events proved the Court a rotten prophet. The earnings of the road continued very high.

In this decision the Supreme Court has given legal support to the crime of fortune-telling, and has given divining and soothsaying a recognized role in arriving at legal decisions.

In this act the Supreme Court has given divining and fortune-telling greater weight in our law than it ever had even among the Romans at the time when these procedures were part of their faith and practice. It has returned American jurisprudence to a status as primitive as that of Medieval law, with its "trial by ordeal". It has nullified the entire code of law that has been built up to protect honest commercial practice. For it is a matter of record that few enterprises survive for more than a generation and most of them terminate bankrupt; and under this decision the Courts could safely divine that the majority of debtors will eventually be bankrupt and order them to defraud their creditors, as in the St. Paul case. The decision has wiped out billions of railroad investments. It is another of the New Deal devices to "distribute wealth" in certain favored directions only.

The NRA proved unwieldly and unmanageable. While it was highly successful in wiping out tens of thousands of small businesses, it failed to permit the wrecking of larger units, the control of which the conspirators sought. The report brought in by the NRA Board of Review and signed, among others, by Clarence Darrow, found that the NRA was being used to foster monopoly. Senator Borah made the same charge on the floor of the Senate. The Supreme Court was called upon to declare the NRA un-Constitutional, which it did on the perfectly correct ground that it was an abdication of its Constitutional powers by Congress. Unfortunately, though this is equally true of virtually all of the New Deal, the packed and biased court has seen fit to so rule only when it serves the interests of the rulers.

With the launching of the NRA the Federal Reserve Board and other banking pressure for prolonging the depression had been relieved slightly. Business began to pick up, but not too much; because that would have upset the plans for extending monopolies. The failure of the NRA to accomplish its purpose called for resumption of the depression. President Roosevelt was put into service to mouth vigorous threats and attacks upon business with the object of smashing the stock market, and banking pressure was resumed to force a new depression in the same manner as had been done in 1929.

The Supreme Court decision wiping out the NRA was made the ground for a propaganda drive for immediate packing of the Supreme Court, instead of waiting to accomplish it gradually as called for by the blueprint of the New Deal. For it was recognized that dictatorship, in addition to being the ultimate goal, was the *sine qua non* of the immediate objectives.

The attitude of the nation and of Congress made it apparent that dictatorship and industrial monopoly could be attained only by the Lenin formula of national bankruptcy. The squandering involved in prolonging the depression, in the Agricultural Allotment Plan, in Relief, and in other deliberately wasteful measures had not irreparably damaged the solvency of the nation. Only war, civil and external, could accomplish this. War was also required to attain world-wide monopoly and fitted into the Imperial scheme.

CHAPTER XIX

ANTI-BRITISH OIL CONSPIRACY SUCCEEDS
U. S. FIGHTS UNOFFICIAL WAR

For the Rockefeller-Standard Oil Empire, a war that would forever break the hold of the antagonistic British Empire on vast oil reserves throughout the world, had become absolutely imperative. Mussolini's acquisition in their interest of the Harrar Province oil fields of Abyssinia, previously related, was a mere stopgap that could not supply all the Mediterranean market.

By far the most important oil reserve from which the Rockefeller-Standard Oil Empire was being blocked by British opposition was Saudi Arabia. In 1914 just prior to World War I, Standard Oil Co. had loaned the Turkish Government thirty-five million dollars. After the war, in 1922 they obtained a concession in Anatolia, Turkey; in 1923, the Mosul concession involved the United States deeply in European and Near-Eastern affairs; and the Admiral Chester grant that had been backed by Kuhn, Loeb and Company precipitated a battle royal with the British interests. Development was begun in 1926. New oil leases were obtained by the Rockefeller interests in Arabia in 1936. But the British still blocked their effective development, despite the fact that the Rockefeller interests had penetrated into control of Royal Dutch and Shell.

To break the impasse the oil interests turned to Germany. Sir Henry Deterding, Chairman of the Board of Royal Dutch, retired to Germany, married a Nazi girl almost forty years his junior, and on their wed-

— 184 —

ding day gave a gift of ten millions to Hitler and the Nazi Party. Standard Oil acquired a 730,000 acre concession in Germany from the North European Oil Company and extended their holdings in the German Dye Trust (I. G. Farbenindustrie). Walter Teagle, President of the Standard Oil of New Jersey and Edsel Ford became Directors of the I. G. Farbenindustrie; and Ivy Lee, Rockefeller's publicity man was retained by the I. G. at $25,000 a year to advise Hitler on Nazi German rearmament. Standard Oil of New Jersey supplied oil to Germany and finally turned over to the Nazis their refineries and accepted millions of harmonicas in payment. Texas Company's shrewd Captain Rieber made a sharper deal for his oil and received full payment in ships, eight of which were delivered before the war, and two after the war. But for that he was ousted with the outcry that he was trading with the enemy.

The plan was to build Hitler up as a menace to England, and smash the British Empire if necesary to gain control of its oil reserves and other resources. It materialized in World War II.

It was not until Hitler arrived at Dunkirk, that the British awoke to a realization that if they did not knuckle down to the Rockefeller Empire, their own would be destroyed. The British made a deal with the Rockefeller-Standard Oil interests to permit a development of the Saudi Arabia field. This was predicated on effecting the entry of the United States into World War II, the United States Navy immediately beginning to convoy British vessels, and the costs of the war being unloaded on the American taxpayers. These were the terms.

Never did Roosevelt follow the dictates of his masters with greater alacrity. His education in Germany, as a youngster, had imbued him with the spirit of Prussian militarism. His prime interest was warships and naval battles. In World War I, F.D.R had not been at the front as were other young men of his age, experiencing the miseries of war. The Dynasty had protected him from that. His war experiences had been *delightful* and *profitable.*

Franklin Delano Roosevelt had dodged the draft and evaded active military service in the war, though he was physically fit, by hanging on to his desk and swivel-chair job provided by the influence of the Dynasty. But he delighted in posing as a war hero, an act that is characteristic of the clan.

Franklin Delano Roosevelt yearned for a war of his own, bigger and brighter than ever, that would memorialize him and carry his name down through history. Peacetime Presidents generally are forgotten by history. On the day of his first inauguration, Roosevelt confided to intimate friends that he hoped to be a War President. He began rebuilding the war organization with which he had surrounded himself in World War I, immediately after his inauguration, making his wartime propagandists, McIntyre and Early, his secretaries. In 1938, after the defeat at the polls of his attempted purge, F.D.R. stated to his intimate asociates: "If I had a war, I could be reelected."

Only war could cover up the crude conspiracy of the New Dealers, and save them from the resentment of the nation.

The internal situation in the U.S., as has been related, demanded from the point of view of the Dynastic conspirators, war. A war emergency would justify a third term, would enable establishment of an absolute dictatorship, and would facilitate welding gigantic trusts and eliminating competition. All who opposed their conspiracy would be labelled traitors. To guard against any miscarriage of their scheme, the conspirators thumbed their noses at the nation and made the candidate of the Republican Party, which they also control, a fake opponent, a New Deal Democrat who was pledged to carry on the conspiracy, "One World", "Me Too" Wendell Willkie.

From the start of his Administration, F.D.R. spared no effort to foment war. On this score he played into the hands of his masters with alacrity. The full extent of Roosevelt's treachery and flaunting of the Constitution by intriguing war and our entry into it, will not be known until the exchange between Roosevelt and his distant cousin Winston Churchill are published. Of special interest would be the full text of the letter in which Churchill stated "between us we can divide the world."

How thoroughly incriminating they are, can be discerned from the criminal treatment accorded Tyler Kent, a loyal American employee of our Embassy in England who sought to expose the conspiracy. In spite of diplomatic immunity which entitled him to a hearing before an American judge and jury, he was turned over to the British for star chamber proceedings and imprisonment. F.D.R. did not dare let his case be heard before an American court. To this day Tyler Kent lives under threat that if he attempts to release or publish the letters, he will be literally or figuratively "bumped off." Roosevelt's conspiracy to foment a war and to get us into it in spite of the opposition of Congress and the nation if it had been adequately publicized and exposed would have resulted in his impeachment.

The Administration is hereby challenged to publish, or release for publication, the full correspondence between Roosevelt and Churchill; and to permit Tyler Kent to publish the correspondence that fell into his hands. We hereby agree to publish them at our own expense, if released.

In 1937, Winston Churchill squarely placed the blame for precipitating the war, in the lap of President Roosevelt. He stated before Parliament that the one contribution President Roosevelt could make to the prevention of war in the world, was to avoid prolonging the depression. Then he stated, the New Deal was deliberately prolonging the depression by its war on individual enterprise and private industry. Within a short time thereafter, President Roosevelt deliberately launched fresh attacks on industry, that had been recovering from depression rapidly, and precipitated a new financial panic.

In view of Churchill's warning, President Roosevelt's precipitation of panic and depression must be regarded as deliberately designed to bring war.

Equally treasonous was the "Union Now" movement in which high New Deal officials took a prominent part. The names of both President Franklin Delano Roosevelt and of Harold Ickes were bandied about in connection with it. "Union Now" demands that the United States return to the British Empire as a colony. It denounces the Revolutionary War as a great error and misunderstanding, and treats George Washington in the light of a traitor to the Empire who is forgiven his "treason". Benedict Arnold on the other hand is regarded by the movement as a great and much misunderstood patriot and hero. Memorials were planned to honor his name. And some agencies closely identified with the New Deal have had written an opera in which Benedict Arnold is portrayed in a heroic role. They planned to produce it shortly prior to our entry into the war.

Streit's "Union Now" is reported to be Princess Elizabeth's principal textbook. It very well might be that. Though Great Britain is virtually an American subsidized colony, "Union Now" demands insolently, on behalf of Britain, that actualities be ignored and the United States cast itself in the role of the most servile of the British colonies. To this, many of the Dynastie rulers of the United States gave their unqualified consent in spirit and deed. In view of the extensive intermarriage with the British nobility, it is not difficult to understand that both their sympathies and their financial interests are with England rather than with the U. S. The allegiance between the Roosevelt-Delano Dynasty and British royalty which has been detailed elsewhere, served to strengthen the tie.

Franklin Delano Roosevelt undertook to fulfill all of the conditions laid down by the British. By an illegal secret order of the President, issued without authorization of Congress, the United States Navy convoyed British and Allied vessels and actively participated in an undeclared war. In short the Dynasty and its allies declared war in the name of F.D.R. personally.

Law, the Johnson Act, forbade the loan of any funds to countries who had defaulted on the World War I debts. This law was evaded and shamefully violated by what was sardonically named "lend lease." Pretendedly it meant that we were lending or leasing materials of war to England and her Allies. From the start England boldly and baldly stated that they have no intention of repaying; and with equal effrontery, United States officials stated that they actually had no intention of asking repayment though the law required it. The Dynasty engaged to finance the war to enlarge the oil reserves of the Rockefeller Empire, with the money and lives of the American taxpayers.

Brazenly false propaganda was fed the country through all the channels of publicity controlled by the Dynasty and its allies—newspapers, periodicals, radio, etc.—by a veritable host of British propagandists spending billions of dollars. All the British expenditures on this false propaganda were later repaid with usurious interest, out of the pockets of the American taxpayers. The Nazi-controlled Hotel Pierre of New York City was filled with such top drawer British propagandists. After the war was over, the British government acknowledged the expenditure of billions on their U. S. propaganda. The objectives of the propaganda was to deceive the American taxpayer into believing that England was fighting the war for the U.S. and that American taxpayers must pay the costs. Later the cost even of the false propaganda was charged to the American taxpayer.

In the meantime the world was amazed at Hitler's failure to make the easy, simple crossing of the English Channel, that could have been made in a few hours. Had there been known the Dunkirk deal between the Rockefeller-Standard Oil interests and the British, the situation would have been understood more readily. For it was common knowledge that as a result of the victory of the I. G. Farbenindustrie (the German Dye Trust) in its feud with the Steel Trust for the control of Nazi Germany, the Rockefeller-Standard Oil interests had a powerful voice in the domination of their creature, Hitler. He was ordered to turn aside from England and attack Germany's ally, Russia. This attack on Russia added the Communist support to England's propaganda pressure to force the U. S. into the war. The Rockefeller support of the Communist elements further insured the Red's support of the war propaganda.

The United States was engaged in an unofficial Dynastic war on the Axis long before the official declaration of war by Congress. Roosevelt and his masters did what they could to provoke Hitler to declare war on the U.S.. But their plans to force Congress to declare war met with greater success in another direction —Pearl Harbor.

President Franklin Delano Roosevelt's treacherous, dastardly and criminal acts involved in getting the United States in the war have been leniently presented by Charles A. Beard in his "President Roosevelt and the Coming of the War 1941: A Study in Appearance and Reality."

CHAPTER XX

"OIL IS THICKER THAN BLOOD"

PEARL HARBOR
A ROOSEVELT-ROCKEFELLER-STANDARD OIL
VICTORY

By the nineteen hundred and twenties the Socony-Vacuum, Standard Oil subsidiaries had gained a virtual monopoly of the market for oil for the lamps of China. It was a monopoly dear to the heart of Rockefeller, of the type he sought to extend to the whole world. Kerosene was sold at prohibitive prices in tiny amounts to fill gift lamps distributed by the Company. But if ever the rich Chinese oil resources were developed such fantastic prices for kerosene even in beautiful tin cans, would be out of the question. It was essential for the monopoly and price structure that no oil be produced in China. The Soongs and the Nationalist Government saw to that. Blunt General Smedley Butler of the United States Marines, after his retirement roared, "All I ever did for twenty-five years in China is watch Standard Oil cans."

All went well until the War Lord of the Shansi province granted a concession to the Japs to drill for oil. The Japs found oil aplenty. This was a serious threat to the Standard Oil monopoly in China. The Chinese Nationalist Government was ordered to seize the War Lord if necessary, cancel the concession and oust the Japs. This was done in 1927.

The Japs did not take kindly to cancellation of their oil concession after spending a hundred million yen on it. Nor did they feel kindly toward the Rockefeller-Standard Oil crowd whom they knew to be responsible. They vowed to come back and seize China, if necessary to get their oil.

The Japs made good their threats and proceeded to seize China in the first Shanghai incident in 1931. And they did not forget the role played by the Rockefeller-Standard Oil crowd in the cancellation of the concessions. They avenged themselves wherever they went by destroying Rockefeller-Standard Oil property first. An illustration of how far the Japs went in destroying Rockefeller-Standard Oil property is the Panay incident. The gunboat Panay was the only representative of the United States Navy in the China Seas. For six years it plied the Yangtze River during the Jap invasions of China but was never molested. Suddenly one day in 1937, the news was blazoned to a shocked world that the Panay had been shelled by the Japs. It has never been told that the reason why the Panay had been shelled, was that it was convoying two Standard Oil tankers. That, the Japs would not tolerate.

The efforts of the Rockefeller-Standard Oil group to protect their property took three directions. First in April 1938, within a short time after the Panay incident, they made the Mitsuis of Japan, who with the Zaibatsu dominated Hiroshito and Japan's policies, their exclusive agents in North China and all conquered territory in Asia. This placed the Rockefeller-Standard Oil group in a position to influence Japan's policies.

But it has always been a Rockefeller policy never to be satisfied with half a loaf when they can get a whole loaf at no expense to themselves. To accomplish a destruction of Japan, it was necessary to bring the American Army to the rescue of their property in China. But it would have been futile for the Rockefeller-Standard Oil interests to ask Congress to declare war on Japan because it was destroying their property in China. Even their numerous agents in Congress could not afford to vote for a war on such grounds. To avoid committing political suicide, they would have to reply: "Go fly your own kite."

Franklin D. Roosevelt had no such fears or scruples. James A. Farley reported in his JIM FARLEY'S STORY (The Roosevelt Years) that Roosevelt brought up early in his first Cabinet meeting his plan to declare war on Japan which was then busy invading China (p. 39). For the background of this scheme of Roosevelt's, one must turn to a carefully suppressed story of national betrayal for private interests that is treason in its ugliest form. It is related by one of the few Rockefeller-subsidized and subverted professors whose spirit of patriotism prevailed, and led him to turn on the conspirators, Professor Harry Elmer Barnes, in his pamphlet THE STRUGGLE AGAINST THE HISTORICAL BLACKOUT.

Professor Barnes relates that Rockefeller attorney and agent, Henry L. Stimson, Secretary of State in the Hoover regime, approached Hoover on behalf of his patron, with a proposition to declare war on Japan to protect Rockefeller-Standard Oil property in China, which the Japs were destroying wherever they went. He promised Hoover, in return, that the campaign of vilification that the conspirators had launched against him, and presumably the depression about which it centered, would cease, and that he would be re-elected President. Hoover has always been a loyal and trusted Rockefeller agent, and member for many years, almost from its inception, of their Council on Foreign Relations. But President Hoover's pacifist religious scruples as a Quaker prevailed, and he refused to agree to join in this patron's war conspiracy (p. 43, 6th ed.). This account by Barnes is cited in full in the author's ROCKEFELLER "Internationalist", The Man Who Misrules The World (p. 362).

Franklin D. Roosevelt, Stimson relates in his ghosted "autobiography" ON ACTIVE SERVICE IN PEACE & WAR (p. 301), was fully in accord with Rockefeller's warmongering. This was an important factor in the Rockefeller support of Roosevelt's candidacy. Roosevelt was delighted and intrigued with the idea of his own war to "immortalize" him. But Roosevelt was restrained by Farley and other Cabinet members. They confronted him with the fact that the Constitution required that a declaration of war be made by Congress; and that neither Congress or the nation were in a mood to go to war. At that time the conspirators had not yet arrived at the point that they now have reached, of thumbing their noses at the Constitution, at Congress and at the people; and they had not yet accomplished the treasonous surrender of our sovereignty to themselves through their agency, the "United" Nations, as a device for evading the Constitution and the law.

If however, Japan could be induced to attack the U.S.—that would be a different story. To accomplish this purpose, it was imperative that the American public should have no suspicion of the significance to the Rockefeller-Standard Oil interests of Japan's aggression on China; and they never were told. This was accomplished by Rockefeller's control of the press and other avenues of publication, and the control of every newspaper and news service of importance in the land. Through the Chase National Bank, the Rockefellers control all the Hearst publications and the International News Service; also the United Press and the

— 192 —

Scripps Howard chain. The Associated Press is entirely under their domination. Arthur Hays Sulzberger of the New York Times is on the Board of Directors of the Rockefeller Foundation since rumors have circulated of his sale of the Times to Rockefeller interests.

Control of the press is the Rockefeller-Standard Oil practice in every land in which they operate. Thus when they sought the French oil monopoly, they purchased three Paris newspapers—Le Matin, Figaro and L'Eclair. Their experience has taught them not to underestimate the power of the press amongst a free people.

They control directly or indirectly, also the important magazines including the Time-Life-Fortune group, the Crowell-Collier group, the Curtis Publications, and many others. They control directly or indirectly all the large book publishing houses. They control also the radio and the motion picture industry. The Chairman of the Pulp and Paper Industry Board is John D. Rockefeller III. Through this complete control of publications they were able to suppress any mention of the damage to their property by the Japs.

Through their control of the Navy and the Government, they were able to prevent any leaks from these sources. When Admiral Yarnell, Commander of the Panay, threatened to return to the United States and tell the American public of the indignity of the United States Navy being used as a convoy for tankers, he was retired; and learned better than to open his mouth on the subject.

Having collaborated with the Dynasty in putting Roosevelt in the White House, the Rockefeller-Standard Oil crowd took over the U.S. Government. The State Department was filled with Standard Oil executives. The Department of the Interior headed by Harold Ickes (attorney for the Rockefeller-Standard Oil interests in the Chicago area) was likewise packed with Rockefeller agents, as were all the rest of the government departments and commissions. For decades the Rockefeller-Standard Oil interests have given berths to retired Army and Navy officers who had proved complacent in the service, to good advantage.

Whereas under President Wilson only several hundred Standard Oil employees infiltrated into the government to take care of their interests in World War I, respect for public sentiment had barred the appointment of a Rockefeller to public office. But by 1933, the lily had been gilded; the Rockefeller name was falsely regarded as synonymous with philanthropy and benevolence, so well had been done the work of Fred T. Gates, Ivy L. Lee and numerous other perverters of public opinion.

Not only was the whole of Franklin D. Roosevelt's Cabinet a Rockefeller-Standard Oil agency, but a Rockefeller, Nelson was appointed to one of the most strategic positions in national defense, Coordinator of Hemispheric Defense. Prior to then, he had been offered by Harry L. Hopkins, Rockefeller almoner and stooge, the job of Assistant Secretary of Commerce, as a trial balloon to test public tolerance of a Rockefeller appointee. Through the office of Coordinator the Rockefeller-Standard Oil interests were able to use the billions of dollars appropriated by Congress for lend-lease to Latin American countries for their defenses, as a pork barrel to bribe or coerce those lands to restore to the Standard Oil, old expropriated concessions or grant them new concessions.

Thus in Mexico, where oil lands had been expropriated during World War I with the aid of Josephus Daniels and Franklin D. Roosevelt the Standard Oil interests were able to secure for themselves $18,000,000 of a $25,000,000 award made to American oil companies for their expropriated properties; and the Standard Oil alone was able to get back the only two concessions in Mexico that they really valued, by an oddly complacent decision of the Mexican Supreme Court. On another occasion Bolivia was notified that she would not get any of the "defense" boodle unless she paid the Standard Oil interests for expropriated lands, a fact that was published in only one American paper, La Prensa of New York.

Nelson Rockefeller's Bureau was manned almost exclusively by Communists who did an excellent job of fostering Communism in Latin America, in collaboration with the O.W.I. It made the United States more enemies in that section of the world than it ever before has had. The Argentine situation and the April 1948 revolt in Colombia that flared up in the face of the Rockefeller agent, Secretary of State Marshall were reactions to the activities of the Rockefeller Empire.

The appointment of Joseph Grew, nephew of John Pierpont Morgan, as Ambassador to Japan was dictated. The plan was to induce the Japs to attack the United States. Grew rapidly earned for himself the name of "friend of Japan." He was of invaluable assistance in aiding their armament. Standard Oil literally poured oil into Japan. Wright Aeronautical and other aviation manufacturers built plants and supplied unlimited numbers of engines and planes. American munitions flowed into Japan in a steady stream. Literally all the scrap on the American market, including the Sixth Avenue El of New York City were shipped into Japan. The United States generously supplied Japan with everything she needed for war. Financing these shipments offered no difficulty. Japan was being given plenty of rope to hang herself.

Despite the growth of her armaments, Japan could not screw up sufficient courage to attack the United States. The conspirators were impatiently waiting and working to bring about an attack on the United States that would force Congress to declare officially the war that the Dynasty already was waging unofficially. Admiral Richardson, who was Chief of Staff of the Pacific Command, testified before a Senate Investigating Committee that President Roosevelt had expressed the wishful thought, at a White House luncheon, October 8, 1940, that *the Japanese sooner or later would make a mistake and we would enter the war.*" Promptly thereafter Admiral Richardson protested once again the splitting of the Pacific Fleet and stationing it at Pearl Harbor, both of which had been done against his advice, in view of the intent expressed by Roosevelt to take steps leading to active hostilities. When Admiral Richardson insistently urged preparing the Pacific Fleet to protect itself, he was relieved of his command and replaced by Admiral Kimmel. The Navy deliberately was barred by Roosevelt from preparing for war.

At the instance of his bosses, Roosevelt followed his childhood yearning to play with warships and naval warfare. He took over, indirectly, command of the Pacific Fleet. Roosevelt did everything that might be calculated to induce the Japs to attack the fleet at Pearl Harbor. He stationed the vessels within the Harbor where they could be bottle-necked and could not possibly be defended. He ordered disregard of any and all warnings of danger and attack that were picked up.

In the meantime, Rockefeller-Soviet dominated and Rockefeller-financed Institute of Pacific Relations had furnished money and spies to the Communist, Richard Sorge spy ring in Japan. The purpose was to induce the Japanese war lords to attack the United States at Pearl Harbor, instead of attacking Rockefeller's Soviet partners, which was the original Japanese plan. The Rockefeller, Red agents in the U. S. State Department, associates of Alger Hiss and the Hal Ware cell, treasonously supplemented the work of the Sorge spy ring.

The Japs were told in effect: "Destroy the United States Fleet at Pearl Harbor, and you have won the war from the start." In the meantime, the Japs who itched to attack were goaded to fury in the field of diplomacy.

This deliberate plan to induce the Japs to attack the United States was common knowledge in diplomatic circles, but it has been regarded as a breach of "ethics" to mention it. But Capt. Oliver Lytteton, Minister of Production in Winston Churchill's Cabinet, stated before Parliament on July 20, 1944:

"Japan was provoked into attacking America at Pearl Harbor. It is a travesty on history to say that America was *forced* into the war."

This is the import of a statement made by Eleanor Roosevelt, as usual sharper in tongue than in wit, in an interview given Kathleen McLaughlin, published in New York Times Magazine, October 8, 1944, about Pearl Harbor.

"December 7, was just like any other D-Day to us. We clustered at the radio and waited for more details —*but it was far from the shock it proved to the country in general. We had expected something of the sort for a long time.*"

Her statement was exceptionally significant. D-Days are known in advance to the High Command. This D-day was known beyond any question to Roosevelt and his entourage. Roosevelt had on his desk a decoded message sent by the Japs to their envoys in Washington, known as the "East Wind Rain" radiogram, which stated that Japan planned to attack Pearl Harbor on the following day, many hours before the attack. But he deliberately betrayed the nation and its defenders and failed to warn them. On the contrary they were under orders to disregard outside danger signals. In all history there never has been a more traitorous act by the head of any nation.

This means that the Dynastic rulers and their pawn,

President Franklin Delano Roosevelt, had courted and precipitated a Jap attack, then deliberately withheld the warning from the armed forces and prevented them from defending themselves. Why? For eight long years the conspirators had worked, prayed and waited for the attack. They would not risk its miscarriage or effectiveness. The motto of the conspirators might have been:

"Oil is thicker than blood."

It was not their own blood that was shed and for them the price was cheap, the blood of 2500 men and a fleet of battleships paid for by the American people. Their lives meant nothing to them. The jeopardy in which they deliberately placed the nation was, as usual, of little concern to the internationally entrenched scoundrels.

The conspirators made little effort to hide their treason. This is made clear by correspondence between two Rockefeller kinsfolks and agents. One of them is Brooks Emeny, husband of Rockefeller's cousin Winifred (who murdered her children and committed suicide), and their agent in the operation of their propaganda agency, the Foreign Policy Association. The other was Congresswoman Frances Bolton, ranking Republican member of the House Foreign Affairs Committee. In a letter to Emeny, Mrs. Bolton acknowledged herself to be "guided" by him and his Rockefeller bosses. And she stated that she and her associates awaited and "celebrated" the December 7 attack on Pearl Harbor.

CHAPTER XXI

F.D.R.'S "NEW DEAL FOR THE MASSES" "SOCIAL SECURITY" AND "LABOR'S GAINS"

The War, which Roosevelt and his Dynastic bosses had worked so systematically to bring about, offered the ideal approach to grooming of the United States and the world for dictatorship and monopoly. The regimentation of industry which the NRA had failed to attain, the war "emergency" made inevitable. Likewise political dictatorship under the Commander-in-Chief was unavoidable and regimentation of the nation within and without the armed forces was a "must."

The wartime regimentation of the nation avoided revealing the true purpose, fostering national and international trusts and monopolies of a private character and *frank* dictatorship. Such "trusts" had been and still were the pet hates of the Marxist, Communist and self-styled "liberal" elements. The error of the NRA and the first New Deal had been that its monopolistic purposes were too obvious to dissemble and that was an important cause for its failure. The conspirators now went to the opposite extreme of pretending to fight the very things that they intended to bring about. That was the truly Machiavellian cunning of the plan that so thoroughly deceived the public regarding purposes of the later Dynastic activities.

The first, peacetime New Deal had openly turned over the latchstring to the public purse to the Dynastic bankers, to Dynastic industrialists and to relatives. They were given the cream of the graft. To the rank and file of the nation, especially to poorer classes, it had thrown a sop in the pattern of the Gracchi and other demagogues of history, in the form of Relief, which was bribery for purchase of votes and a spoils system on a vaster and more corrupt scale than has been dreamed of or dared in all of human history. The mob was given the skimmed milk of the graft.

Historically there was nothing in Roosevelt's, or Bismarck's, New Deal that was not an integral part of the New Deal launched by the Gracchi in ancient Rome. There was nothing missing in FDR's program of the laws of Rome except one. In Rome the receipt of Relief was made a hereditary privilege for 500 years.

There was, however, an added wrinkle to FDR's appeal to the mob that was uncalled for in Rome's. He offered to restore prosperity by abolishing prohibition. It was soon found, as was expected by the more sober citizenry, that prosperity was thereby restored to the liquor industries and vendors only; and the balance of the community was richer only in glow—but poorer in purse. The Dynasty and its allies are heavily interested in the liquor industries. They grew richer. Their depression was relieved, as in all other instances where the Dynasty was involved. For the rest of the nation the depression rolled on unrelieved by the flow of liquor, except in spirits.

The unemployed were placed on Relief through the WPA, the PWA, and a host of alphabetic and constantly changing bureaucratic agencies which in their multiplicity and confusion justified numerous irregularities which were introduced by deliberate plan. The dole was openly designed to discourage people from working so as to hold down the production that would arise from greater employment. Relief agencies such as the WPA were frankly created and administered for the purpose of purchasing or extracting supporting votes from the recipients.

Politically influential reliefers got more in Relief than they had earned ever before in their lives; and they lived on the fat of the land. But the great minority received scarcely enough to hold body and soul together. They lived on the verge of starvation, seeing neither butter nor meat for week after week. Malnutrition among them rose to heights which had never before been seen in the history of the country.

In 1934, the author reported on the basis of schoolchildren visiting New York Ciy Board of Health eye clinics, most of whom were on Relief, that more than a sixth were suffering of malnutrition that was so severe that it seriously impaired their vision. The particular type of malnutrition involved was a deficiency of vitamin A which previously had been known to exist on so wide a scale only in poverty stricken China. Following the appearance of this report, the author's scientifc publications were stopped by a rigid censorship, to prevent the facts becoming known. Two years later after temporary restoration of employment had resulted in improved diets and material improvement in nutrition, the Administration and social service agencies acknowledged the existence of the conditions which the author had described.

Workers under NRA were extended a minimum wage of $12 to $15 a week and kudoes were rendered to the "right of collective bargaining." They were also extended the fraud of "social security" and the claptrap of Bismarck's Made-in-Germany "New Deal." In return for payments deducted from their wages, certain classes of workers are offered first, a pittance of unemployment insurance which often did not equal the Relief dole; and second, a pension after reaching the age of sixty-five that is not enough to starve on respectably. It is made certain that the pensioners will starve, in the case of the average individual with no private income, by barring them from even those shabby "benefits" if they earn an adequate supplementary sum by continuing to work beyond pensionable age.

In return for the payments made, the worker has no legally secured rights. What rights may redound to him are subject to the constantly changing rules and regulations of the Social Security bureaucrats. The bureaucrats' only interest is to provide social security for themselves in the form of jobs. Under the regulations which they set up from time to time, fewer and fewer workers are eligible for pensioning. Thus a man totally and permanently blinded to-day is entitled to neither a pension nor the return of his money unless he is sixty-five years of age and has worked and paid his assessments up to retirement. Since most blind folk can not get jobs, they are ineligible for benefits. The same is true of many folk over forty who in normal times can not secure employment. Death benefits or return of money paid in are denied in an ever wider group of cases by bureaucratic rules that change from day to day.

An ever larger proportion of the contributors to the fund never receive any return—not even a refund of contributions. In the case of private insurance companies the courts have ruled that to fail to pay benefits due, or else, to return the premiums paid in, constitutes fraud. But government agencies including the Social Security Bureau may and do practice these frauds with impunity while the "liberal" political donkeys bray about workers' benefits, and the even more assinine electorate believe them.

The most stupid aspect of the humbug and fraud of "Social Security" is the fact that the money collected from the workers must be spent on current government expenses and only tokens of the liability for these funds in the form of government bonds are left in the S.S. treasury. Under our present scarcity-economy set-up, the failure to spend most of the Social Security funds immediately, would cause contraction of the currency volume; and that in turn would cause progressively deepening depression and increasing unemployment. Unemployment prior to retirement would bar the contributor from enjoying the benefits of Social Security unless the unemployed were placed on a dole and their security payments made for them out of the dole. The dole would have to be paid in part out of Social Security funds by the sale of Government bonds to the fund. As a consequence of the diminishing employment, however, the contributions to the Social Security fund would diminish, thus steadily reducing the amount available for purchase of bonds and payment of doles. The same progressive contraction would prevail in industry and the taxes derived therefrom. Eventually the Social Security fund, the government and industry would all be bankrupt. Therefore the Government must spend the Social Security funds as soon as it receives them.

But now that the Government has accepted its *"duty"* to spend all of the Social Security funds currently, to avoid paralyzing our scarcity-economy monetary system, other hydra-headed evil consequences appear. First, the forced increased expenditures by the Government designed to put the money collected for Social Security, back into circulation, in order to avoid contraction of the currency volume and depression, results in inflation. Inflation causes a rise in cost of government and therefore a rise in taxes. Increased taxes means further inflation and higher prices. This inflation is aggravated and bankruptcy hastened by the necessity of currently raising taxes to raise money for repayment of the bonds placed in the Social Security vaults in order to provide for payment of pensions and for the interest on the bonds. Thus there is set into operation a vicious spiral of constant, uncontrolled inflation with eventual bankruptcy of the Nation.

The absurdity of the Social Security situation rises to the highest zenith when one stops to consider that the pensioners can find no security in either money or bonds; nor can they clothe or shelter themselves in them. Security rests only in having available for purchase necessities of life at all times. Droughts and other upsets make it necessary to produce always at maximum capacity, and to set up continuous reserves and surpluses to make sure that necessities of life at all times will be available. But reserves and surpluses, in our present speculative economic set-up spell a drop in prices, a loss of employment in production because of dropping out of marginal producers, and the wiping out of surpluses.

In short in a scarcity economy, such as our normal economy, the surpluses which insure security can not be attained. Under the New Deal economy that restricts production and plows under crops, the Administration is destroying the reserves that would have freed us of the necessity of hungering for food, clothing and housing (in the form of rationing). It destroys real security, while taxing the nation for pretended security.

The credits which are being set up in the Social Security books in Washington for the moneys taken from the workers present no security whatsoever. They offer only a mirage of security.

This fraud has been possible because the gullible and unthinking public, hear and believe what the politicians say, but are too dull to perceive that they do the very opposite.

The absurd inadequacy and undependability of the New Deal's Social Security program is vividly portrayed and attested by the fact that many powerful unions —including United Mine Workers, International Ladies' Garment Workers—have spurned its provisions. They have established pension and retirement systems that more closely approach adequacy and are less completely fraudulent, with funds raised as a private tax by assessments levied upon employers and industries.

When it had made its war official, the Dynasty carried on its skullduggery behind the front of real and pretended war needs, of sham "soak the Rich" class warfare and of Bismarxian pro-laborism. That was labelled the second New Deal.

The needs of war offered a pretext for shamelessly betraying the security of the United States in favor of the interests of the far flung Rockefeller Empire. The story has been related of the Rockefeller-Standard-Oil I. G. Farbenindustrie conspiracy to deprive United States and the Allies of rubber which would have resulted in an Axis victory, had it not been exposed and checked. But this is only one of the conspiracies centering about essentials of war and peace which menace national prosperity and security.

Tin is one of the prime necessities of modern life. It is absolutely essential for national existence, defense and for war. Despite the fact that tin may be mined in many parts of the world including the United States, a British and Dutch cartel conspire to monopolize the tin industry of the world by suppressing its production elsewhere, with every device at their command and at the command of their governments. The tin which they produce the Tin Cartel ration out at exorbitant prices to the countries of the world. They deliberately and systematically discourage or block the production of tin by corrupt machinations to prevent competition and hold prices at an exorbitant level.

The United States is particularly rich in tin. Production of tin was undertaken in the United States by the

British tin interests when Cornwall tin ran low in the 1860's just before the alluvial Malay deposits came into production. It was mined by them in the State of South Dakota on property that now belongs to the Dakota Tin and Gold Company. From this property there was sent to England for refining, shiploads of high grade tin oxide (cassiterite) ore.

Shortly thereafter, the British discovered the commercial possibilities of alluvial ore in the Malay Peninsula, with its cheap labor. They undertook to discredit and paralyze competitive tin production for the purpose of maintaining their monopoly. In the United States they found ready allies in political circles. Boycott of American and other tin was required of industries whose products were admitted to the British and Dutch markets on a favorable basis. Support of the Tin Cartel was required of companies such as the Rockeeller-Standard Oil interests that sought to operate or produce in British or Dutch possessions.

The success of the operations of the Tin Cartel in maintaining a world scarcity of tin almost won the war for Germany and Japan. The stockpile of tin in the United States was so small that bearings for aviation engines had to be made with silver as a poor substitute for tin. Failure of these silver alloy bearings caused numerous crashes and deaths.

Some tin was made available for the United States by the Tin Cartel in partnership with the Rockefeller interests, from the Patino Bolivian tin mines. This tin ore is so highly impure that it is impossible to refine it by ordinary methods or to the ordinary grade of purity. The U.S. Government built for the Cartel-Rockefeller interests a special refinery in Texas for the refining of this ore at a cost of many million dollars; and it paid so high a price and bonus for the inferior Bolivian ore that Patino Mines stock earned more per year than the price of little over five dollars a share at which it sold at the start of the War.

Even under the stress of war, however, the U.S. government did whatever it could to discourage production of the higher grade American tin. Thus the Dakota Tin and Gold Company shipped one ton of high grade alluvial tin to the Metal Reserve Board, and was paid twenty-nine cents a pound. This was less than the actual cost of production at the time. But the payments made to Bolivia constitute a small fraction of the cost of their tin. Enemy submarine action made shipping dangerous and costly in money and lives. It also made the flow of imported supplies precarious. Shipping space had to be diverted to tin from other necessities. The Bolivian tin was therefore far more costly than the actual price paid.

Even if the government had subsidized the domestic production of tin to the extent of paying ten times the Bolivian price, it would have been worth-while in terms of national security and saving of lives. But high subsidy is not necessary. American tin, in such case as the Dakota Tin and Gold Company, could be produced at virtually no cost, as a by-product in the production of sodium feldspar, which is a valuable commercial product, if adequate financial support were given in starting production.Either directly or through the SEC, the Government has barred the financing of American mining and tin production. British propaganda, supported by U.S. Government agencies, has persistently and falsely discredited American tin because it could readily supply all the needs of the United States at prices far lower than the Cartel's. The Rockefeller-Patino tin interests have been subsidized heavily by the New Deal. Overtures were made to Roosevelt, Wallace, the Army, the Navy and various New Deal officials to help the American tin industry get on its feet with RFC loans of the same type as was extended to Rockefeller Bolivian tin producers and refineries, to help it provide the tin that was so direly needed in our war effort, and the lack of which was costing many lives. The Company was flatly rebuffed. American tin was not wanted, officers of the Company were told, even if lack of it meant loss of lives. The reasons stated were quite frank. Rockefeller's agent, Henry Wallace, stated that he wanted no competition with the British-Dutch tin cartel, or with the Rockefeller-Patino interests. Cordell Hull, who it was rumored had a sizeable investment in the British Tin Cartel stocks, vigorously opposed any encouragement of American tin production. On April 23, 1948 the International Tin Study Group conference, representing the Tin Cartel reported that there would be, according to their plans, a shortage of 20,-000 to 40,000 tons of tin a year between 1948 and 1950 with no provision for stockpiling for war.

The desire of the Dynasty to leave the United States dependent upon foreign sources of tin, columbium, tantalum, and of other essential minerals and commodities, as in the case of rubber, clearly indicates that the safety and security of the United States means little to them. It appears to make clear that they care little if the United States wins or is defeated in war, so long as their own selfish purposes are served. It also indicates that they have a community of interests with enemy lands that would make them secure even in case of an enemy victory. And as a matter of fact, either complete exhaustion of the United States or its eventual military defeat, or both, seems to be regarded by them as almost a *sine qua non* for the destruction of democracy in the U. S.

It can be predicted with reasonable certainty that in event of war with the Soviets, the East Indies and probably also the Bolivian sources of tin will fall into Russia's hands at the very start of hostilities. Russia has been very busy buying up our sources of strategic minerals with "Lend Lease" funds supplied them from the U. S. Treasury by the Dynasty.

The sham "soak the rich" program is improperly labelled. It is really a "soak certain rich" program. Its purpose is to maintain a monopoly of wealth by preventing any working man from becoming rich through his efforts. This is accomplished by imposition of progressively higher taxes on everything that a man makes by working. But the wealthy are protected in their wealth, and the speculative fraternity are fostered, by various loopholes in the tax law, and by the provisions of the capital gains tax. The wealthiest interests escape taxation by the United States completely by the provision of the law that exempts from taxes any money made by Americans in foreign lands. This has served to stimulate the flight of capital of the wealthy from the United States and to foster, with American funds, foreign competitive industry.

The Labor Baron agents of the Dynasty enjoy tax exemption that is conferred on the unions whose funds they control. Thus there is developed an ever tightening monopoly of wealth by the Dynasty. This monopoly is being tightened at the insistence of the Labor Barons, supposedly on behalf of the workers and as a part of their Marxist program.

The NRA function of wrecking industries that are not controlled by the conspirators was assigned to the Office of Price Control. At the top of the OPA were put such men as advertising agent Chester Bowles, who posed as the white hope of the Communists but could be trusted by the Dynasty and the Rockefellers to protect their interests. The lesser offices of the OPA were deliberately filled with Communists and their sympathizers who were encouraged to run riot in their savage anti-capitalist "production for use and not for profit" fanaticism. They were left to vent their destructive mania on small property owners and the industries that the conspirators sought to destroy or suppress and take over into their monopolies.

The OPA Office of Rent Control offers an excellent illustration of the operation and consequences of the OPA. The personnel consisted of rabid Communists and crooked real estate brokers. All of them were absolute dictators. All of them, down to the lowliest clerk were a law-unto-themselves as far as concerns the landlord. From their maliciously destructive acts there is no appeal. The employed brokers worked in collusion with friends to depress the value of property which they wished to acquire at forced sale. They placed rentals at so low a level as to inflict losses on the owners, that compelled sales. The Communist employees had but one purpose—to foster Communism by disrupting and destroying production of housing and of every other necessity of life. By deliberately setting prices and rents so low as to inflict bankrupting losses they blocked production and provision of housing. They then blamed the havoc which they had wrought on Capitalism; and advanced more Communism as the only remedy.

The OPA and CIO revolutionary unionism, and their successors, have been the chief agencies of Communism and of the Dynasty's conspiracy for dictatorship and supermonopoly. Since the procedure of the OPA pretended to base rents on comparative values that had prevailed in years prior, comparison was a matter of judgement at best, and arbitrary, when at the worst. The landlord had no recourse. The landlord under their procedure is criminal suspect in advance and he has no recourse and no opportunity to defend himself against the falsest allegations. Under the law, the landlord was, and still is, robbed of his right of contract, is required to carry the whole cost and burden for the government of subsidizing low rents, while paying constantly rising taxes and operating expenses. In short, the landlord is faced with the confiscation of his property without any process, not in the interest of the nation but of private individuals. The entire situation is un-

Constitutional and plainly dishonest. It is legitimatized thievery.

The housing shortage which now plagues the nation is a deliberately planned consequence of this rent control policy. Preservation of their jobs was almost as cogent a force in that policy, as are the desire to inflict damages on property holders and the other motives that have been mentioned. Employees of the OPA Office of Rent Control openly acknowledged that the permanence of their jobs depended upon creating and maintaining a housing shortage. They planned to force the creation of permanent housing administration which would take them over and make their jobs permanent. This they plan to accomplish through the Taft-Ellender-Wagner Housing Bill, which is designed to Communize ("nationalize") housing.

If the courts had not been so completely packed and corrupt, it would be possible for the landlords to recover from the Government the losses which it has inflicted on them. When the Government undertakes legitimately to subsidize, the burden must be borne by the taxpayer and the subsidies paid out of the Treasury. Landlords who have been forced to privately subsidize low rents have a legitimate claim on the Treasury for the losses inflicted on them that will be upheld by honest courts.

Complementing the OPA and price control in destroying competition and bolstering monopolies, rationing was extremely effective. Years of "New Deal" scarcity economy had stripped the nation of all commodity reserves and had reduced production of raw materials to a low ebb. This situation served to justify rationing of commodities. But in every instance the rationing was made to serve, as in the case of sugar, the monopolistic purposes of the Dynasty.

In the case of oil and petroleum products, however, rationing was completely unjustified. Various state and national agencies, such as the Railroad Commission in Texas, and voluntary prorationing agreements entered into by the industry, had served to reduce the U. S. oil production to a mere fraction of the potential production. The excuse offered for this procedure was the desire to conserve the life of the fields. But the real reason was that the Standard Oil and other major companies did not wish to pay the higher price for American oil when they could buy, or steal, Venezuelan or other oil for a mere fraction of the American price.

By the influx of foreign oil and restriction of oil production, before the OPA and by price control during the war, the price of oil was kept at so low a level that it did not pay the American producer to continue black oil and marginal production, or to seek new production.

The nation's distribution facilities up to the time of the war were geared to the importation of foreign oil by tankers. During the war a large proportion of the tankers were sunk by submarine warfare. But even that did not imply any real need for rationing of oil and gasoline during the war. For the number of cars on the road was so severely cut down by restriction of auto and tire production that there would have been ample fuel to go around, if the production and distribution of oil had not been disrupted deliberately.

As a result of rationing, numerous producers and distributors of gasoline and oil were forced out of business or were compelled to sell their businesses to the Standard Oil and other larger companies, most of them Rockefeller controlled, that could hold out. At the end of the war the monopoly of oil was tighter than ever. The artificial shortage of oil was maintained by the shipment to Russia and to the Rockefeller-Standard Oil development in Saudi Arabia and other foreign lands of most of the available equipment for production and distribution of oil. As a consequence the United States now freeze in winter because of lack of oil and other fuels, industries are paralyzed and must shut down at times, rationing is being brought back, and in case of war, a shortage of oil and gas may spell disaster and defeat. Russia when she seizes Saudi Arabia and Iran will have more oil than the United States thanks to the activities of the Rockefeller Empire. But the profits of the monopoly have become enormous because of the shortage.

The most amazingly ingenious and ingenuous sham incorporated by the Dynasty in its New Deal is its mechanism for regimenting labor under their own aegis through "labor leaders" and its use for establishing monopolies that are entirely within the law. Wagner's subservience to the Rockefeller-Standard Oil interests makes it clear that the Wagner Labor Relations Act is designed to serve their purposes. It epitomizes and points up the warfare of Labor on Capital in so truly a Bismarxian sense   that Wagner has earned for himself the title of "America's Bismarck", a noble title for a pawn.

The Supreme Court decision wiping out the NRA was mock obeisance to public sentiment against monopolies in restraint of trade, through control of machinery, that has been built up through decades., With equal diligence there had been built up by Marxist agencies and pseudo "liberals" a sentiment in favor of union monopolies of labor. It required little astuteness to discern that industry could be monopolized even more completely by control of labor than by control of machinery.

The Roosevelt-Delano Dynasty, FDR and the New Deal, demanded through the National Labor Relations Board, of certain industries not controlled by them or their allies, that they turn over management, or share it with the Labor Barons of the unions involved. As a result Roosevelt was hailed as a "champion of Labor". This pose contrasts sharply with the harsh and ruthless attitude of the Dynasty towards the workers in the industries which they control.

A number of members of the Dynasty, including FDR, and his uncle Frederic A. Delano, shared ownership of the Graceton Coal Co. and of the Vintondale Colliery Co. which operates a mine at Vintondale, Cambria County, Pa. The production of the mines was sold through the Delano Coal Co. which drained off most of the earnings.

Launched about 1892, the Company built over 200 homes and employed about 400 men. The town was completely owned and rigidly controlled by the Company. Strangers could not enter town without the permission of the superintendent of the Company. Armed guards patrolled the town. Workers dared not discuss conditions in the mine with strangers. They were compelled to buy at the Company's store at high prices.

The Company persistently fought unionization with violence. In 1922, the UMW was enjoined by the Company from holding a meeting in town on property owned by the union. In 1933, after Roosevelt's inauguration and his adoption of a friendly policy towards labor unions, as a political device, the mine was organized by the UMW.

On March 18, 1940, the Vinton Collieries Co. shut down the mine, locked out the workers and left without paying them $40,000 in wages due them, after sneaking out 86 carloads of coal under a large guard.

The Company's store was shut down and its stock of food left to rot, while the workers and their families were left destitute and hungry. The Company refused to sell the food in its store to the workers. Eventually the miners were placed on Relief and they were furnished some items of food by the Federal Surplus Commodities Corp.

There is no record that Eleanor R. ever made one of her "welfare" visits to this mine, of the type that she made to the West Virginia mines, that were so widely publicized, or that she ever extended them any of her notorious "charity". Maybe it struck too close to home?

The fostering of labor unionism on a vast and unprecedented scale by the Dynasty and the Rockefeller Empire is completely understandable. By doing so they have completely regimented labor under their own control through their own appointed agents, provocateurs and dictators, more pleasantly labelled "labor leaders". This they have done through the Wagner Labor Relations Act and other "New Deal" labor legislation, which have robbed workers of their freedom and their right to work at a vocation of their own choice. This right the Dynasts have farmed out to the goons, racketeers, ward heelers and zealots, the "labor leaders" who are their vassal agents. They would be more correctly named "Labor Barons", for they serve in the same capacity as do barons in feudal states.

Under the franchise of the Wagner Act the Dynasty extended to the Labor Barons a series of so-called "rights" that flagrantly violate the rights that are supposedly guaranteed to the nation at large by the Constitution and the Bill of Rights. These special "rights" of the Labor Barons, that are equally enjoyed by the Dynasty include the following among others:

1. The "right" to extort from vassal workers a private tax for the privilege of working.

2. The "right" to dictate who may work, when he may work, and to virtually enslave the worker.

3. The "right" to practice blackmail and extortion on all employers and industries, and to levy unlimited assessments on them.

4. The "right" to wage unlimited class warfare on the rest of the community for their own special interests and to sabotage the nation at large.

5. The "right" to mercilessly profiteer, to exploit communities and to deprive them of the very necessities of life, whenever it suits their purpose.

6. The "right" to betray the country and to traitorously traffic with its enemies—as is instanced by the negotiations of John L. Lewis with Hitler, and the CIO-PAC betrayal of our nation to Communism and Russia.

7. The "right" to conspire to restrain trade.

8. The "right" to disrupt industry and to destroy whole industries.

9. The "right" to bring whole communities, and if they desire, the whole nation, to verge of starvation by strikes and sabotage.

10. The "right" to throw out of work and deprive of a livelihood, employees of whole groups of industries whenever, however, and as often as they choose.

11. The "right" to precipitate inflation, panic, depression and unemployment on as wide a scale as they choose.

12. The "right" to destroy the Constitution and the government and to deliver the United States to foreign powers.

13. The "right" to engineer staggering taxation on the community at large while they themselves are tax-free.

14. The "right" to bribe and corrupt public officials, and to buy elections.

The Labor Barons and their henchmen—gangsters, goons, ex-convicts, convicts and intellects prostituted to them—have been extended these "rights" on the pretense of giving "protection", in the true gangster or baronial sense, to workers. The more moronic element believe that the unions provide the higher wages, the employment and the standard of living that now prevail. It requires only a very mediocre memory to reveal how false is this claim.

Labor unions rose to relatively as great power in World War I and its aftermath, as they now enjoy. They then did not prevent depression and unemployment, or provide for it. On the contrary, they forced wages during the post-war era to such extortionate heights, and restricted production so much, as to force collapse of commerce and industry and to price workers out of their jobs. They forced an inflation so high that the unions themselves called a buyer's strike against the purchase of the very merchandise produced at the higher wages.

With unions equally strong in the 30's and now, the difference in the situation accounts for higher employment at this time. Industry was prostrate in the 30's and could provide no employment. It is strong and prosperous now, and therefore provides jobs. Strong industry provides employment. Strong and arrogant unions weaken industry and destroy employment.

The Labor Barons deliberately collaborated with the Dynasty and precipitated the depression of the 30's. The objective of the right wing Labor Baron is to control or destroy; and many of them have gained control of industries in their domains. The objective of the left wing and subversive Labor Baron is to destroy the U.S. Government and to create an American Soviet over which he hopes to be Commissar.

To cover up their crimes, the Labor Barons have employed prostituted professors of economics and statisticians to throw dust in the eyes of the public and to falsely place the blame for the depression on capitalists and industry. The latter have been too stupidly disorganized to refute the false charges levelled against them.

What is more disastrous for the nation, is the fact that these "economists" who are prostituted to Labor Barons and most of them frankly Communists, have deluded the public into taking larger doses of the same quack medicine that killed the golden goose of prosperity in the 1920's—ever higher wages for ever less work. Their pretended purpose is "pump priming" and increasing the purchasing power of the workers. At a time when the United States and the world at large are crying for greater production of the necessities of life, they are imposing a shortening of the work-week and a restriction of production. This is clearly a part and parcel of their wrecking program of Communization of the United States through national bankruptcy. As might be expected, the result of their activities is a rapidly mounting inflation.

The Labor Barons and their Dynastic overlords could readily bring on another depression now, if they are not checked. That would be fatal to human freedom. Freedom would be lost to the Dynasty through the agency of the "managed economy"-Labor Baron clique, who use Communism as their bait. Depression as a step to revolution and overthrow of our government is the deliberate and avowed objective of the tactics of the labor movement, according to an article published by left - wing, Maxim Gorki Institute - trained, Victor Reuther of the UAW.

It is difficult to understand how anyone can be so

stupid as to believe that the Labor Barons and their Dynastic patrons are serving the interests of the workers, or of the nation, by inflicting upon them the miseries and deprivations of inflation and depression; or that they are serving them by restricting production, by production and work rules, by featherbedding, by conspiracy with specific employers or by numerous devices that they are free under the law to employ with impunity. Are any Labor Barons so brazen as to openly assert that in preventing workers from getting homes, cars, refrigerators, and other necessities and luxuries, they are serving the interest of the workers? Have any of them the temerity to allege that they are protecting workers by pricing them out of jobs and forcing them into unemployment as they are doing in the movie industry, the housing industry, and many others, through ever increasing wage demands; or that they are protecting workers by chain strikes that keep hosts of workers unemployed for months on end, and wipe out their savings and impoverish them?

The record reveals the Labor Barons as the most ruthless exploiters and betrayers of workers, who spring into action and demand a cut of wages and profits when industry offers employment; then they expel the workers for non-payment of dues when employment is no longer available to them.

Pretendedly in the interests of the workers, the vassals of the Labor Barons, the Dynastic patrons extend the following so-called "rights":

1. The "right to work"—when, as, and if the Labor Baron wishes them to work. As a corollary to the "right to work" there is claimed the "property right" in a job. This means in principle that when an employer gives a man a job, that man acquires a share in the business, which is tantamount to confiscation of the employer's property. This is one phase of the idea that has been incorporated into our law, to the effect that any man who gives employment to another man and provides him with a living, is an enemy of society, a criminal suspect who is guilty of any and every crime until he proves himself innocent; and that he must be hounded, harassed and penalized at every turn.

2. The so-called "right to strike" consists of the right to violate the Constitutional rights of the others—the "right" to deprive the owner of the use of his property, the "right" to restrain trade, the "right" to use force and violence on the person and property of others, the

"right" to assault, maim and murder, the "right" to deny others the "right to work" and earn a living, the "right" to endanger the health, safety, and lives of whole communities, and numerous other wrongs and crimes that when perpetrated by or under the direction of a Labor Baron are strangely converted, by a perversion of our laws, into "rights".

The "right to strike" is neither used or intended primarily to benefit the worker. So-called organizational strikes, called by almost all Labor Barons annually under normal circumstances, are intended to assert the authority of Labor Barons over their vassal workers, to force them into line and to pay arrears in dues and special assessments including those levied for the strikes in question. They are primarily directed against the worker; and only secondarily against the employer and the community.

Strikes are sources of revenue for the Labor Baron. They serve to dramatize him and put him before the public. In normal times strikes are the Labor Baron's chief function. The union member, or serf, loses wages during the period of strikes and can only be the loser. But the Labor Baron has asserted his authority and gained for himself notoriety and added income.

3. The "right to collective bargaining" which means the "right" of coercion, blackmail, extortion and holdup of industry by the Dynastic politicians through their agents, the Labor Barons, in the pretended interest of the worker. These holdups of industry continue until high wages completely wipe out profits, shut down or bankrupt industry, and destroy employment. At the same time they force steady inflation. Ultimately they serve merely to impoverish the worker. Water can not be drawn from a stone, nor can wages be paid by industry that has no earnings for any length of time. These are the objectives sought by the Dynasty in their conspiracy to effect monopoly and dictatorship.

The dramatic effectiveness of the sponsorship of even the most Communist and subversive Labor Barons by the Dynasty and the Rockefeller Empire, is illustrated by the current developments in the New York City Transit situation. The success of the Rockefeller interests in getting New York City to bail them out of their transit investments through their subversive, Red agent, Fiorella LaGuardia, and their objective of increasing fares before they openly resume control of the companies has been related. Within one week after the prediction had been made, the fare on the subways of New York City had been doubled from a nickel to a dime by order of Rockefeller's hand-picked Mayor William O'Dwyer in a farcical performance that had all the elements of a Gilbert and Sullivan comedy, except the music.

From the start the New York City subway systems were ruthlessly looted by its financiers. Through dummy, exclusive purchasing agencies with a capitalization of a few thousands they drained off many millions of dollars. They paid themselves series of enormous dividends ranging up to 100%. They then unloaded the highly watered securities on the public, and after the panic of 1907, bought back the bonds for a mere fraction of their face value. With subway unification engineereed by their agent, LaGuardia, they were repaid full face value on their bonds, giving the Rockefeller interests alone a profit of $150,000,000 at the expense of the taxpayers. In the meantime their own agents in the Transit Commission continued in control of the lines for the purpose of mismanaging them and creating a public outcry that would require improvement, extension and eventual reversion to private control.

A fare increase affected so many voters that politicians dared not advocate it. The five cent fare was a political shibboleth. Most vociferous in their opposition to an increased fare were the Communists, the Red American Labor Party and the left wing unions. To overcome their opposition, the control of the transit workers was turned over to the radical Transport Workers Union, CIO headed by the crimson City Councilman Michael J. Quill, its International President. Repeated strikes were called by the union that were settled by wage increases. In all of these strikes the union demanded wage increases *without a rise in fares* and the politicians all paid homage to the five cent fare.

Early in 1948, New York City was presented with a budget demand of more than one billion dollars. It superimposed on the grotesque corruption and waste of the LaGuardia regime the added figure of relatively modest Tammany graft. Subsequent events make it apparent that the budget was deliberately padded so as to threaten New York City with bankruptcy, as an excuse for the next fare move that was calculated to absolve all politicians involved, of any blame for the fare increase that was made to appear imperative. The Republicans at Albany refused to pass a bill increasing the fare outright, but did pass one permitting Mayor O'Dwyer and his City Council to increase the fare. Piously and with great ostentation, O'Dwyer protested that he had no intention of increasing the fare and passed the buck.

Very conveniently, City Councilman Michael J. Quill, of the Transport Workers Union called another strike demanding a wage increase. Mayor O'Dwyer played his act. He said that he forbade the strike; and that there could be no wage increase without a fare rise. Councilman Quill took the cue and issued an ultimatum on April 13, 1948 that his union would strike if the fares were *not increased* promptly.

Thus the responsibility for the fare increase was put squarely on the shoulders of the most troublesome of the opposition. The Rockefeller Empire won another victory through the agency of unions and Communists sponsored by them, and the politicians who fronted for it were left free to engage in other skullduggery.

The advantage of using unions to set up monopolies in restraint of trade has been demonstrated repeatedly. Thus Petrillo, the Czar of Music, suppressed television by interdicting the use of music, stopped phonograph recordings for months, suppressed popular music on the radio for a time, and systematically racketeers and levies a toll of protection money on every musical industry. The people of the nation are denied modern fireproof or prefabricated housing, and for the major part are denied any housing within their means, by conspiracies in restraint of trade by the building unions that are implemented by their overlord politicians through building codes. The nation is also denied food fresh from the farms at reasonable costs by a conspiracy engaged in by Teamsters' unions under the aegis of financial and political overlords. It has resulted in a constantly higher price in every populated section of the country on all foods and necessities of life. In the case of the Rockefeller-controlled Milk Trust, their Milkmen's Union has served as an excuse for repeatedly raising the price of milk to extortionate heights.

The Wagner Labor Relations Act and accessory labor legislation has imposed on the United States every phase of the destructive class warfare that Bismarck designed for the enslavement of labor and the disruption of the industry and defense of nations that Germany would have to defeat to attain a conquest of "Deutschland uber Alles". As in the case of every country that succumbed to Bismarck-propagandized Marxism this subversion was accomplished by agents subsidized by the very people who were to be victimized by it. In the United States the sponsor of the key legislation was a kin of the very man who had formulated the plan for Bismarck, Adolph Wagner; and the principal subsidizer was John D. Rockefeller, a descendant of a Hessian, who aspired to outdo Bismarck in the conquest of the world.

Through the Wagner Act there finally has been brought about in the United States the beginnings of a true feudal state masked by the trappings of democracy. The blueprint of Nickerson has been outdone. Both labor and the bulk of the rank and file of the populace have been reduced to serfdom by Labor Barons and their Dynastic masters. This serfdom is ironically labelled "Labor's *Gains*".

When all is said and done, the greatest boon that the Dynasty offered the American people through Franklin Delano Roosevelt was the opportunity to shed their blood and dissipate their wealth for its private purposes and for world-wide extension of the Rockefeller Empire and its oil reserves.

CHAPTER XXII

F.D.R.'S NEW DEAL FOR ROCKEFELLER EMPIRE

SAUDI ARABIA, PALESTINE AND THE "TRUMAN PLAN"

Through President Franklin Delano Roosevelt's New Deal and his bright new World War II, the Dynasty gained many victories for the Rockefeller Empire. The greatest prize of all was the rich oil fields of the Near East, especially Saudi Arabia.

All of the territory that lies between the Gulf of Aden and the Red Sea, the Black and Caspian Seas at the North, the Mediterranean Sea at the West and the

Persian Gulf at the East, is a vast oil basin. Large concessions in the southern part of this region had been granted between 1935 and 1937 to British interests headed by Sir W. Fraser and C. S. Gulbenkian and were turned over to a series of companies controlled by them including Petroleum Concessions Ltd., Petroleum Development (Oman and Dhofar) Ltd., Petroleum Development (Palestine) Ltd., Petroleum Development (Qatar) Ltd., Petroleum Development (Transjordan) Ltd., Petroleum Development (Trucial Coast) Ltd., and Petroleum Development (Western Arabia) Ltd. Hitler's war on England had gravely endangered these concessions.

Our entry into the war had rescued them and had assured the Rockefeller dominated Aramco the right to develop Saudi Arabian oil for Standard Oil of California's and Texas Company's joint venture, Cal-Tex.

The $30,000,000 which the United States Treasury gave Ibn Saud for the support of himself and his 450 wives and their progeny, to maintain the Rockefeller-Standard Oil interests in his good graces, cost the American people twenty cents a head. In addition King Ibn Saud got a "loan" of $25,000,000 of taxpayers' money from the Export-Import Bank to build a railroad from his capitol across the desert to his summer palace at Rayadh, and numerous gifts from the American taxpayers ranging from multi-million dollar airplanes to sight-seeing tours to the United States for himself, his many princes, and their numerous retinues.

For the millions of taxpayers' money poured into his lap by the United States, King Ibn Saud did offer to them in return, a very suggestive, and under the circumstances, a premonitory and appropriate token gift. He presented America's Queen Eleanor (Roosevelt) with a jewel becrusted, solid gold crown. Eleanor accepted this crown with peculiar alacrity, but it was given little publicity.

After they secured payment for their concession by the United States Treasury, the Rockefeller Empire then ordered their New Deal agents in 1941 to begin the construction for them of a pipe line in Saudi Arabia at the expense of the American taxpayer. This required the diversion of pipe sorely needed for the war effort and for the heating of homes on the Eastern seaboard that were without fuel and heat. Though it was frankly stated by the oil interests that the pipe line in Saudi Arabia could not play any part in the war and would not be completed until five years after the war, pipe was to be diverted from the war effort at top priorities and shipped.

A bill was introduced in Congress appropriating $165,000,000 for this Rockefeller-Standard Oil chore. The outcry against the bill was so great that it was dropped.

The Rockefeller Standard Oil interests once again planted one of their vice-presidents and kinsmen, Jimmy Moffett, in the government, as Housing Administrator. He was given the assignment of "pressuring" Roosevelt into handing over the $165,000,000 to the Rockefeller interests for the development of Saudi Arabia. For this he was promised a commission of 5%.

Moffett succeeded in getting Roosevelt to hand over the millions. But he was defrauded out of his commission. He sued the Rockefeller interests for the commission, and was given an award of more than a million dollars by the court. But his adversaries had the verdict reversed by one of their "kept" judges. He decreed that it was against public policy to permit an agent to profit from the exercise of influence on an official. He left it to be inferred, however, that it was quite legitimate for them to enjoy the benefit of such "influence" and welsh on their deal.

In the following year President Roosevelt gave the Rockefeller interests the $165,000,000 out of special, secret appropriations given him by Congress for use in the war effort, for which he was required to render no accounts. It was used for surveys and preparatory work for the pipe line. In addition the United States Army was assigned to do part of the task and to build an airfield and base at Dhahran, the construction of which by soldier labor battalions survived the war. Under the contract with Ibn Saud, the base will have to be turned over to the Saudi Arabia in February, 1949, shortly after its completion at the cost of more than six millions to the United States taxpayers.

Col. John Zott, a West Point graduate Army officer, was assigned the task of geologizing and developing Saudi Arabian oil. He was first sent by the Army to the University of Pennsylvania for training in oil technology, and then placed in charge of the Saudi Arabian venture. His command consisted of draftees. It was assigned the task of drilling the oilfield, and bringing it into production for the Rockefeller Standard Oil interests at the expense of the taxpayers.

Two drafted United States soldiers who were kept in the service after the termination of the war to labor on the fields protested to Congressman Phillip J. Philbin who denounced this "quasi-private" undertaking for the Rockefeller Empire at the cost of the American public, with drafted American soldiers. The air base is close-by the oilfields.

A number of gross misrepresentations were involved in the negotiations with the New Dealers to induce them to take the burden of Saudi Arabian concessions off the shoulders of the Rockefeller-Standard Oil interests, according to testimony before a Congressional Committee investigating the deal. First, it was misrepresented that the oil was fit for use by the U. S. Navy. The Naval Laboratory reported, however, that the oil was of inferior grade and unsuited for use in Navy boilers. Though it was condemned, its purchase was arranged for by oilman, Admiral Andrew F. Carter, then executive officer of the Army-Navy Petroleum Board and now employed by Overseas Tank Corporation a subsidiary of Cal-Tex Company, Aramco's owner. The purchase was made by his brother, Admiral William J. Carter, Chief of the Bureau of Supplies and Accounts. In charge of the price negotiations were Lt. John Walsh, now employed by the Standard Oil of New Jersey and Lt. D. Bodenschatz, now with General Petroleum Company. What use the Navy made of this inferior oil, if any, has not been revealed.

Aside from the false representation regarding the quality of the oil and its value to the Navy, misrepresentation was made regarding the price that would be charged the Navy for it. Despite the fact that the U.S. taxpayers financed the deal, the price that the Navy was to pay was the same as would be charged the British Navy; 40 cents a barrel for fuel oil, and 75 cents a barrel for Diesel oil. Instead the U. S. Navy was charged $1.05 for fuel oil and $1.68 for Diesel oil, more than double. Senator Brewster, chairman of the Senate Investigating Committee stated that these prices involved an overpayment of $68,000,000.

The ownership of the Saudi Arabian concession is vested in the Standard Oil of California and the Texas Company, through a jointly owned company, Cal-Tex. The operating company is a subsidiary, the Arabian-American Oil Company, called briefly Aramco. The

Cal-Tex Company is reported to be about to sell a 40% interest in the field to the Standard Oil of New Jersey and Socony Vacuum Oil for a sum stated as more than a quarter of a billion dollars.

Aramco is now shipping from Ras Tanura more than 350,000 barrels of oil a day, and the shipments are rapidly increasing. The value of the shipments amounts to an income of almost a million dollars a day for the Rockefeller Empire. The cost of this oil to them is very low, involving a royalty to King Ibn Saud that is reported to be 23 cents a barrel. The profits to the Standard Oil of California and the Texas Company on the Saudi Arabian oil are enormous. But they are completely exempt from taxes on those profits. Thus the Treasury Department has aided the Rockefeller Empire in evading taxes on profits made on moneys given it by the American taxpayers.

The cost of the Rockefeller Empire's Saudi Arabian oil to the American people is tragically high. It cost them two World Wars, hundreds of billions of dollars, tens of thousands of lives and hundreds of thousands of maimed and crippled—the expense of obtaining the oil fields for the Rockefeller Empire. If the U. S. had paid the Rockefeller Empire ten times as much as their profits from the fields, it would have gotten off cheaply, for it would have saved its citizens the untold miseries of the wars and billions of dollars.

But the U. S. is not yet through paying, the full tragic price of the Rockefeller Empire's Saudi Arabian oil. World War III, the continuation of World Wars I and II, centers just as they did, about Saudi Arabian oil. For Saudi Arabia lies close-by Russia, and possibly is part of the same basin that includes the Baku oil fields. Russia wants Saudi Arabian oil and in fact needs it, if she is going to seek to conquer the world.

The Rockefeller Empire has done business on an extensive scale with Russia and may even be said to have dominated Russia in some respects. There never has been any major disagreements between Russia, when dominated by Stalin, and the Rockefeller Empire since they started doing business together. At the Paris Conference, the U. S. voted with Soviet Russia and the Slavic block, against England, on the question of Roumanian oil. Even as recently as April 1948, the Rockefellers honored Russia with an exhibition depicting the glories of Soviet Russia and Communism by celebrating the 30th Anniversary of Russia under Communism at their Museum of Science and Industry in Rockefeller Center. And Nelson Rockefeller amazed the members of the Thursday Club by there entertaining the Russian emissary Andrei Gromyko. It was probably the Empire's "kiss of death" signalizing their order to his government to recall him.

The Rockefellers have no quarrel with Communism. On the contrary, as has been related, their General Education Fund and Rockefeller Foundation have been among the chief supporters of Communism in the United States and in other lands. They have planted Communist teachers and professors in every school, college and university in the land. Few of the Communist front organizations of note have failed to secure a subsidy from the Rockefeller "philanthropies". The most recent of them to come to the lime-light as subversive activities were the American-Soviet Science Society (harboring Dr. Condon) which is suspect in connection with the leaks of atomic bomb information to Soviet Russia. The Rockefellers financed it to the tune of $25,000. They also subsidized with $20,000, Broom, the publication of Hans Eisler who was recently deported as one of the key Communist agents in the United States.

They have fallen in line with Bismarck's clever scheme to use Communism to foster dictatorships and monopolies. They appreciate, as did Bismarck, that the concept of Communism held by the moronic elements is absolutely false. The moron thinks of Communism as a State in which everyone shares alike. Actually Communism is a State which owns everything and everyone, in which, with one exception, everyone has nothing and is equally poor, in which the problem of poverty is solved by making everyone possessionless. The moron regards the State as something abstract, apart from men. But in reality the State is a single man or a group of men. Therefore the greater the power given the State, the greater is the power of that man or of a group of men.

Since the Communist State owns and controls everything and everyone, it is the most perfect type of Dictatorship—a Super-Capitalist Super-Dictatorship that outdoes in its perfection anything that is offered by Nazism, Fascism or New Dealism. From the point of view of the Rockefeller Empire, the Communist State is most perfect, if the man of their own choice be at its head. At any rate it is the shortest route to Dictatorship in Democracies and in attaining it there can always be the pretense of improving on democracy.

The quarrel of the Rockefeller Empire is not with Communism but with a Russia dominated by Molotov, who will not do business with them and who threatens their Saudi Arabia, the gem in their diadem; but with a Russia that, now that they have broken the back of the British Empire, is their only serious rival for world-wide imperialism.

The Rockefeller Empire dictated the setting up of the United Nations after World War II, primarily to establish a community of interest with Russia. They were willing to give Russia anything she asked for, within reason provided the U. S. taxpayers could be made to bear the burden. They were willing to give her, via the United Nations a fifty square mile base in Westchester and Connecticut, within striking distance of every strategic United States East coast industry. Since fifty square miles is a larger area than would be required to house some ten thousand employees, it is obvious that the area was intended to serve the purpose of a military base. In short they were willing to extend Russia a military base in the United States and a forum for propaganda. A committee headed by the Jugo-Slav Communist Stoian Gabrilovich, and completely manned by Communists, were permitted to select the site. John D. Rockefeller Jr. offered his home at Pocantico to the United Nations.

The Committee demanded full extra-territorial rights an insult that not even China is now willing to accept. But it was granted.

Russia demanded the power of veto. That also was granted.

When public indignation, first stirred up by the author, among the residents of the district who were to be expropriated, blocked the granting of this site, the Russians, maneuvering shrewdly pretended to favor Geneva. The Rockefellers whom this move made anxious, frantically offered the United Nations a site in the heart of New York City, that had been assembeld for another purpose, at a cost of eight million dollars. This suited the purpose of the Russians and was grabbed.

Russia had demanded through President Roosevelt at Yalta and Teheran the Balkan States, Western Germany, Poland, Austria, Jugoslavia, Mongolia, Manchuria, Korea and Sakhalin and numerous other territories. President Roosevelt mouthed the Empire's agreement alternately with mouthings of the non-existent Atlantic Charter that guaranteed autonomy to those very states. The effect was almost as if Charley McCarthy had two Edgar Bergens.

Russia demanded disarmament of the United States and withdrawal of its troops from Europe and Asia. Communist agents openly agitated for it in the United States and abroad. It was granted.

Russia demanded continuance of "lend-lease" of material of war and of equipment for war production from the U. S. after the end of the war. It was granted.

Russia demanded a let-down and disruption of the defenses of the U. S. It was granted.

All of these requests were granted at the behest of the Rockefeller Empire because they cost it nothing. The U. S. taxpayer paid the bills. Those demands it classed as within reason.

The basic motive of the Rockefeller Empire interest in the United Nations and appeasing Russia was revealed by their spokesman in the State Department as world oil control. This was embodied in a New York Times special article published on August 17, 1946, reporting a broadcast made by them on the National Broadcasting Company's "University of the Air". The State Department "experts", loaned it by the Rockefeller-Standard Oil interests, proposed an International Petroleum Authority under the United Nations. Naturally this was represented to be in the interest of the U. S. to relieve its oil "shortage", and not of the Rockefeller Empire to increase its monopoly and profits. The following month, on September 6th, 1946, a variant of this scheme was offered by Howard A. Cowden, President of the Consumers' Cooperative Association.

The United Nations is the prototype of the Parliament of the Rockefeller Empire after the pattern of Nickerson's *American Rich*—a mere "advisory body", a debating society, all talk and no action, for "letting off steam."

In short, pending world-wide dictatorship by the Empire, they seek to bring about an Oil Cartel under the auspices of the U.N. The Rockefeller entente with Russia in opposition to England despite all the surface antagonism, came out into the open at the Paris Conference on September 21, 1946, when the U. S. voted with Russia and the Slavic block against the British Empire on Roumanian oil. The same community of interests was responsible for their ousting of Churchill when, after his speech before Parliament announcing that he "would not preside over the dissolution of the British Empire", he began blocking afresh the development of Saudi Arabia. Churchill was promptly ousted and the Marxist Labor Party, that stands so close to the Soviet, was put in power.

But when Russia merely threatened to reach out for Rockefeller Empire's darling Saudi Arabia, that was entirely beyond all reason. The Empire is prepared to fight for its Saudi Arabian oil with the last American life and the last American dollar.

The entire foreign policy of the State Department, as might be expected from its personnel, is warped to protect Rockefeller's Saudi Arabian oil. President Roosevelt, when he needed the Jewish vote to win his fourth term, supported the commercially motivated Zionist claims to Palestine based upon their Biblical documented conquest of it from the Arabs. While Roosevelt mouthed this program to the stupid but fanatic Zionist element for their vote, his Rockefeller dominated State Department penned for him a letter to his "great and good friend" and Rockefeller's, King Abdullah, a leader of the anti-Jewish Arabian forces in Palestine, assuring him that no decision would be made with regard to Palestine without consulting with the Arabs, or that was hostile to them. This situation is laden with additional interest for the Rockefeller Empire by the fact that all of Palestine is virtually a proved oil field. These acts are attributed to Roosevelt's duplicity. But it is questionable that a mouthpiece, a Charley McCarthy, can be guilty of duplicity, for he is merely a tool.

With an election in sight, the U. S. supported in the U.N. the Palestine compromise, partition. Then the Communist-inspired Stern Gang cut the Haifa pipe line of the Iraq Petroleum Company on March 28, 1947, as a protest against the execution of the assassin Dov Gruner. Burt Hull, President of the Texas Pipe Line Company, who had been assigned the task of building the Saudi Arabian pipe line, undertook to negotiate with the Jewish Agency to avert any further damage to the pipe line as a condition prerequisite to laying the Saudi Arabian pipe line through the Jewish corridor that the partition plan created through Palestine. The rabid Communists in the Jewish Agency prevailed over the more rational head of the Agency.

They said that they would cut the pipe line whenever it suited their purpose. That attitude doomed the plan of a Jewish state. Election or no election, President Truman demanded that the U.N. follow the Rockefeller State Department and abandon partition or a Jewish state.

At this point it might be noted that it is probably not a matter of accident that the granddaughter of John D. Rockefeller is named Lucy Truman Aldrich.

Under the "Truman policy", Russia's goodwill is being purchased on behalf of the Rockefeller Empire with the U.S. taxpayers' money through such devices as the Greek and Turkish loan "to stop Communism" and the Marshall Plan for the same purpose. At the same time the bankruptcy of the U.S.A. that is intended to bring dictatorship, is being hastened.

The pattern that is being followed is a variant of that used after World War I. Then foregn bonds of every conceivable land were sold to the American public. When they became worthless, a short time later, a Congressional investigation revealed that a major portion of the "loaned" money had never reached the lands for which the bonds were issued. It had stuck to the fingers of the top-flight, Dynastic bankers. The wariness of the American investing public and the Johnson Act forbade a repetition of the bond sales. "Lend-lease", government loans and the Marshall Plan are serving to drain off the money from the purses of theAmerican public into those of the Dynastic bankers and the Rockefeller Empire. Some of these moneys are serving to pay off Russia for staying out of Saudi Arabia— a form of international blackmail.

The mechanics of these loans is made clear by the Greek "loan" of $400,000,000 "to fight Communism". If fighting Communism was the true object of this loan, the purpose would have been served better by shipments of arms and munitions from our huge war surplus. For wars are still fought with shells and not with dollar bills. If it was the intent to stop Communism, the U. S. would not have sent some of its notorious Reds to Greece for that purpose—headed by New Dealers, Griswold and Eleanor Roosevelt's kin Ambassador MacVeagh. For when the program began, there were but a few scattered bands of Communist guerillas in Northern Greece. But after several months of "stopping Communism" and the expenditure of the whole loan, a Communist government controlled all of northern Greece. But just as if it had been pre-arranged, the Communists stopped short of the Mediterranean, the life line of the Rockefeller Empire and their Saudi Arabian oil.

But, in these days seven hundred millions are mere chicken feed and are totally insufficient for respectable international bribers. That requires billions. Marshall, Chief of Staff, who participated in the betrayal of Pearl Harbor, the best Secretary of State the Rockefeller Empire ever has had, executed the master plan for drawing billions from American purses to finance the Empire's program for international bribery. Following instructions, he asked the nations of the world at large how many dollars they would like to loot from the United States Treasury "to fight Communism". Their imaginations were cramped and they asked for a "trifling" sixteen billion dollars over a period of five years. (Russia is addicted to five year plans.) The disappointingly small sum requested has been amplified by Imperial generosity which insists upon extending a few billions to China and a half billion to South American countries.

To insure the support of the Marshall looting of the United States, good use was made of the sham anti-Communistic drive which has been taken over by the most notorious Communist fellow-travelers, who now follow the party-line and pose as anti-Communists. Soviet Russia is ever willing to cooperate in drawing off the wealth and resources of the United States and has undertaken to increase the popularity of the Marshall Boodle Fund by pretending to be opposed to it. The success of the plan with the American public is a tribute to their childishness. Russia will receive the tribute of the Rockefeller Empire paid by the American taxpayers, while the latter will be blissfully deceived in the belief that they are contributing to "stopping Communism".

If the Rockeller Empire should by any chance withhold the tribute, Russia would collect it indirectly, as she has the UNRRA aid, by seizing the countries that have received the aid.

The half billion offered to South America gave rise to an amusing incident which is revelatory of the true purposes of the loans. At the Inter-American Conference, in Bogota, Colombia, Secretary Marshall announced at the April 8, 1948 session, that the United States was prepared to extend an unsolicited bribe of five hundred million dollars to them. This announcement was greeted coldly with neither applause or comment. The press reported that Marshall was "shocked" by the reception his announcement received and commented that it was probably due to the sum, a mere half billion being regarded as inadequate.

The real reason for the attitude of Latin America to this offer of American taxpayers' moneys on behalf of the Rockefeller Empire is their sad past experience with similar "gifts". Nelson Rockefeller's Committee for Inter-Hemispheric Defense had been used effectively to club Latin America into granting concessions to the Rockefeller Empire and to implant Communism. They had learned to shun Rockefeller "philanthropy" as a costly affair, even when extended through U. S. Government agencies. That was the real significance to the answer which Marshall received on the following day when the Communists themselves staged a rebellion against the Rockefeller control of Colombia, wrecked the Conference and forced the delegates to flee for their lives.

At the International Socialist Conference on European Recovery held at Sanderstead, England, Hugh Dalton, Laborite and former Chancellor of the Exchequer on March 22, 1948, pointed out the true complexion of the Marshall Plan. He noted that the government of practically all sixteen European nations directly involved in the Marshall Plan, were completely or almost completely Socialist. i. e. Marxist. He intimated that Russia would be expected to participate in the Plan that was designed so fully to support Marxism.

The real significance of the Marshall Plan is a Rockefeller Empire compromise with Soviet Russia, offering a partnership and splitting of the world into two spheres. It is a counterpart of the Russian-German alliance of Hitler's; and it recalls the temporary Rockefeller Empire partnership with the Mitsui that was dictated by expediency. Russia is being bribed to stay out of Saudi Arabia until the United States can replace the armaments that were so treacherously and treasonably scrapped for political advantage. In large part it was given to Russia as part of the Empire's "pay-off". Some of it is still being shipped to Russia, while Congress is preparing to appropriate billions for its replacement. The Empire brooks no compromises if it can fight at no expense to itself.

Throughout the process of financing of Saudi Arabia by American taxpayers there has been advanced the utterly false allegation that U. S. national security demands its development. *The truth is exactly the reverse.* The development of the Saudi Arabian oil fields is the greatest menace to the security of the U.S.A. For, as has been stated, Saudi Arabia lies a short distance from the Russian border and in event of war would rapidly fall into the hands of Russia. The enormous production of its oil fields would relieve the Soviets of the limitations in the conduct of war posed by their meagre oil supply, and would enable them to wage war indefinitely. Availability of Saudi Arabian oil might be the deciding factor in inducing Russia to make war on the U. S.

By the same process of providing Russia with adequate Saudi Arabian oil, the Empire by deliberate plan is reducing the capacity of the U. S. for oil production. At its dictate, the U. S. is allowing the shipment to both Saudi Arabia and Russia of pipe, casing, drilling equipment and an endless array of material and equipment essential to the production and transport of oil. This is almost paralyzing the United States oil industry and is entirely responsible for the continuous domestic shortage of oil and petroleum products that has resulted in cold, fuelless homes, illness, restrictions or stoppage of industry and transportation, and threatens restoration of gasoline rationing — in other words a restriction of the entire American economy geared to oil.

A deliberate effort is being made by the Rockefeller-Standard Oil interests to create a shortage of oil reaching the consumer market. H. J. Porter, President of the Texas Independent Producers and Royalty Owners Association stated in a telegram to Representative Alvin Weichel, on June 28, 1947:

"Above ground stocks of crude (oil) are actually 15 million barrels above this time last year . . . any spot shortages are the result of insufficient oil being refined".

He stated that American steel is being used to build pipe-lines in Russia and the Middle East despite its desperate need in the United States to bring oil to independent refineries.

The purpose of the Empire in engineering this shortage is to justify the import of Saudi Arabian oil into the U. S. without payment of duty. They do not want

to use American crude oil which costs them many times
the price of Saudi Arabian oil and leaves them less
enormous profits. For, the price situation of petroleum
products is based on the price of American crude oil
plus the taxes involved in American production and
refining. On Saudi Arabian oil subsidized by the American taxpayer, they have to pay no taxes to the U. S.,
which further enhances their profits. By blocking the
flow of American crude oil to the refineries and the
market, they create an artificial shortage which main-
tains the price structure for their cheap Saudi Arabian oil. In the meantime the military power and security of the U. S. are undermined. The land is placed
in multiple jeopardy, in order that their profits will
accrue.

During the summer of 1947, the Standard Oil Company of New Jersey and Socony-Vacuum Oil Company
announced to the press that they were preparing to
purchase crude oil in Saudi Arabia and join the Texas
Company in importing it to the United States as a
public service. They said that this public service was
non-profit-making because of the 10½ cents duty per
barrel and the $1.21 shipping costs. The implication
of the story is that such public service should not be
handicapped by a duty, that the oil should be admitted duty-free. No mention was made of the fact that
cheaper oil at lower shipping cost is available in Venezuela but is not being used, for Imperial reasons. Nor
did the story make any mention of the fact that the
Saudi Arabian oil was being produced largely at the
expense of the American taxpayer.

About six months later, December 17, 1947, Socony-
Vacuum announced the arrival of a third tanker cargo
of 166,449 barrels of Saudi Arabian oil at their refinery
in Paulboro, N. J., "to help alleviate the shortage of
fuel oil and gasoline in the East". The arrival of a
fourth tanker was announced three days later.

On March 27, 1948, nine months after it was established that the shipment of pipe abroad was paralyzing the oil industry of the U. S., a Congressional subcommittee spokesman investigating black markets announced to the press that pipe was being shipped out
of the country by the shipload. They brought to light
one stockpile of millions of feet of pipe awaiting shipment to Russia. Subsequently it was revealed that
thousands of tons of machinery for the manufacture
of munitions and planes, hundreds of aviation engines,

and an endless array of new Army and Navy equipment has been shipped to Russia or is being shipped under "lend lease", at the very time when Truman announced to the world the adoption of the Marshall Plan "to stop Russia's aggression" and the plan to rearm of the U. S. for that purpose.

The program presented by the Russian situation is the same as was presented by the Japanese situation in the ten years prior to Pearl Harbor. Russia is being ruthlessly helped to rearm for war on the U. S. by the Empire and its puppets, American officials. Once again the country is deliberately placed in grave jeopardy this time, in order to encourage the Russians to attack and to precipitate war. A policy of talking roughly for the benefit of the American voter, and dealing softly to appease Russia has been adopted. Protests against these shipments to Russia have proved ineffective.

These facts incidently explain why the post-war prosecution of the officers of the German Dye Trust has failed "because of lack of evidence." Dillon, Read & Company, allies of the Dynasty, was one of the banking houses through which was done much of the financing of the German munitions industry, of Krupps and the I. G. Farbenindustrie. James V. Forrestal, Roosevelt's appointee, now Secretary of Defense, was then head of Dillon, Read & Company. William H. Draper, former vice-president of Dillon, Read & Company, is Under-Secretary of the Army. Draper, in 1945, as a brigadier general subordinate to the Commander in Germany, General Lucius Clay, stated that (from the point of view of Dillon Read interests?) he regarded the policy of destroying the German munition industry an error. For this he was reprimanded by General Clay, who pointed out that in event of war, the German munitions industry will fall into the hands of Russia.

Secretary Forrestal thereupon promoted his former partner in Dillon Read, to a partnership in a bigger concern, to the post of Undersecretary of the U. S. Army. Phillip Hawkins, Draper's son-in-law, was made Chief of Property in the American Military Government in Germany. In this post he promptly isued an order sparing the Dillon Read financed munition and dye works from dismantlement. Thus is the Empire acting to arm Russia for war with us, just as it helped to prepare Japan for Pearl Harbor. Howard Ambruster in a book published by the Beechhurst Press in April

1947, labelled these maneuvers "Treason Peace."

The full extent of the treachery of the Rockefeller Empire in its quest for oil and power was illustrated by current events in Palestine. Their American agents, Truman and all the other candidates for the Presidency, who faced an election, recognized the Israel government but maintain an embargo on arms which might insure the wiping out of the Israelis. The pretext for maintaining the embargo is that another of the agencies of the Rockefeller Empire, the United Nations, had not lifted the embargo. Their right hand evidently does not know what their left hand is doing.

In the meantime the Rockefeller Empire was instigating and arming the Arabs through its allies, Bevins and the British Labor Government. The poverty-stricken Arabs demand less than the customary $12\frac{1}{2}\%$ royalty on their oil; and despite their reputations as sharp traders, they are more readily swindled out of the money which they are paid for the oil, so that the net cost to the Empire is zero. King Abdullah of benighted and backward Transjordania was used as their tool in carrying out the plan of seizing Jerusalem and oil-rich Southern Palestine. This might have insured the British a military and air base near the Suez Canal in lieu of Egypt from which they had been ousted by Rockefeller-Soviet agent Nasser. King Abdullah's troops were trained and armed under a treaty with England, well in advance of Britain's withdrawal; and authentic reports indicate that they had Abdulah's soldiers planted in Jerusalem and other strategic points in Palestine well in advance.

The Arabs have been instigated in their action by the Rockefeller Empire, by Nazi agents, by the British and by Russia. The instigators have paid little heed to the menace of a Holy War which might easily be stirred up among the ever-martial Mohammedans, that in years to come may threaten conquest of Europe and war on Christianity by them. Such a war of the Orient on the Occident long has been predicted.

The financing of the development of the Rockefeller Empire's Saudi Arabian fields was also engineered by Secretary of Defense Forrestal's firm. Dillon, Read & Co. and by its senior partner Clarence Dillon, nè Stenbock.

If by any chance Russia should trap and imprison the American Army in Central Europe, or attack elsewhere, the story would be bad. For the U. S. is virtually stripped of the magnificent defenses built up during the war that are now largely turned over to Russia. An ultimate American defeat is part of the plans for attaining dictatorship and might serve the purposes of the Dynasts, if and when they make their own peace with Russia.

The good will of the Red's is one of the objectives of the Empire's support of the darling of the subversives and traitors, Henry A. Wallace. It is reported that his salary as editor of the *New Republic* as well as his campaign expenses have been defrayed by Michael Straight, Anglophile son of Willard Straight of J. P. Morgan and Company, "Jock" Whitney and Nelson Rockefeller. In Wallace's support, British propagandists have once again joined hands with the Rockefellers. The *New Republic* is published by Westrim Ltd. a corporation financed through Mrs. Leonard Elmhirst of London, the widow of Willard Straight, a former partner of Morgan & Co., for the British radicals. Her son, Michael Straight, former "adviser on economics" to Rockefeller Empire's U. S. State Department and protege of U. S. Supreme Court Justice Felix Frankfurter, has boasted:

"The New Deal is more dynamic than Fascism and more revolutionary than Communism."

Associated with Wallace as co-editors of the magazine, are a group of editors who have been closely identified with Communist front organizations and Communist "transmission belts" as Earl Browder testified under oath. These include: Bruce Bliven, Edward C. Lindeman, Helen Fuller, Stan Young, Elizabeth Hulin, George Soule and Malcolm Cowley. Cowley is also editor of SOVIET RUSSIA TO-DAY and contributor to the NEW MASSES and the DAILY WORKER. Phillip Murray, president of the CIO has openly charged that Wallace's third party movement was launched by the Communists. The Communist party confirms it. Its important support comes from the Rockefellers.

This would not be the first time that the Rockefeller-Standard Oil interests have drawn the United States into a war on their behalf, and at the same time, betrayed the country to its enemies by double-dealing. They were indicted in the second year of World War II by Assistant Attorney General Thurman Arnold, for deliberately blocking the production of synthetic rubber. Under their influence, Jesse Jones had persistently refused to stockpile crude rubber and tin for the oncoming war despite the obvious need and the demands of the military. Such stockpiling would involve a violation of an agreement with the Dutch-British Cartels under which the Rockefeller-Standard Oil interests participate in East Indies oil production. But in this war emergency, the British and Dutch interests were identical with ours, and they undoubtedly would have welcomed our stockpiling rubber and tin under these circumstances. Nevertheless none was stored.

As if this situation created by the interests of the Rockefeller-Standard Oil crowd was not bad enough, Thurman Arnold's indictment proved that the Rockefeller-Standard Oil interests were also blocking the production of synthetic rubber by withholding the use of the patents which they shared with I. G. Farbenindustrie, the German Dye Trust. The indictment did not make it clear that the Rockefeller-Standard Oil interests and their Chase National Bank owned and controlled the majority interest in the German Dye Trust. Nor did the indictment make it clear that at the very time of these acts, Nelson Rockefeller occupied the post of Coordinator of Hemispheric Defense, an ultra-strategic one for the safety of the U. S.; and that high policy-making government posts in the hundreds and possibly in the thousands were held, and strategic government departments were controlled by officers of the Rockefeller-Standard Oil Companies "loaned" to the government. It is interesting to note the name of Rockefeller did not appear in the indictment though he controls the Company.

The Standard Oil of New Jersey pleaded that its agreement with I. G. Farbenindustrie barred their permitting the use of synthetic rubber patents by the United States or the Allies. In effect they pleaded guilty to conspiring with Germany to prevent the use by the U. S. Government of synthetic rubber processes. Without the synthetic rubber prepared by these processes, the war inevitably would have been lost. Caught red-handed in their treason, they pleaded guilty to the indictment. They agreed to release the patents and processes for use by the U. S. barely in time to save the situation. None of the traitors was shot. That indicates how far more binding and protective is loyalty to the Rockefeller-Standard Oil Empire than to the U.S.A. The conclusion that the defeat of the Allies would have made no difference to the conspirators is sustained by the fact that they had extended their full support and cooperation to Hitler and the Nazis. Thurman Arnold was relieved of his post shortly after the incident.

Senator Joseph C. O'Mahoney of Wyoming, when discussing the Saudi Arabian deals of the Rockefeller Empire in a radio interview on February 2, 1947, stated:

"It is but a step from giant combinations of this kind to the authoritarian state."

In these machinations the Sidney Hillmans, Harry Hopkinses and their ilk, were mere puppets and stooges of the Rockefeller Empire — red herrings drawn across the trail.

CHAPTER XXIII

ROOSEVELT'S ODD AILMENTS
AND HIS STRANGE DEATH

Mention has been made of F. D. R.'s attack of encephalomyelitis and the stigmata which it left in its train. Both his physical and mental health were seriously and permanently impaired by it. The uncontrollable temper, the attacks of excitement with wild laughing, and of depression and high suggestibility are among the sequella that might be expected after the disease. Newspaper correspondents reported episodes of unreasoned and sustained uproarious laughter of the same type that startled guests at the Du Pont wedding and led Eleanor to pack him up and send him home. Tubbing and hydrotherapy are effectively used in these conditions.

At Teheran Roosevelt and Churchill met with Stalin to confirm the division of the World between them. During the conference, Roosevelt had been prevailed upon by the Russians to stay at the Russian Embassy because the Russians said, the American Embassy was not safe. At the Russian Embassy, it is reported, a special courtesy was extended to the guests. They were assigned a special waiter who served them exclusively. It was later discovered that the waiter was a physician who specialized in the science of poisoning, toxicology. The use of doctors under Russia's state medical system in disposing of persons whom the powers-that-be wished out of the way, by poisoning them, has been attested to in the Moscow purge trails. Dr. Levine testified that he had been ordered by his superiors to poison Maxim Gorki and had done so.

Shortly after their departure, Winston Churchill became extremely ill. He was hurried to Egypt where he was so sick that his death was expected momentarily. But his life was saved by a protege of his, Sir Arthur Fleming, the discoverer of penicillin, whom it is reported, he had sent through medical school as a reward for saving his life from drowning.

Roosevelt also was extremely ill on his return. He was unable to walk or stand unassisted, and never recovered his strength. His disability bore a striking resemblance to poisoning with a form of curare, an Indian arrow poison that had engaged the interest of Russian scientists. He wasted steadily thereafter.

In informed circles there is told a tale of an Oriental poison handed down from the days of Genghis Khan, that causes a slow, steady wasting and delayed death. Its administration is spoken of in terms of "passing the silver cord". Reputedly it has been Stalin's favorite method of unobstrusively purging folks that stood in the way. Lenin, after he had decided to oust Stalin, died such a death. Likewise Krassin wasted away in the same manner. Rumors reached this country before Roosevelt's return that the "silver cord" had been passed to him and other conferees by Stalin.

The motion pictures of Roosevelt debarking from a cruiser on his return from Teheran, in December 1943, revealed him to be a very sick man. He had lost considerable weight, and was quite emaciated. The black mole over his left eyebrow, that had constantly been a feature in his photographs, stuck out of his head like a horn.

It takes no great medical skill to diagnose the character of the growth over President Roosevelt's left eyebrow. It had the characteristic appearance and behavior of a mole turned malignant and rapidly growing, a type of cancer, or sarcoma, known as melanosarcoma.

The dishonesty that characterized the reports issued by the President's medical attendants is revealed by a statement which he himself gave the Press. Vice Admiral McIntire makes no mention of the rapidly growing mole that had become malignant, in the book that was ghosted for him by one of the veteran perverters of the truth for political purposes, otherwise known as "publicity man", George Creel, under the title WHITE HOUSE PHYSICIAN (G. P. Putman's Sons, N.Y., 1946). He mentions, instead, a relatively minor condition: "a nagging inflammation of the bronchial tubes" which he reports troubled Roosevelt during the 1943 Xmas celebration at Hyde Park.

Adm. McIntire's efforts to delude the Press and the public about the state of health of his patient, were frustrated by a statement issued by Roosevelt himself to Press correspondents on February 4, 1944, that was published in the New York Times on the following day (p. 17, col. 7). He revealed that he had had an "operation to remove a wen on his head". But McIntire and his consultants had made no mention of the operation in their bulletins, which they had issued as supposedly honest reports to their employers, the nation, on the condition of the patient.

Residents of Ormond Beach, Florida, reported that in January, 1944, they had seen President Roosevelt there with a bandage about his head, obviously convalescing from an operation, at the estate of John D. Rockefeller. It is highly probable that it was at that time there was removed the melanosarcoma (one of the most malignant forms of cancer) that had developed in the mole over Roosevelt's left eyebrow.

From the time of Roosevelt's return from Teheran, until January 6, 1945, more than a year later, Press photographers were ordered not to take, or publish, any photographs of the ailing President, except when specifically permitted to do so by the White House. Few exceptions were made.

What could have been the reason for that order?

It long has been the custom for the world dictatorship conspirators to use doubles for the men that, as their agents, they place at the heads of governments. This is clearly illustrated by the widely published report of the experience of the German medical consultant who was summoned to Moscow to examine Stalin, in the year before he died. The physician was taken to a hospital ward, where he was confronted with seven men. All of the men resembled Stalin sufficiently to be mistaken for him. This childish maneuver was intended, evidently, to delude the physician as to whom he was treating.

Likewise, Hitler and Mussolini had their doubles.

One of the doubles for President Franklin Delano Roosevelt, who acknowledged that he had acted on public occasions as "Roosevelt", appeared with the author on the Tom Duggan Television program on Station KCOP, Los Angeles, in November, 1957. He was the Warner Bros. actor, Captain Jack Young, of Norwood, Ontario and Beverly Hills, California. Capt. Young stated on the program that after he had been given the assignment to double for Roosevelt in 1941, he had spent several months as a guest in the White House, studying the President's speech, actions and mannerisms, until he learned to imitate them perfectly. He stated that in addition to his public appearances in the role of "President", he had been featured in that role by Warner Bros., in the movies "Yankee Doodle Dandy", "Mission To Moscow" and "This Is The Army"; and by 20th Century Fox, in "Woodrow Wilson". Capt. Young delighted his audience by imitating Roosevelt and his "again and again" speech.

Undoubtedly, the doubles served the conspirators as puppets quite as well as did their originals.

It is quite obvious that such robust doubles as Capt. Young could not play the role of the aged, wasted, emaciated and deathly sick Roosevelt who returned from Teheran. He is too robust. But there is reason to believe that, subsequently, other doubles assumed the role of the dying President, and carried it off well.

In the months following the original operation announced by Roosevelt, Drew Pearson reported in his radio broadcasts that the President had had two additional operations, supposedly for "wens", that were done at the Bethesda Naval Hospital. During those months there were relatively long periods of time when the Press correspondents who constantly surrounded Roosevelt, and had virtually lived at his side, as well as other close associates, were completely cut off from any communication with the President. Indeed, it is open to question if any of them ever saw him, in person, again. Elaborate efforts were made by the conspirators to keep the public from learning of the vanishing of the President from the public scene.

Gen. Dwight D. Eisenhower, for instance, was reported to have had an audience with the President, by the N.Y. Times on January 18, 1944 (p. 40, Col. 5). A Press conference was also announced by the Times, on January 19 (p. 5, Col. 6). But these followed a shock-breaking announcement in its columns of January 15 (p. 9, col. 6 that "Roosevelt" had lost ten pounds. This might well have been a maneuver to cover up the use of one of the doubles to play the role of "President".

The February 25, 1944 N.Y. Times carried (p. 17, col. 7) a strange dateline and even more curious headline that read as follows: "With Pres. Roosevelt, Feb. 24. PRESIDENT HOLDS ALOOF FROM PRESS". The dispatch relates that the correspondents had been informed that *his presence could not be recognized, he was absent from the city, and no questions would be entertained by the President.* It was emphasized that the dispatch did not come from the Press correspondents "who continually stay near the President" because the correspondents had not been permitted to take the trip.

The absence of Roosevelt from the White House was covered up by statements issued by various persons concerning the state of health of the President, whose whereabouts was shrouded in mystery. On March 25, however, it was announced that the President had left the White House *for the first time after his prolonged illness..*

In the meantime, something had occurred that is of special interest in connection with the situation. On March 21, 1944, the N.Y. Times (p. 19, Col. 3) reported that Winthrop Rutherfurd, a distant kinsman of Roosevelt's, had died on March 19, at his estate in Aiken, S.C. That there may have been some connection between Roosevelt's disappearance from the public eye and this death at Aiken, is brought up by a revelation of Grace Tully, Roosevelt's secretary, in her biography entitled F. D. R. MY BOSS.

Miss Tully exposed the fact that the widow, Mrs. Winthrop Rutherfurd, nee Lucy Mercer, was present at Georggia Warm Springs at the time that "Roosevelt's" death was announced—more than a year later.

Prior to her marriage in 1920, Lucy Mercer had been in the employ of the Roosevelts. She had attracted the roving eye, that is so characteristic of the clan, of Franklin D. Roosevelt. In the true family tradition, that was followed more recently by his son Jimmy, FDR had indulged in a kiss-and-tell romance with his attractive employee—and then cavalierly blabbed about it to his spouse, Eleanor.

Miss Mercer left the Roosevelt employ, married shortly thereafter and presented her aged husband with a daughter to take a place beside her five stepchildren. Curiously, Eleanor Roosevelt makes no mention of these intriguing matters in her supposed utterly candid biographies!

Visits of the President, clandestinely, to the Rutherfurd New Jersey estate on several previous occasions, that were kept from public ken by censorship, are related by Westbrook Pegler, in his King Features column dispatched from Washington on December 22, 1949.

It seems hardly probable that Mrs. Winthrop Rutherfurd would have been present at Georgia Warm Springs, visiting an admirer whom she had spurned—Franklin D. Roosevelt—within a year after the death of her husband. It is highly improbable that she would have brazenly employed an artist, Mrs. Elizabeth Shoumatoff, to paint the portrait of a former lover, FDR, as stated by Miss Tully. Since Mrs. Shoumatoff had been commissioned to do portraits of several members of the Rutherfurd family, it appears more probable that she and Mrs. Rutherfurd were present at Georgia Warm Springs with a member of the Rutherfurd family. Is it possible that the more aged Winthrop Rutherfurd was substituted for the dying President in the early months of 1944, when the latter vanished from the public scene?

The author interviewed Mrs. Shoumatoff at her Fifth Ave. apartment, in the early 1950's. Her story was a strange one. She stated that she had done a portrait in water color, years earlier, of a younger Roosevelt, which she had in her apartment, and showed me. It showed FDR, who had managed to evade the draft and military service, striking a pose as a "fighting man", a naval officer. She had nothing to show for a portrait of the Warm Springs invalid.

For keeping her secret, concerning the nature of which she was not specific, Mrs. Shoumatoff related, Eleanor Roosevelt had offered, after the death at Warm Springs, to hang that portrait at the Hyde Park "shrine" for a period of time; and promised that at the end of the period she would pay her handsomely (my recollection was that the sum specified was $50,000, a really handsome bribe) for the portrait and make it a permanent part of the exhibit. However, Mrs. Shoumatoff related, at the end of a year, after the myth of the "Roosevelt" death had become too firmly established in the minds of us "peasants" to dislodge, Eleanor Roosevelt curtly returned the portrait to the artist with not even a "thank you", and welshed on the deal in characteristic Roosevelt style.

This affair may give some clue as to who was the double who campaigned for Roosevelt in 1944, who went to Yalta with Alger Hiss for the "One World", Rockefeller-Soviet conspirators; and who it was that died so mysteriously at Georgia Warm Springs.

In spite of censorship and propaganda, it was fairly widely suspected that the man who campaigned as Democratic candidate in 1944 was not Roosevelt. Fulton Lewis Jr. informed the author that he attended one of the few personal appearances of the "candidate" in the campaign—the foreign policy speech that was delivered to a rowdy bootlegger- and racketeer-infested Teamsters' Union convention in New York. The appearance, speech, diction, enunciation and mannerisms of the speaker were so different from those of Franklin Delano Roosevelt, Mr. Lewis related, that he approached Presidential secretary, Steve Early, and asked him who had substituted for Roosevelt in delivering the speech. Early took Lewis aside, shushed him, and tried to pass off the question by alleging: "The President has had too many drinks".

The fact that it was some one other than the President who delivered the "fireside talks" during the campaign was evident to every critical listener; and it can be discerned from the recordings of them.

The order prohibiting the taking or publishing of a photograph of the President that had been issued to the Press in December, 1943, was countermanded on January 6, 1945. The Press photographers were ordered to take, for publication, a photograph of "President Roosevelt broadcasting his message on the state of the Nation". But contrary to the practise that had previously prevailed, they were not permitted to take any "closeups", or to publish enlargements of the "President's" features; and were required to take only distant views from across the chamber. As a consequence, the face of the broadcaster was so small, in the picture, that the features could not be discerned in the prints. In published reproductions of the picture, printed with screening, the details were entirely indistinguishable; and accurate identification of the subject was impossible.

The author purchased an enlargement of the photograph taken by the Associated Press photographer, together with a number of closeup portraits taken in years prior. It is reproduced here, together with the earlier photos known to be those of F. D. Roosevelt. The enlargement reveals the fact that the person making the January 6 broadcast on the state of the nation could not possibly be mistaken for Roosevelt. The differences in the features are such that neither age nor disease can effect, viz:

1. The ears presented by the two, differ in shape.
2. The position of the ears on the heads differ.
3. The shapes of the heads and of the hairlines differ.
4. The shapes and color values of the eyes differ.
5. The shapes of the noses differ.
6. The broadcaster presents a butterfly eruption over the saddle of the nose that is typical of pellagra. This arises from heavy drinking without an adequate diet, that results in a deficiency of Vitamin B. Since Roosevelt drank liberally, but also ate heartily, he never presented any pellagratous signs.
7. The broadcaster is edentulous, presenting only two long, rounded upper incisor teeth. Roosevelt had a full set of short, irregular, angular teeth and his physicians never reported that any tooth extractions were done on the President, though they would have been certain to report it because it would have helped explain their patient's difficulties without creating any alarm.
8. The shape of the two chins differ in a manner that no disease could bring about.
9. The ratio of the width of the cheek bones to the height of the skull, which is an anthropometric index that does not vary with disease, differs widely in the two photographs.
10. The mole that Roosevelt had presented on his forehead over the left eyebrow, for many years is absent in the broadcaster, but in its place there is a scar at the site, through the eyebrow. The impression given by the picture, is that the scar was deliberately created by an incision through the eyebrow, in the effort to make the deception more perfect.

The enlarged photograph of the broadcaster makes it quite evident that both the photographers and the nation were duped. The conspirators evidently trusted that their deception in palming off a double would be insured success by the barring of close-ups.

It is reasonably certain that no such chances would

have been taken by the conspirators if Roosevelt was alive and competent mentally. It therefore appears to be a certainty that President Roosevelt was either dead, or incompetent mentally, on January 6, 1945; and that since the same person appears in the photographs released from the Yalta conference, it evidently was the double who attended that conference. Winston Churchill remarked in his autobiography about how strangely different a person was the "Roosevelt" who attended the Yalta conference. There is reason to believe that he was aware of the fact that he was dealing with a double. The Communists, undoubtedly, had been informed of the deception by their Axis partners, and were fully aware of it. This may explain the demand on the part of the Soviet Ambassador following the death that the coffin be opened and he be permitted to view the remains, on behalf of his government. The request was denied. Both the request and its denial are quite extraordinary. It creates the impression that Stalin and the Soviets were trying to make sure of the elimination of a trusted agent; or that they were checking to make sure of a purge.

Strange as were the features and circumstances of Roosevelt's illness and operations, the circumstances of the death at Georgia Warm Springs were even stranger. These make it obvious that there is more to the situation than meets the eye, and that gross deception has been practiced on the nation. They have given rise, quite naturally, to many rumors that could and can be set at rest, and should be, by the legally required postmortem on the remains. But all demands made upon the authorities for compliance with Federal and State laws which require an autopsy in the case of sudden deaths of unexpected nature, to eliminate the possibility of murder and foul-play, have been ignored.

The sudden and unexpected nature of the death is attested to by the statements and actions of President Roosevelt's personal physician who was assigned by the Navy to be in constant attendance on him, Vice Admiral Ross T. McIntire. He was not present in Georgia Warm Springs at the time of the death. This fact makes it highly probable, almost a certainty, that the person who died there *was not President Roosevelt.*

The alibi that the professional perverter of the truth for public deception, otherwise known as "public relations counsellor", assigned by the Government to fashion the Doctor's published story to suit their purposes, and to protect those involved, is so weak that it merely serves to fully confirm the justified suspicions. Ghost-writer, George Creel represents the Doctor as asserting: that tests proved him (Ed. i.e. Roosevelt) organically sound ... (p. 238). His heart was their principal concern ... The signs counted on for diagnosis of the condition of the cerebral arteries, were absent.

There emerges, quite obviously, from this statement the fact that whoever it was that died at Georgia Warm Springs, did die a sudden and unexpected death from a cause that might be surmised, or guessed, but could not be definitely established except by a postmortem. In such cases the laws of every State in the Union, and the Federal laws, require a postmortem for the purpose of definitely and positively determining the cause of the death, and for elimination of the possibility of murder or foul-play. This means that the burial of the Georgia Warm Springs victim without a postmortem was a flagrant and deliberate violation of the law. Consequently, it raises a grave suspicion of assassination, or murder, of the victim. And to this date, no move has been made by law enforcement agencies to dispel that suspicion in spite of a public demand made by the author!

Ghost-writer Creel has acknowledged on behalf of Dr. McIntire that an autopsy was in order; but alleges that it would serve no useful purpose. (p. 239) This allegation is preposterously false. It would serve the obvious and most important purpose of complying with the law that was enacted for the purpose of guarding against murder —which is a highly useful purpose. The postmortem, if it had been performed, would have determined that the "cerebral hemorrhage" that is given as the cause of death in the death certificate had not been brought about deliberately by any one of a number of means, for the purpose of murder.

The hemorrhage might have been caused by a fracture of the skull. It might have been due to an assassin's bullet, the point of entry of which, as happens at times, was not evidenced by any external mark, but might have been discovered at autopsy. It might have been caused by the administration of a poison, such as dicoumarol, that favors the development of hemorrhages, that might have been administered either for the purpose of accomplishing a murder, or carelessly administered by the treating physician in excessive amounts. Or the hemorrhage might have been caused by a brain tumor, or a metastasis to the brain of a mole become cancerous; and this undeniably would be a most useful bit of information for the nation to know—with its evidence that there was a pathologic basis of mental impairment, in the brain of the nation's ruler who had done so much to change the structure and administration of its government. It would open to question the decrees and orders he was supposed to have signed. And finally it might have revealed that the remains were that of an impostor, of a double, who had been used by conspirators to accomplish their malign purposes.

NO AUTOPSY WAS MORE DEFINITELY REQUIRED BY LAW, AND NONE COULD SERVE A BETTER PURPOSE, THAN ONE MADE ON THE REMAINS OF THE GEORGIA WARM SPRINGS VICTIM!

An explanation of the possible cause for the failure to perform an autopsy on the corpse may lie in the report that emanates from a local clergyman who chanced on the death scene. He reported that the death had been caused by a bullet through the skull from behind forward, that had blown away the victim's face. This would also serve to explain why the body never was laid out in state.

A survey made at an undertakers' convention in the South, a year or two after the death, reported that no undertaker had been found who would acknowledge that he had embalmed the remains. However, Mr. Patterson, of H. M. Patterson & Son, of Atlanta, Georgia, more recently informed the author, in August, 1958, that he had embalmed the body before it had entrained from Atlanta for Washington, accompanied by soldiers, sailors and marines as pall-bearers.

Before it was shipped, the coffin was sealed. And it was never again opened, even for the family services. The GI's who accompanied the body had instructions to shoot anyone who attempted to open the coffin. In Washington, those who came to view the remains, saw only the unopened coffin. While in broadcasts to the Armed Forces Elmer Davis, Chief of the Office of War "Intelligence", falsely alleged that the body lay in state, the buddies of the deluded GI's stood guard about the coffin to make sure that no one could view the remains by opening the coffin. The sealed coffin was placed in the East Room of the White House, where services were held on April 14 with Rev. Angus Dun, bishop of the Episcopal diocese of Washington officiating.

On the same afternoon, the sealed coffin was shipped, under armed guard, to the funeral parlor of Auchmoody, of Fishkill, N.Y. Mr. Auchmoody informed the author that he was given strict orders not to dare to open the coffin, and was told that the armed guard was under orders to shoot anyone who would attempt to open it.

On the following day, April 15, the unopened coffin was buried with military honors. These were anomalous in view of the fact that FDR had carefully avoided and evaded draft into active military service though he inflicted it gleefully on others. The coffin was buried in the garden of the Roosevelt Hyde Park estate. Rev. George W. Anthony, rector of St. James' Episcopal Church at Hyde Park, officiated. For a long time, armed GI's with drawn bayonets stood guard, day and night, over this country grave. They were succeeded by National Park Service guards.

By way of sharp contrast, let us consider the status of the tomb of FDR's closest relative among the U.S. Presidents, Ulysses S. Grant. Grant's tomb is located at 125th St. and Riverside Drive, in Harlem, one of the most crime-ridden sections of the land. But never has any armed guard been posted over his tomb.

The situation stresses the questions: WHAT ARE THE CONSPIRATORS TRYING SO DESPERATELY TO HIDE? WHO LIES BURIED AT HYDE PARK?

The postmortem that is required by the law that was flaunted in the burial, would help, at even this late date, to supply the answers. Dentures could be compared with the records of the President's dentist. They could suffice for identification of the skeleton. The presence of bullet holes in the skull, or their absence, would set at rest that story, and would dispel some of the mystery.

The author made a public demand for the disinterring of the remains and their postmortem examination upon the public officials who are required to enforce the law that is designed to discourage and expose murder and foul-play. The demand was served on Thomas E. Dewey, who was then Governor of the State of New York, in which the burial took place. It was published in the N.Y. Enquirer. But no more has been done about investigation of the death in compliance with the law, than was done in another activity of the same breed of conspirators, back in Civil War days, when they engineered the assassination of Abraham Lincoln.

An effort was made to cover up the irregularity, failure to perform a portmortem, in the death certificate signed at Georgia Warm Springs by Dr. Howard T. Bruenn of the U.S. Naval Hospital, Bethesda, Md. that is here reproduced. He stated as the primary cause of death, "cerebral hemorrhage". As contributory cause, to which the death should be charged, he names "arterio sclerosis". This representation is proved utterly false, however, by the statement made by ghost-writer Creel in the name of Dr. McIntire, to the effect that the patient *did not have* either extremely high blood pressure or generalized arteriosclerosis, or any signs that would lead one to suspect damage to the cerebral arteries (p.244). This completely belies the death certificate and further stresses the legal requirement for autopsy that was disregarded.

Eleanor Roosevelt, in an effort to cover up the fact that the body did not lie in state, as custom requires, made the obviously false allegation, in one of her publications, that it was not the custom in the Roosevelt family. This was belied, however, by the fact that the President's own mother, Sara Delano Roosevelt, lay in state on the order of her son.

It indicates something very peculiar in the situation, that the Roosevelts, with their love of ostentation, missed the chance for a display of public adoration. And Eleanor Roosevelt has added considerable fuel to the fire of suspicion concerning the death of her husband by her later confession to the truth of the matter, in an article of hers that was published in the February 8, 1958, issue of the Saturday Evening Post, entitled ON MY OWN (pp. 69-70). She alleges that on the day following the Hyde Park burial, son Jimmy belatedly found in a safe, the directions left by the President for the arrangements of his funeral. She says that Roosevelt had *directed that his body lie in state* in Washington, in the Capitol. But, she relates, by some curious chance, *all other of his instructions had been followed exactly.*

This story bears all the earmarks of some of her other fiction. For, as above said, it is utterly inconceivable that the Roosevelts, with their love of self-aggrandizement and their exhibitionist delight in public homage, would

County file NO.: 4979

DEPARTMENT OF COMMERCE
BUREAU OF THE CENSUS

CERTIFICATE OF DEATH
GEORGIA DEPARTMENT OF PUBLIC HEALTH

State File No.

L. R. File No.

1. Place of Death
(a) County Meriwether   Midde Dist. No. 704
(b) City or Town Warm Springs, Ga
(If Outside City or Town Limits, Write Rural)
Name of Hosp. or Institution
(d) Length of Stay Hosp. or Institution   In This Community

2. Usual Residence of Deceased
(a) State Georgia   (b) County Meriwether
(c) City or Town Warm Springs, Georgia
(If Outside City or Town Limits, Write Rural)
(d) R.F.D. and Box No.
(e) Citizen of Foreign Country? (Yes or No) If Yes, Name of Country

3. Full Name Franklin Delano Roosevelt

If Veteran Name War   Social Security Number

PERSONAL AND STATISTICAL PARTICULARS   MEDICAL CERTIFICATION

4. Sex Male   5. Race white   6. Marital Status Married S. M. W. D.
7. If Married or Widowed Give Name of Spouse Eleanor Roosevelt
8. Age 63 Years   Months   Days   If less than 24 hrs. Hrs. Min.
9. Date of Birth 1-30-1882 Mo. Day Year   Birth Place Hyde Park, N.Y.
10. Usual Occupation President of United States of America
11. Industry or Business

Father
12. Name James Roosevelt
13. Birthplace Hyde Park, N.Y.

Mother
14. Maiden Name Sarah Delano
15. Birth Place Nurburgh, N.Y.

16. Informant Own Signature F.W.Patterson
17. Informant's P. O. Address 1020 Spring St, N W

18. Burial, Cremation or Removal Burial   (a) Date 4-15-45
19. P. O. Address of Place of Burial Hyde Park, N.Y.
20. Signature of Person Burying Body H.M. Patterson & Son
21. P. O. Address of Undertaker Atlanta, Ga   Date Filed with L R 4/13/1945
22. Registrar's Own Signature Hiram A. Hadaway

22. Date of Death April 12 19 45 Time 3:35 P. M.
24. I hereby certify that I attended the deceased who died on the above date. I last saw H 1ma live on April 12, 19 45
Primary Cause of Death Cerebral Hemorrhage   Duration
Contributory Causes Arterio Sclerosis

Operation
Date of Operation   Diagnosis: Clinical, Lab., X-Ray (Check)   Was Autopsy Performed?
25. If death was due to external violence please answer the following questions:
(a) Accident, Suicide, Homicide (Specify)   (b) Date of Occurrence
(c) Place of Accident   (city) (county) (state)
(d) Industry, Public Place   Where: Home, Farm.   While at Work
(e) Means of Injury

26. Physician's Own Signature Howard T.Bruenn M.D.
Physician's P. O. Address U.S.N.H.Bethesda, Md.   Date Signed 4/13/1945

CERTIFIED COPY

State of Georgia
County of Meriwether

I hereby certify that the foregoing is a true and correct copy of a record on file in this office.

(Signed)

John Heal

SEAL   RCA 1109

Certified Copy Of Roosevelt's Death Certificate

"Contributory Causes (to which this death should be charged) Arterio Sclerosis" belies statement made by George Creel in the book he ghost-wrote for Roosevelt's personal physician, Vice Admiral McIntire.

have missed the chance for a display of public adulation. One is forced to the conclusion that there must have been a very compelling reason for not opening the coffin, to permit the body to lie in state.

In death, as in life, Roosevelt and his fellow conspirators disdained, defied and violated the law. His burial without an autopsy was a flagrant violation, a criminal act. Under the law, persons responsible for such illicit burials are subject to criminal prosecution. For they might well prove to be accessories to murder.

The nation is entitled to every precaution to make sure that the control of its destinies is not usurped by conspirators acting through the agency of an incompetent, or a bogus "President". Every G.I. is subjected to many procedures such as finger-printing, photographing, intelligence tests and so forth, to make certain of his identity and competence. It can not be said that a random G.I. is more important in the conduct of national affairs than the President is supposed to be. Obviously it is far more important for the nation that the identity and the competence of the President be established repeatedly and with absolute certainty—both in life and in death.

Too often in our past history, have the reins of our Government been taken over by conspirators of the Illuminist-Communist, Rockefeller-Soviet breed, during periods of incompetence of the President. Such incident occurred when President Grover Cleveland was carried off to sea for an operation for removal of a cancerous palate. Another far more disastrous incident was the control of the nation by the conspirators during the period of physical and mental incompetence of President Wilson, after his apoplectic stroke. This was facilitated by the cooperation of his second wife whom he wedded under curious circumstances. And it happened once again throughout the regime of Franklin Delano Roosevelt. The rapid advance of the conspiracy to destroy our Constitution, in the two latter cases illustrates the advantage to the conspirators of *adopting measures that insure the incompetence of the President.*

It has been reported that the Russian Ambassador demanded, on official order of his government, that the casket be opened and that he be permitted to view the body; and that this request was denied. Both the request and its denial must be regarded as extraordinary. The Russians might have suspected that the body was not that of Roosevelt, as rumors allege. This raises the question: "Why was it so important to the Russians to make positive that Roosevelt was dead?" Could it be that he was a tool who had served his purpose and, with Churchill, would be an annoyance in the way of future plans? Could it be that Russia planned alleging secret agreements that might be denied? Could it be merely the scientific interest of a toxicologist? Or had Stalin found Roosevelt's obsequiousness coupled with his betrayal of his own country a disgusting annoyance?

There is more in this situation than meets the eye. Ample excuse is given for rumors, however wild. And credence will continue to be given them until the body is disinterred and autopsied. Failure to do so indicates a desire to hide something that may be of serious import to the nation.

It has become a standing practice in this country to protect the interests that control the country by denying the nation and the world at large information on the state of the President's health. This was done in the case of Grover Cleveland's cancer of the palate, Wilson's apoplexy and F.D.R.'s various ailments. That would be of no moment if the President's powers and influence were checked and limited as provided in the Constitution. But those checks have been steadily and progressively eliminated and in many respects the President's power has become more absolute than that of most kings. Illnesses which incapacitate the President enable the group that controls him to work their will on the nation in his name. That is a very strong temptation that may actually endanger the President's life at times of disagreement with his bosses. In a way the secrecy regarding the ailments of the President illustrates and stresses how much the office has assumed the aura of monarchy.

Certainly the health of Commander in Chief of the Armed Forces, a title in which Roosevelt took great delight and a role which he had insisted on playing, is of more vital significance to the nation than the health of a mere private. But the private is compelled to undergo a rigid physical and mental examination before he is accepted for service; and he must continue to be revealed fit by subsequent examinations so long as he remains in the service. Psychopathic conditions call for compulsory relief from duty and discharge. The nation can not demand less of so important figure as its Commander in Chief. Nevertheless twice in a quarter of a century, the helm of the nation's ship of state has been held by paralytics who were mental and physical wrecks, Wilson and Roosevelt.

The safety and security of the nation demands that never again shall its destiny be controlled by agencies operating through the impotent hands of a prostrated executive. The nation must demand as rigid medical examinations and as fit a physical and mental condition of its chief executive as it demands of the lowest soldier. There is danger enough in the domination and control of a healthy executive by malign forces. With a diseased executive it is certain, and fraught with grave peril for the nation. It should never happen again. The nation should require by law periodic physical examination of the President and honest reports to it of the findings. Disabling mental and physical conditions, by law should disqualify the incumbent and require his replacement.

The deception perpetrated on the public in regard to Roosevelt's health is characteristic of that which prevailed in all matters during his Administration.

CHAPTER XXIV

MORAL CONSEQUENCES OF NEW DEAL JUVENILE DELINQUENCY

One of the gravest injuries done the nation by the Marxist New Deal is the decay that it has wrought in the people's moral fibre. There has been a certain measure of decay, some rotten apples in the barrel, from the start. Gradual and insidious changes were brought about by legal and political termites, the disciples of Bismarxian propaganda, who have gnawed at the law and Constitution. This slow process was accelerated in Wilson's Administration. But in Roosevelt's regime, an overnight abrogation of the Constitution was effected on the grounds that it was antiquated. There developed a total disregard of all law by the very public officers who were sworn to uphold it. A destructive transformation was effected in the entire governmental organization that has converted it into the worst type of tyrannic autocracy in which the whim and caprice of every petty bureaucrat is a dictate from which there is no appeal.

In short, government by law and Constitution have ceased to exist. The United States has become as tyranny-ridden and corrupt a land as those of the pashas and viziers. Citizens have no longer any legally defined rights or privileges. There has been substituted for government by law, dictation by insolent, autocratic and irresponsible bureaucrats from whose arbitrary and unprincipled dictates there is no appeal; and rule by favoritism and an unabashedly dishonest officialdom. As a consequence of the disregard of principle and law, the practice of law has degenerated to the practice of "reaching" and bribing key bureaucrats.

This conception has gone so far, even in our courts, that New Dealers themselves are beginning to protest against it. Thus U. S. Supreme Court Justice Felix Frankfurter, one of the sponsors of the New Deal placed on the Bench in connection with the packing of the Court, protested against the open collusion involved in the decision handed down by Judge Ben Moore in the CIO test case of the provision of the Taft Hartley Law on the use of union funds for campaign purposes. This section of the law is intended to prevent partial disfranchisement of some members of the unions by compelling them to contribute through union campaign funds to the election of candidates favored by the Labor Barons but opposed by themselves. Undoubtedly an element of this protest was directed to the failure of Judge Moore to disqualify himself because his old firm is employed by the United Mine Workers, CIO.

Equality before the law has ceased to exist. Such equality is decried as *unfair* and *inconsiderate of "human rights"*. The average employer, the landlord, the investor and the person who has saved his money are criminally suspect and are held guilty in many directions, even if proved innocent. But the laborer, the poor and the improvident are generally held innocent no matter what they do — if they do not transgress against Dynastic interests or Labor Barons.

Property rights have virtually ceased to exist for the average citizen. In the quest for monopoly and dictatorship via Communism, labelled "New Deal", there has been spurned the sound commonsense counsel of Abraham Lincoln to a delegation of union officials who called on him after the New York Draft Riots:

"Property is the fruit of labor; property is desirable; is a positive good in the world. That some should be rich shows that others may be rich, and hence is just encouragement to industry and enterprise. Let not him who is houseless pull down the house of another, but let him labor diligently and build one for himself, thus by example assuring his own shall be safe from violence when built".

In these few commonsense statements applying the

"Golden Rule" to property rights, Lincoln reduced to absurdity the fundamental Marxist and New Deal doctrines on property rights. But the Dynasty's malevolent purposes are better served by Marx's insane concepts, which they propagandize and foster in law.

Where there is no honesty in government, none can be expected in private life. Diligent, industrious, principled and provident individuals who provide employment, housing and other necessities of life for their fellow-men are pilloried by law and the government, as criminals on a priori grounds. They are deprived of the benefit of justice and honesty, and the protection of Constitution or law, by corrupt, demagogue officials and servile, venal and self-serving judiciary. In many instances, such as rent control laws, landlords are declared guilty of violating, retroactively, laws which did not exist at the time of the acts in question; and viciously are penalized therefore. A form of "lettre de cachet" has become a favorite "New Deal" device for dealing with those not in its favor.

The dishonesty of the situation is so patent it can not be overlooked by the rising generation. It is a natural consequence that juveniles hold in contempt law, honesty and decency that are so shabbily treated by their elders. Rampant juvenile delinquency is an inevitable result. The corruption, shiftiness, immorality and dishonesty of high public officials, from the President down, adds powerful stimulus to the delinquency of the younger generation.

When the President of the United States brazenly and unabashedly lies to the whole nation in fireside chats, then when he is confronted with his lies adopts the Jesuitic attitude that "the end justifies the means", and is acclaimed for the brazenness of his lying by a servile entourage and press, he is not encouraging honesty in the younger generation. When his folks deport themselves scandalously and with depravity, they are not setting an example of morality for impressionable youngsters.

Children can not be expected to grow up honest, moral and law-abiding when they see about them in public life nothing but dishonesty, corruption and contempt of decency and law; and when they are taught to believe that all public officials must be expected to be crooks. It is useless to appoint commissions to study the prevention of juvenile delinquency, as long as this situation prevails.

A child is not as devious in his mental processes as are so many of its elders. When a man is robbed of his earnings and wealth by law on the pretense of "distributing wealth", they recognize the arrant thievery involved. Rightly they can not see that such thieving is different from thieving on any other pretext. Youngsters are not capable of the casuistry that differentiates between holdups of the nation by corrupt autocrats who have seized its government, and the mugging and if necessary, killing of a man on the street to steal his possessions. They too engage in "distributing wealth" in their favorite direction, themselves.

When Labor Barons, goons, racketeers and thugs have the full blessing of the law in their systematic holdups and betrayal of the nation, what is more natural than that the youth should seek to emulate them in their preying on the community? Why work for a mere wage when by strong-arm tactics one can attain the "eminent" and "enviable" rank of Labor Baron, or his satellite, stand above law and order, levy tribute from both labor and industry, and dictate to the nation?

When impressionable youngsters see their teachers and professors employed as fronts by Labor Barons who dishonestly seek to force industry to pay workers for work that they have not done—by featherbedding, by "portal to portal" pay claims, and seek to bankrupt industry by assessments and levies, by restrictions and work rules, by disregard of property rights and law, and by fake wage claims; when they hear those self-same professors undertake to ethically justify this blackmail; and when they see the prostituted professors cynically appointed "neutral arbitrators" or "commissioners representing the public" in situations that involve them, they are not learning honesty or principle.

When children witness prostitutes engaged in the practice of their art while being maintained on public charity and Relief in hotels on a higher scale of living than can be attained by the average worker ($500 a month and more) and their occupation and mode of life condoned and commended by government "welfare" agencies; when they see crooks and swindlers aided in repaying their thefts with government Relief funds; and when they see people who can afford mink coats and cars, shamelessly receiving aid from Relief agencies—they are being offered little inducement or example to lead honest decent lives.

In short, a life of dishonesty, immorality, crime, force and violence, rather than that of a law-abiding citizen, has become the highest attainable ambition of the youth of the nation. Is it not natural that violence and crime are steadily increasing, and that the world is fast travelling the road to rule by force that prevailed in the Middle Ages?

If force and violence are to be the rule of life of the New Deal, wherein lies its vaunted security? Can there be any security under such a rule, except for the strong-arm man and the thug when at the height of his strength and virility? Are not Marxism and its corollary, the New Deal, rapidly carrying society back to its most primitive state of slavery to force?

Only a return to the principle and freedom of true democracy can save the nation from this atavism.

CHAPTER XXV

PREDICTION OF COMING EVENTS

It is safe to predict that if any of the candidates now in the public eye, or any prominent political figure in any of the parties, is nominated presidential candidate, there will be no change in national policy. While lip service will be given to democracy, and Communism berated, the Bismarxian road to dictatorship and monarchy, will be followed steadily until every vestige of freedom eventually is wiped out. The United States will continue to be betrayed and sold out, and the Rockefeller Empire will be served to the last draftee and the last American dollar.

This prediction is based on the fact that every candidate thus far mentioned is a hand picked agent of the Dynasty, or of the Rockefeller Empire, or of both. Three of the Republican candidates, Robert A. Taft, Thomas Dewey and Douglas MacArthur are derived from the Roosevelt-Delano Dynasty, are more or less remotely related to Roosevelt, and are responsive to the same Dynastic and Rockefeller influences. They are in ultimate analysis, quite as completely, or more completely New Dealish, as Franklin Delano Roosevelt himself.

Taft's relationship to Roosevelt and the Dynasty already has been related. Like his father he is the product of the Rockefeller-dominated Ohio Republican political machine which Mark Hanna built. Except in a few instances, his record has revealed him to be a weak and ineffective rubber-stamp of the New Deal who shammed an opposition that demanded nothing more than slight modification for the record. His law firm has been attorney and adviser, according to Danton Walker, to Jack Kroll, National Chairman of the CIO-PAC; and apparently his record has been satisfactory to them. The Taft-Hartley Act which bears his name, he did the best he could to emasculate in favor of the left wing, CIO elements; and he ruined a basically sound and excellent bill drawn up by Hartley. As the Act stands, it accepts in principle all the gross violations of the Constitution, the Bill of Rights, justice and honesty that prevail in labor law and practice. He has served the labor elements and apostles of class warfare well, and deserves their gratitude and support instead of their opprobrium.

Further evidence of Taft's Marxist, New Deal mentality are to be found in his bill to socialize medical care and in his housing bill, the Taft-Ellender-Wagner Bill. In the latter his name is significantly coupled with that of one of Rockefeller's principal legislative agents and the staunchest friend of subversives, Senator Robert F. Wagner. No doubt Taft fancies himself as a great compromiser. But principle can not be compromised. Taft's nomination or election would bolster the Dynasty's pretensions to hereditary rulership in the land and serve to affirm that practice so dangerous to democracy.

Both Thomas Dewey and his wife are related to the Roosevelt-Delano clan. His wife is reported to be a fifth cousin of President Roosevelt through Jefferson Davis. The Rockefellers financed Dewey from the start of his career as running mate of their agent, LaGuardia, on their left-wing Fusion ticket. He served them well, as has been related, in diverting attention from really important issues by his dramatic, pre-fabricated prosecution of the white slave and "numbers" rackets. Dewey campaigned on LaGuardia's left-wing platform and was completely in accord with his pose of radicalism and his subserviency to the Rockefeller interests.

When he left the office of District Attorney of New York County and returned to private practice, Dewey was retained by several labor unions including the garment workers'. The platform on which he campaigned

for the governorship of New York was distinctly leftist and appealed to the radical and subversive elements. He called to his side as advisers, the Labor
Barons Dubinsky and Hochman.

As Governor, Dewey had his eye on the White
House. He showed a lack of creative intelligence applied to the problems which confront the community
and the nation; and was satisfied to court both his
masters, the Rockefellers who largely financed his campaign, and the radical and labor elements who employed him and whose vote he seeks. He is a political
agent, and not of the calibre of the statesman and
leader that the nation and the world require. His election would insure the steady advancement of the
schemes of the Dynasty and of the Rockefeller Empire for the establishment of dictatorship and monarchy. In his presidential campaign in 1944 Dewey merely offered the nation a more virtuous "New Deal" than
that of Cousin Franklin Delano Roosevelt. But the public were rightly sceptic when they saw the same
Rockefeller-Labor Baron sponsorship of his and Roosevelt's nominations.

General Douglas McArthur is a capable general. But
his rise to the position of Chief of Staff of the Army
was not attained without a record of amenability to
Dynastic and Imperial dictates and designs. As dictator
of Japan his disciplinarian attitude has spelled success. To the radical elements, who have reviled him for
his handling of their numbers in the Veterans' March
on Washington during the Hoover regime, he has en-
deared himself by enabling them to foist their unions
and their New Deal on Japan. From this it can be con-
cluded that MacArthur would continue to favor the
same elements, would continue the Dynasty and its allies in power and carry forward their plans for dictatorship. These are not the qualifications of an American President.

Senator Vandenberg principal advocate on the Republican side of the Senate of the Rockefeller Empire
was dubbed by the Gridiron Club "vacillating Van".
For years he staunchly opposed betraying the United
States to further private interests in foreign lands and
was therefore labelled "isolationist". But he could be
depended upon to follow and implement the policy of
the Empire. There was no vacillation from its dictates.
After the Dunkirk deal, Vandenberg shifted overnight
and became one of the most rabid internationalists

and interventionists. Shifting from a position of opposition to all the frauds and inequities of the New Deal, he became one of its most dependable and staunch supporters. Obviously Vandenberg has but one principle and firm conviction—obedience to the dictates of the Imperial allies of the Dynasty.

Harold Stassen's metamorphosis is even more striking. He started off as a rabid left-winger, fellow-traveller and darling of the Reds. He was largely responsible for putting over on the nation through the Republican Party, the fraudulent candidacy of "One World", "Me Too' New Dealer, Wendell Willkie, as a fake opposition to F.D.R. He did so on behalf of his bosses and sponsors, the Rockefeller-Morgan-Dynastic interests. They are now supporting and financing him as a phony opponent of Truman. He is as completely their puppet as cousin Truman. They can not lose no matter which way the election goes. If elected he can be depended on to betray the nation once again to the interests of the Rockefeller Empire.

He closely followed the Communist party line and went went to Moscow to do obeisance and lick the boots of Joseph Stalin. He returned to the United States and suggested that the nation bow to Stalin as he himself had done. When Communism began to grow unpopular in the United States and the Communist Party line was to denounce Communism, Stassen proclaimed himself rabidly anti-Communist. By curious chance the shift coincided with the reversal of the policy of the Rockefeller Empire towards Russia.

A study of the list of contributors to the fund that has supported Stassen, and his family, through several years of campaigning for the presidential nomination reveals that they are identified with the banking interests closely associated with the Rockefeller-Morgan-Dynastic group including Reeve Schley, President of the Chase National Bank, the young Rockefellers, the Vanderbilts, the Whitneys, and the millionaire pro-Communist, "Mission to Moscow" Joe Davis. Stassen is now the most open of the candidates in advocating the program of the Rockefeller Empire—immediate belligerency against Russia. Of all the presidential candidates, Stassen would probably prove to be the most pliant to the dangerously subversive Dynastic and Imperial interests, and the most destructive to human freedom and the security and independence of the United States.

The other Republican candidates that have been

paraded before the public eye are of about equal quality and equally tools of the Dynastic and Rockefeller interests. One of the most important of the Rockefeller agents in the Republican Party is its adviser on foreign affairs who so strongly dominates Vandenberg and Dewey, John Foster Dulles. Through his wife, Janet Pomeroy Avery, Dulles is related to the Rockefellers. He is a senior partner in the Wall Street legal firm, Sullivan and Cromwell, and Vice-President of the Association of the Bar of New York City, member of the New York State Banking Board, Chairman of the Bank of New York, and of the International Nickel Company. He is the liaison member between the Carnegie Endowment for International Peace, of which he is Chairman, and the Rockefeller Foundation of which he is trustee. He was on the Peace Commission and the Supreme Economic Council of the World War I and United States Delegate to the San Francisco, London and New York United Nations Assemblies, and to the London and Moscow meetings of the Council of Foreign Ministers after World War II. He ably represents the Rockefeller Imperial interests as an agent of the United States. Closely associated with him is his fellow trustee of the Rockefeller Foundation, John J. McCloy of the Rockefeller law firm Milbank, Tweed, Hope, Hadley and McCloy. He is head of the International Bank that was set up in accord with the Bretton Woods plan to finance the foreign activities of the Rockefeller Empire at the expense of the American taxpayer.

On the Democratic side, the picture is even uglier with regard to President Truman. It has been mentioned that it is more than a mere coincidence that the name of the grand-daughter of Senator W. Aldrich, and John D. Jr's kinswoman, is Lucy *Truman* Aldrich. Truman's change of character since he entered the White House is well nigh that of the Jekyll and Hyde, split personality type. Whatever may have been his prior associations and activities, Truman was outstanding in the Senate for the courage that he manifested in fearlessly attacking and exposing corruption even in his own Party. He made himself feared as a power for good and respected for his Americanism.

As an occupant of the White House, Truman underwent a metamorphosis and a deterioration of character that would be unbelievable if not so manifest. Almost incredibly, despite the strength of character which he had previously manifested, he became a craven puppet of the very subversive and traitorous groups that previously he had fought with the utmost vigor. This indicates the tremendous pressure which the Dynasty and the Rockefeller Empire exert on a President.

The pressure on the President is materially enhanced in its effectiveness by the fact that the President of the United States is not paid sufficient to support his family; and meeting his expenses as Chief Executive is impossible on the salary that he is paid, unless he can draw on a private source of income—legitimate or illegitimate. Rather than face the disgrace of proclaiming his poverty, an incumbent is apt to prefer to accept loans, gifts or bribes. The donors of these advances generally manage to get what they want in the way of public favors. Two groups of citizens are now in the position to make such gifts without being severely penalized by the Treasury Department. One is the very wealthy especially those who derive tax-exempt income from outside the country. The others are the tax exempt Labor Barons, whose private tax on the American workers and industries runs into billions, and their allies, subversive propagandists. It is significant that the voices of these groups have been servilely heeded by the White House.

The Presidential salary of $75,000 is meagre pay today for the president of a second rate industrial concern. Many clowns and numerous showfolk earn several times that sum. When income taxes are deducted there is left less than $28,000, or less than $2500 a month. Such low pay for an office that makes so many costly demands, bars any honest but poor man from accepting the presidency, even if the opportunity should offer.

Wisdom dictates that the President of the United States should be paid a salary that is commensurate with the responsibility, dignity and expenses that go with that office, and that would put him in a position in which corruption and bribery would offer no temptation. The President of the United States should receive a minimum salary of $5,000,000 a year in the form of a tax exempt trust fund yielding him an annuity. This would place him on a par with the King of England and other chief executives. It would also provide a pension after leaving office that would reduce the temptation to seek repeated re-election, or to debase the presidency by undignified or sordid activities on leaving office. Until something of that nature is done, it is impossible for a poor man to be President of the United States and remain honest and American.

The most horrible possibilities of nomination on the Democratic ticket are the sons of Franklin Delano Roosevelt who are eagerly scrambling for it. That would mean the evils of the New Deal intensified to the *nth* degree; the openly corrupt offers made by the Democratic Party in the 1944 campaign to sell Presidential favors at $1000 per block would be regarded as virtue in comparison with what might then be expected. Nickerson's blueprint of electively attained hereditary monarchy would be an accomplished fact spelling the end to freedom and democracy. The U. S. would be irrevocably a wholly owned subsidiary of the Rockefeller Empire.

This **brings to the fore** the fact that if freedom is to survive in the United States control of nominations must be taken out of the hands of private cliques and parties and placed in the hands of the people. The betrayal of the nation by the Dynasty and the Rockefeller Empire has been accomplished by their control of the nominating machinery of all parties. This has reduced the right of franchise to the absurdity of choosing between two or more puppets of the same masters.

Campaigns for nomination and election must be financed in the future out of the public treasury. Every man who seeks to serve the public must be given an opportunity to offer himself and his program to the people. Unless that can be accomplished, dictatorship is inevitable.

World War III with Russia for which preparations are already under way, probably will not break out into open violence in the near future unless one of three things happens:

1. Open attack on our occupation troops on a scale that cannot be ignored. Minor attacks and restrictions have occurred, but they are being ignored.

2. A move by Russia threatening the Rockefeller Empire's Saudi Arabian oil fields. Such a move on the part of Russia before the completion of the pipeline and other developments would hardly be wisdom or good judgement on the part of the Communists. If they bide their time, they will get a completely developed oil empire. In the meantime Russia will collect direct and indirect bribes through the Marshall Plan

and will continue to expand in zones which the Rockefeller Empire yielded her through Roosevelt at Yalta, Teheran and Casablanca through secret agreements.

3. Revolutionary pressure and popular discontent within Russia may force her masters to go to war without regard to potential losses.

Ultimately Russia is forced by her ideology to either destroy all other forms of government or to be vanquished. That is the goal that her masters have set for her. The Rockefeller Empire, on the other hand, has set for itself an equally ambitious goal, when, as and if it can get the United States and other lands to fight their war.

They seek "One World", a Rockefeller-Standard Oil controlled world and Empire. Their propagandists shout that there can be no peace, they will allow no peace, until "One World" is theirs. They are as insistent as are the Soviets on this point. Since oil can be found in all parts of the world, a monopoly of oil is impossible without a complete and absolute control of the world.

This war can be averted in only one manner. An example must be given to the world of a surplus economy; an economy of plenty in which everyone will have all that he requires and is willing to work for; an economy which will give its people all the things that the Communists and other brands of Marxists pretend to secure but fail to do in practice. How this could be done within the framework of present law, as a full development of the economy envisaged and implied by the Constitution and by a truly American plan, will be pointed out in the last chapter.

The pretenses of "fighting Communism" by pouring billions of dollars of American taxpayers' money into Europe is absurd. Faith is not a matter of dollars and cents. On the contrary the very meaning of faith is a disregard of material advantage or the dictates of daily experiences. Those whose faith is Communism will no more change their faith for a dollar or for food, than those whose faith is Christianity. Some may pretend to change their faith in Communism for material advantage, but their conversion is more transient than the advantage gained. Such pretended changes in faith are part of the present day Communist party line. On the other hand a pretended increase of faith in Communism is the favorite device of foreign lands for grabbing important participation in the global handout of the Truman administration on behalf of the Rockefeller Empire.

A successful surplus economy would reduce Communism to absurdity. It would undermine the faith of Russia and the Communists in their Marxist scarcity economy that is a hopeless failure. Since Communism is virtually a religious faith with most of its adherents, only such destruction of their false faith would dispel their illusions, bring the world back to an even keel, and make wars useless.

War is an absolute necessity for the continued maintenance of our present scarcity economies and for the support of the scarcity monetary system, whether that economy be Communist, Socialist, Nazi, Fascist or the speculative or "Gold Standard" economy we call Capitalism. In any managed, or speculative, scarcity economy, surpluses of men and materials develop in spite of all efforts at suppression, because of the bounty of Nature and the vagary of its moods. War is essential to wipe out these surpluses of humans and materials, in order to reestablish scarcity—to maintain the sanctity of "management" in the role of *deus ex machina*..

Instead of attempting to solve the grave problems of scarcity economy that deprives a large segment of the nation and of the world of necessities of life and makes war essential, the Truman Administration is deliberately undertaking to intensify the situation. The objective is ruinous inflation, leading to national bankruptcy and dictatorship or monarchy.

No stone was left unturned by the Roosevelt Administration to bring about inflation. For the so-called "economists" saw in inflation the remedy for depression. Production and surplus were the dragons that the Agricultural Allotment plan, the NRA and the whole New Deal vigorously fought. The price of gold was raised from $20 to $35 an ounce. Restriction of production was designed to force inflation. Enormous Relief handouts, pensions, Allotment Plan payments to farmers and other wasteful expenditures coupled with heavy taxation were employed to stimulate inflation.

The Treasury and the Federal Reserve Bank adopted an "easy money policy" and stimulated expansion of credit to bring about inflation. With the outbreak of the war, billions of "Lend-Lease" handouts to foreign lands and staggering military expenditures were coupled with a program of confiscatory taxation and steadily higher wage increases, to bring about inflation. During the war this inflation was masked by price control which was a sham completely negated by the transfer of goods from regular market to the "black market".

At the end of the war the Administration was forced by public outcry to take cognizance of damage wrought by the inflation that it had brought on with full deliberation and intent. On various specious grounds, with tongue in cheek, the Government then applied to the process of "fighting inflation" the same measures that it had adopted, in bringing it on. Since employment was at an all-time high there was little or no excuse for great Relief expenditures. Neverthless recent exposures in New York City have revealed that the Relief agencies were urged to pour out public funds. Prostitutes were subsidized as highly as $600 a month and housed in hotels by Relief agencies while they plied their trade. Criminals and wastrels were given aid amounting to more than honest men can earn. Since enormous expenditures could not be made on the pretense of "Relief" resort was taken to other methods of pouring out the wealth of the land. "Lend-Lease" was continued for years after the close of the war on a vast scale that cost billions. Much of it went to arm Russia. More American wealth and resources were poured out of the country into the laps of any taker with a foreign front, through relief agencies, the UNRRA, Export Bank loans, R. F. C. loans and an endless chain of devices topped by the Marshall Boodle Plan "to stop Communism".

Little of this money goes abroad. Most of the appropriations are drained out of the pockets of the taxpayers into those of the Dynastic and Imperial bankers. One glance at the glowing faces in the photographs of the Congressmen surrounding the President as he signs such an enormous "pork-barrel" bill as the Marshall Plan appropriation raises the question, "How much are they getting out of it, as a 'kick-back'?". They are too addicted to "pork-barrel" to be so happy handing out taxpayers' moneys without participation.

President Truman deliberately stepped out of line to advocate the C.I.O.-Communist Front program of repeated wage increases. Soldiers' bonuses were paid. Taxes were continued at an unconscionable level. Intensification of price control and harassment of legitimate enterprise forced ever more business into extortionate "black markets" that drove to sky-rocketing levels the prices that actually had to be paid for merchandise in contrast with the official fixed price at which no merchandise could be purchased.

Even to an imbecilic mentality, it should be obvious that all these pretended "measures for fighting inflation" are designed and intended to do the reverse—to force constantly greater inflation and a steady rise in price of the necessities of life. Taxes must be added to prices. The higher the taxes go, the higher prices must follow. The pretense of increasing taxes "to fight inflation by keeping money out of circulation", is the height of absurdity. For inflation is the increase in price of necessities of life, and only a plentiful supply of those commodities can keep prices low and prevent inflation. But commodities can not be plentiful if the Government agencies constantly purchase all available necessities of life for shipment overseas through various competing agencies. The Government is deliberately forcing to a higher level of inflation, the necessities of life by its constant purchase of all commodities in sight at ever higher prices; and by supporting the speculative markets whenever prices settle to lower levels. Likewise speculation by key government officials on the basis of inside information does not constitute "fighting inflation". The continuous restriction of production of necessities of life in the interests of maintained scarcity likewise constitutes deliberate forcing of inflation while pretending to "fight inflation".

What is the purpose of this thoroughly dishonest and malicious policy of the Government to bring about constantly higher inflation while pretending to fight it? Where will it lead?

The Truman Administration, like that of Roosevelt, is undertaking to follow the Lenin formula and force dictatorship through bankruptcy. By direct and indirect taxation it is taking between a third and a half of the nation's income. As the percentage rises higher, ever more persons will be forced into straightened circumstances and bankruptcy. Finally, when a sufficient number of taxpayers and a sufficiently large proportion of the productive capacity of the nation has been bankrupted, the government itself will be bankrupt. The nation will be faced with the alternative of seizing private wealth and industry, as was done by the Communists in Russia; or concentrating wealth directly in the hands of the ultra-wealthy whose fortunes will have escaped taxation through various loopholes written into the law, in which case the pattern will be that of Fascist Italy and Nazi Germany. In either case dictatorship will eventuate, as planned. The blight of wanton waste and of oppressive and confiscatory taxes is being depended upon to impoverish all but the Dynastic rulers and their allies. The Rockefeller Empire will then reign supreme.

To accomplish this ruin, the waste and destruction of another war may be needed, because of the great wealth of the nation. That war is in the making. And if military defeat is necessary to accomplish their purpose, the nation's malevolent rulers can be depended upon to traitorously engineer it. The U. S. will then have been sold into bondage to the largest, most ruthless and most hypocritic Empire that the world has ever known. For in all the process of engineering this sell-out, the wealth of the nation will have been drained off into the coffers of its behind-the-scene rulers.

The nation must demand a New Deal of its political parties and compel it. If necessary it must smash the monopolistic control of nominations. All the prostituted, chronic political candidates must be discarded. A true American who will not sell out his country, must be nominated and elected, if the U. S. is to remain free. Any honest American among our hundred and fifty million population will serve the purpose and make a better president than the stooges of the Dynasty and Rockefeller Empire. The U. S. must have a President who thinks and acts in terms of "America first, last and always" and who will not be afraid to be called an "isolationist" when that term is used synonymously with patriotism and protecting the interests of America.

CHAPTER XXVI

THE REMEDY — A SURPLUS ECONOMY
THE MASSACHUSETTS YANKEE PLAN

A conspiracy to destroy democracy might have been motivated either by lust for power or by fear of destruction and ruin. In the case of John D. Rockefeller both factors were involved. Initially fear played a larger role than the Napoleonic complex. But as Standard Oil grew and flourished, conquest became a predominant factor; but fear still loomed large.

John D.'s fear of want, amidst all his wealth, is evinced by the penurious and penny-pinching training he gave his children. His fear of being crushed by the weight of his own wealth and public resentment against it, is evidenced by his pretense of philanthropy. In the present Rockefeller Empire, this fear has been compensated for and supplanted by a Napoleonic complex.

There is security neither for the rich nor for the poor in any of the present scarcity economies. But today these fears should be as anachronistic as the scarcity economies which give rise to them.

In the past, not so many decades ago, there gripped the whole world a historic fear — the fear of want and starvation. It was very real. It arose from the inability of mankind to produce enough food and other necessities of life. Periodic droughts, or disasters, produced famines of the type that still scourge China, India and Russia, even in this modern era. In times of famine the short supply of necessities caused a rise in their prices. Only the rich and more fortunate who could find food and other necessities, and had the money to purchase them, could manage to survive. Supply and demand operated with direct and overwhelming force in influencing the prices of commodities in times of shortage.

Today the same fear grips the world under circumstances that make it very strange. Modern science and technology have so tremendously increased the world's productive capacity of necessities of life that the usual fear is no longer production of too little food and necessities of life but production of too much, in most parts of the world.

Though man's life-span has been extended to little less than the "three score and ten", it is a curious fact that modern-day society looks little beyond the immediate present under its present economic organization. The production of food, and other necessities, in excess of its immediate needs has repercussions and sequelae that are as drastic and, ultimately, are identical with those produced by shortages in primitive society. It matters not that an excess over immediate needs is essential to provide for tomorrow, to furnish a reserve against times of disaster and shortage. It matters not that such reserves are essential for security and for continued existence of man and society. Such excessive production of necessities, however slight, is labelled "overproduction".

"Overproduction" is converted by a perversion of the economic organization of society whether it be Capitalist or Communist (Super-Capitalist), into a major disaster. It leads to a drop in prices because of competition of producers in attempting to dispose of their production immediately, in order to "make them liquid". That means to sell them immediately to convert them into money.

The rush of all producers to sell causes a drop in prices. The function of carrying over the momentary surpluses is relegated to speculators, whose purchasing capacity is limited and who are forced to seek a profit by buying cheaply. Sellers compete with one another and force prices down. As a consequence the marginal producer sustains losses and drops out of production. That sets in operation a vicious cycle of reduced production, unemployment, lowered consumption, lowered prices, a further drop in production and so endlessly. The eventual outcome is production of less food and necessities than the nation requires, the same condition as was faced in the less advanced stages of society, and the wiping out of surpluses that spell security.

This situation comes about solely as a result of the mechanics of faulty economic organization of society, which is designed as a cut-throat, starvation, race suicide scarcity economy. It leaves but three alternatives — sustaining prices either by a monopoly which means private enforcement of scarcity, public enforcement of scarcity by a "managed economy", or a scarcity resulting from the interaction of supply, price and production. Fear of too little results from fear of too much.

The remedy for this absurd situation requires clear, untrammelled and unequivocal thought on the subject of the economic organization of society. In final analysis it is thought and ideas which rule the world. Unfortunately, there has been so little thought given to the problem, that the solutions that have been offered whatever their labels, especially if they be Communism or Fascism, are in their ultimate form merely identical aggravations of the evils of our traditional system.

Any quest for a solution must begin with a clear and concise expression of the problem.

What is the axiomatically basic function of Government? The reply is obvious:

Without life, there can be no government.

Therefore the basic function of government is *to enable its citizenry to live.*

Since raw materials of the necessities of life are essential for existence, the corollary basic functions of government requisite for its continuity are:

First: To make available stores and reserves of the necessities of life both for immediate needs and against times of disaster.

Second: To make it possible for its citzenry to obtain the wherewithal to purchase those necessities.

No government now undertakes to perform these basic functions except in the case of emergency and war. The reason for this is obviously that the character of the economic organization of society bars the way. The idea which is the cornerstone of that economic organization is the so-called "law of supply and demand."

The fallaciousness of this "law" is most simply revealed by the illustration used in elementary textbooks on economics for the very purpose of demonstrating its validity. It reads:

Three men are stranded on a desert island. Only one of them has barely enough of the necessities of life for his own needs. Consequently, the economist relates, the price of those necessities would rise to a high level. For the demand exceeds the supply and scarcity lends value, he reasons.

But the conclusion which the economist draws is obviously fallacious. Any man who under those circumstances would undertake to sell the irreplaceable commodities which he requires for the preservation of his own life, as a matter of business, would be either stupidly avaricious or insane. He might share them with his fellows as a matter of humanity; but to trade in them would be equivalent to trading in his own life.

Quite as absurd is it for nations to permit their commerce in the necessities of life to be dominated by the supposed operation of the "law of supply and demand." It is absurd not only because it means a scarcity economy that is rendered entirely needless by the abundance which man can now derive from Nature; but also because it bars the government from performing its function of making available to its citzenry the raw materials of the necessities of life by enabling the creation of reserves and surpluses.

The idea of a "supply and demand" economy is even more absurd because it exists only for today and gives not a thought to tomorrow. The demand of a nation for the necessities of life, like population, remains relatively constant. Likewise, though vagaries of Nature may cause variations of supply from year to year, the average productivity of the land remains constant. Even primitive man realized this clearly, as is illustrated in the Biblical story of Joseph and Pharaoh.

In reality, a study of the events of the past twenty years reveals that it is neither supply nor demand that determines prices of the raw materials of the necessitis of life. This becomes apparent from the fact that the price of wheat was ten times higher during 1919, when there was a bumper crop, than it was in 1932, when there was an actual shortage. These facts impelled Professor Warren, the Cornell authority on chicken and "New-Deal" economics, to advance the explanation that it is the relation of the supply and demand of a commodity to the supply and demand of gold that determines prices. But this is a rather complicated formula for the simple fact that *it is neither supply nor demand but speculation* that determines prices.

Speculation prevents the setting up of surpluses of the necessities of life, which constitute the only real security for the nation and the individual. The holding of reserves by the government or by individuals acts on the speculative market as an excess supply, and depresses prices. Drop in price reduces profits and forces a reduction in production, which in turn forces using up of reserves.

Applied to labor and human values, as justified by Karl Marx's Socialism, by Communism and by labor unionism, the so-called "law" is even more destructive. In its converse expression, "scarcity alone lends value," the "law" demands restriction of the supply of human beings. The term "social" cannot be applied to such an organization which makes man serve it as victim and sacrifice. The birth control movement, the purges of Hitler and Stalin, the merciless condemnation to misery and death of refugees, the destruction of the livelihoods and futures of younger generations, national and racial antagonisms—sacrifices to the Moloch of human scarcity—are all natural outgrowths of such economic concepts.

Roseate and sanguine peace discussions always ignore what human experience has proved invariably true: that war is an absolute necessity for the maintenance of scarcity economies and is made inevitable by them. Under scarcity economies a certain portion of the people of a nation, and of the nations of the world must do without a sufficiency of the necessities of life, must live a submarginal existence, and in some cases must actually starve—because scarcity economies mean that there must not be enough to go around, if values are to be maintained. It is inevitable that violence breeds among the groups that are condemned to want or starvation, and if and when those groups become sufficiently large, war readily emerges from their struggles for survival.

The factor that precipitates war, however, is the necessity of destroying accumulated surpluses of both men and materials in order to avert complete breakdown of the scarcity economy. For inevitably the vicious inverted spiral of lowered production, resulting in lowered employment, which results in turn in lowered consumption, that involves again a further lowering of production to maintain scarcity and value, ultimately brings about the state of widespread unemployment that means a surplus of labor, as well as surpluses of commodities. This cycle generally reaches its climax at intervals of about a quarter of a century. As a consequence of the intolerable stagnation, unemployment and hunger that results from it, war is eagerly sought by nations as a solution of the impasse created by politicians, on the counsel of malicious propagandists or of stupid fools who parade as "professors of economics".

Side by side with the more active destructive forces operating in scarcity economies actively to destroy surpluses of men and materials, there operates a slower, more insidious but even more basic destructive force —voluntary birth control and race suicide. It is this factor that has been responsible for the destruction of every empire and every civilization in history. Individuals either can not afford to have children as a consequence of the cost of living in relation to earnings under a scarcity economy, or else they voluntarily undertake to avoid bringing children into a world already cluttered with large numbers of unemployed. They thus aid in the effort to attain a scarcity of human beings. Since such voluntary efforts at birth control are usually adopted by folks of a higher level of intelligence and culture, the consequence is a lowering of both the population and its level of intelligence.

There are two types of scarcity economies.

Gold Standard, or Laissez-Faire, type of scarcity economy makes no effort to restrict, or manage, production directly. It operates through the interplay of gold supply and production: with a fixed volume of gold as the basis of value, the more there is produced of commodities and necessities of life, the less they are worth as measured against the fixed supply of gold. Or if the supply of gold is restricted by manipulation or speculation, the price of commodities and necessities of life can be forced down without regard to the adequacy of the supply. Naturally when the price is forced down below the level of the cost of production, production falls off because it no longer pays to produce; discontinued production means unemployment with consequent lessened consumption; and that in turn means further reduction in production and repetition of the vicious cycle. Consequently, under the gold standard economy, the breakdown that leads to depressions and wars is precipitated by prosperity and by the approach of production to adequacy.

"Managed" economies are manipulated to attain the most rigid form of scarcity economy whether they be Fascist, Communist or "New Deal". The motive of these types of economy are variously expressed for ideologic or propaganda purposes. Thus the Fascists make no humanitarian representations for their managed scarcity economies but frankly advocate them to serve the purposes of the State. The so-called Liberal, i.e. the Communist, New Deal and Labor economies, profess to manage their economies for the purpose of preventing the accumulation of reserves and surpluses in order to avoid unemployment that they regard as the inevitable consequence of "overproduction." Their shibboleths are "Production for use not for profit" and "Labor must get all that it produces". The fallacy of this type of thinking is obvious: Use is in itself a form of profit; but for the maintenance of an economy other forms of profit are essential: there must be the profit to provide for the maintenance of surplus and reserves against times of need, which is the only true form of security; and the profit that must repay human ingenuity for its task of creating and must provide for production and maintenance of other machinery of production. Without these forms of profit, an economy must inevitably break down.

The obvious remedy of the evils of a scarcity economy is to remedy the basic defect — the more there is produced, the less it is worth. This would make it possible to set up the surpluses and reserves that spell security without destroying thereby the price of the commodities — a surplus economy.

To accomplish this purpose, fortunately, it is not necessary to resort to another of those economic experiments that have trifled with, and endangered, the lives and livelihoods of many millions of people that have characterized the 'New Deal" in the past decade. The setting up of vast surpluses and reserves without depressing the price of the commodity involved has been accomplished for long periods of time in the case of one commodity — gold. Vast surpluses of gold have been stored up without depressing its price. Even when the production of gold was lowest, in 1929, its real overproduction relative to the amounts required for technologic uses was more than 90% of the total production. This overproduction has been buried in a hole in the ground at Fort Knox. So far as goes the nation's actual need of it for fabrication into necessary devices, it can remain in that hole forever, or until some technologic use for gold is discovered that requires the large surplus that has been built up in the course of world history. (This amounts to a block of gold about the size of a thirty foot cube that could be contained in the average thirty-five foot, three story building.) In spite of this real overproduction the price of gold actually has been raised by the New Deal.

The mechanism that has defied the speculative influence of supply and demand on the price of gold is the monetization of gold. It has been accomplished by the Currency Act of March 14, 1900 and its recent amendments.

Through the Currency Act, the nation alleges that it regards gold as absolutely essential for the existence of the nation — that it can not live without gold, it can not eat or drink without gold, it can not clothe itself without gold, it can not shelter itself without gold. These allegations implied in the Act, are obviously false. Nevertheless, the Act provides that in order to stimulate the production of gold to the nation's maximum capacity, no producer of gold shall have to rely upon speculators for marketing his production. It provides that all gold produced would be stored by the Treasury and warehouse receipts, in the form of gold notes, shall be issued for it at a fixed price, originally a dollar for each 25.8 grains of gold. The result has been complete stabilization of the price of gold no matter how great the overproduction; and the creation of a huge surplus of useless gold without impairing its market price.

Despite the allegations implied in the Currency Act, gold is not essential for human existence. If the men stranded on a desert island had all the gold in the world and all the money in the world with them, they would still starve to death. King Midas who mythology tells us was endowed with the gift he prayed for — that everything he touched be converted to gold — nevertheless starved to death. What then gives gold and money based on gold their value?

Obviously the only thing that gives gold, or any form of money, its value is solely its acceptance in exchange for the things required for existence: food, clothing, shelter and other necessities and luxuries. When gold or money can not buy these things it has no value. Therefore the only real security behind gold and money, that give them their value, are the raw materials from which the necessities of life can be made.

Though gold, silver and the national debt are the basis of the currency issued by the Treasury, that money constitutes only a small fraction of exchange medium of the nation. Currency created by the private banker constitutes the bulk of the currency in use. In 1929, for each dollar created by the Treasury on the basis of gold, the private banker created two hundred dollars. Without credit currency, the nation's business would come to a standstill.

The bulk of that credit currency is created by the private banker, when he desires to create it, on the basis of the things that people require for their existence. Therefore the real basis for this credit currency and the security behind it is the raw and fabricated materials constituting the necessities of life.

This credit currency is produced in violation of the Constitution and law. The Constitution states that Congress alone shall have the power to issue money and determine its value. It prescribes gold and silver as the basis for money. Credit currency and its creation by private bankers are implicitly prohibited by the Constitution.

This situation was brought about by the efforts of Alexander Hamilton, at the behest of George Washington, to win over the Tory elements, such as the Roosevelts, to the support of the Constitution. They insisted upon retaining the control over the real wealth of the land, the raw materials of the necessities of life, through the device of private banking credit, and the speculative manipulation it made possible. This was granted them and the limitation of the monetary powers of Congress was written into the Constitution. Though the exclusive "power to issue money and define its value" was reserved to Congress, this provision of the Constitution was disregarded from the very start. Consistently since, the real security behind money and wealth, the nation's commodities, has been ignored by the law, and the currency based upon that wealth is denied the status of legal tender.

Before this had been done, however, the Colony of Massachusetts Bay had coped with the problem of inflation and had arrived at a true Yankee commonsense solution of the problem. Massachusetts, like the rest of the Colonies, had sought to evade its obligations to the Continental Army, the payment of wages and pensions to volunteers, by the issue of unsecured paper money. The money rapidly became so worthless as to give rise to the expression "not worth a Continental"; and the Colonial governments were bankrupt.

By 1780 the number of returned, unpaid veterans of the Colony of Massachusetts Bay had grown large. They threatened to seize the government if they were not paid. This was an emergency that stirred Yankee ingenuity to its full depths.

The Massachusetts Yankees reasoned soundly that the best way to stabilize prices and stop inflation was by direct action rather than by roundabout methods. They defined money in terms of the things that folks wished to purchase with it, the staple necessities of life. In that manner the lender would be sure to receive back the same purchasing power as he had loaned. They therefore defined the money in terms of the staple commodities produced in the Colony — beef, corn, sheep's wool and sole leather. These notes, a reproduction of one of which appears on the frontispiece, were issued in 1780 and came due in 1784. They were accepted as legal tender.

While this monetary plan prevailed, Massachusetts alone among the Colonies prospered. By 1784 it had been agreed that currency would be issued by the Federal Government. The Massachusetts Yankee staple product notes were redeemed at the same value at which they were issued. Yankee staple notes were the only currency ever redeemed at the value at which they were issued by any American governmental agency. All the other forms of currency issued were either wiped out completely, like the greenbacks, or were so tremendously inflated like the Continental and the Roosevelt dollar, that they were redeemed at a mere fraction of their value at issuance.

The only measure that can block the wiping out of the major part of the wealth of the rank and file of Americans by this conspiracy is re-adoption of the Yankee staple product currency base. Since the only real security that lies behind the dollar and gives it its value is its acceptance in exchange for the raw or fabricated staples constituting the necessities of life and luxuries, it is essential that the fact be recognized. Money must be based upon those staples directly just as it is now based upon gold and silver directly. The staples that constitute the raw materials of the necessities of life can be kept in storage, with modern technology, almost as safely as can gold.

Widening the monetary base to include all staples that can be stored over periods of years would mean the inclusion in the base of the grains, such as wheat, corn, and soybeans; the elements, such as uranium, copper, tantalum, coal, tin and sulphur; minerals such as feldspar and phosphates; petroleum oil; the fibres, such as cotton, wool, hemp, rayon and silk; leather; rubber, and a wide array of other staples. The large number of staples included in the base would serve to prevent unbalancing the economy by a rush into production of the staples that were thus made liquid wealth. The liquidity of the staples would serve to stabilize the values of products fabricated from them. The entire economy would be stabilized and the dread of production of the staple necessities for fear of "overproduction" would vanish. The nation's economy will recognize what common sense teaches the individual: intrinsic values are not impaired by the amounts produced; momentary excesses in production over immediate utilization of staples, do not constitute overproduction from the viewpoint of long term needs; folks need not starve and want, as when rationing prevailed, if there is at hand too much of necessities, but they must starve if there is too little.

It is questionable if in a constantly expanding economy and steadily maintained prosperity, that such a program makes inevitable, there can be any tremendous actual overproduction. But even if there should chance to be such an overproduction in some staple or another, any losses implied could be written off by a slight increase in seigniorage or taxes, and would involve no significant loss. Since free exchange of staples between the nations of the world would become possible as a result of stabilized values, such excessive surpluses should be few and far between.

The Yankee staple product currency would enable the government to perform the first of its axiomatically basic functions — the setting up of surpluses and reserves to insure the citizenry against want and starvation. It would also make possible its performance of the second function — enabling the citzenry to obtain the wherewithal to purchase. For when production of staples can be expanded to the maximum capacity, and the production has become liquid wealth, there is inevitably stimulation of the entire economy by the increased wealth. This would make for greater employment. More important still, widening the currency base and the monetization of staples, would enable a government to put an end to unemployment by creating absolute freedom of employment. Without this freedom, all other types of freedom assured citizens by documents—freedom of life, liberty and pursuit of happiness—are meaningless. For without the absolute right to employment and to earn an adequate living the citizen cannot even enjoy the freedom of life.

Until the government has created and given substance to the ideal of freedom of employment that is implied by our Constitution, we cannot claim to have fulfilled its letter, nor can we claim to be a democracy.

By freedom of employment is not meant the "right to organize" into labor unions. For that implies the substitution of one form of coercion, economic, by another, that of labor unions.

Freedom of employment also can not be effected by placing a host of persons on the Government payroll. Quite as ominous as the Relief rolls is the steady growth of the number of government employees, and the spectacle of hordes seeking Civil Service employment because it alone offers security of employment to many. Government employees, as a rule, do not produce or increase the resources of a land but deplete it. Parasitic bureaucratic systems eventually destroy the lands on which they prey.

Freedom of employment can be produced only by a social organization which gives man the freedom of choice between accepting employment offered him by another or of creating adequately profitable employmnt for himself.

That a form of social organization which creates freedom of employment is possible, is indicated by the fact that our law and government do create it in one direction. Under our present law, the men who can go out and pan gold in sufficient amounts are given freedom of employment that is adequately and assuredly profitable. No matter how many men engage in the production of gold, no matter how much is produced, its price remains unaltered. They can be certain that if they can pan a definite amount of gold they will have enough for all their needs. This contrasts sharply with what would happen if an equal number of men engaged in any other form of production; for them the more they produced the less it would be worth.

It is truly absurd that gold should be the only commodity the production of which, and the producers of which, are adequately protected by a law which gives form to the dictates of our Constitution. For it alone among the commodities is useless—so useless that it is taken out of one hole in the ground and buried in another at Fort Knox.

The monetization of gold has created freedom of employment and has also tremendously stimulated employment and wages in its production. Widening the monetary base to include a wide array of commodities, the staple products that are the raw materials of the necessities of life, would obviously stimulate employment in many different directions.

Creating freedom of employment in directions other than self-employment in producing gold is not popular with the Labor Barons and their "Liberal" henchmen. It would wipe out any excuse for their activities. They therefore allege that freedom of employment can not exist because, they say, "sixty families and a few hundred companies own and control all the machinery of production". This is a Marxist myth that is proved obviously false by an examination of what, in ultimate analysis, constitutes the basic machinery of production. Some glibly state that labor is a basic machinery of production. But labor as often destroys as it produces; unthinking and plodding labor may produce little; and monkeys labor all day long and produce no wealth. It is the thing that differentiates man and monkey that constitutes the most important basic machinery of production.

The ultimate machineries of production are two—human ingenuity, and the earth and elements, which are the sources of the raw materials. It would be ridiculous to pretend that any six hundred families or ten thousand corporations have a monopoly of human ingenuity. The elements are relatively uncontrolled. Of the other machinery of production, the land, this group controls scarcely one percent in the United States. The largest owner of land in the United States is the Government, the people themselves. The governments control well over fifty percent of the nation's land. Over twenty percent are included in the Federal parks and reservations alone.

With regard to government lands there exists in the United States a curious situation. They are carried on the Government's ledger as liabilities together with the many billions of debt. As they are handled today they are really liabilities. They produce nothing, cost much to maintain and police, and eventually are given away to speculators or to homesteaders on the speculation that they will be able to hold out.

But this land situation is unquestionably absurd. The land could be converted readily into a very real asset that would salvage the nation's solvency and credit by a very wide margin if the disposition of the Crown Lands of England were followed as an example. The Crown Lands are usually not alienated from the Crown, but are leased for production for a percentage of what is produced in some instances.

Following the example of England, the United States could lease its lands for production and thus convert them into assets. With the widening of the currency base to include the staple products, it could go even further. It could utilize these lands for the creation of true freedom of employment. It could offer to lease to all who care to do so, as much land as each individual can work, for the production of staple products, at a rental consisting of a percentage of the production. Instead of frittering away the national wealth on a dole system, and stimulating sloth and shiftlessness, it could undertake to lend the money for financing purchase of machinery of production with the proviso that the loans be amortized in kind with a part of the staples produced. The incorporation of staples in the monetary base under the Yankee plan would make this possible.

Under the Yankee plan no depression or unemployment could ever exist. A bit of commonsense thinking makes clear the irrationality of these problems. The consideration of them has been so stereotyped, that no one has stopped to reflect that the unemployed, like the rest of mankind, require their share of the necessities and luxuries of life. In producing those items for themselves lies the obvious solution of their unemployment.

The Antigonish movement that has converted a pauperized group of fishing villages in Newfoundland into a prosperous and model community, attests to the potentialities of such a solution. It contrasts sharply with the persistent accentuation of the unemployment problem that has resulted from the plans of the subversive, radical and "New Deal" groups that are more bent upon stimulating class hatred and wars than employment, prosperity and peace. The country was well on the way to arriving at such a solution in the barter plans of 1933, when the advent of the "New Deal" put a stop to the rational solution, resuscitated the banks and then rescued the old economic setup which repeatedly has proved unworkable.

Such a plan would satisfy every legitimate element in the community. It protects those that have, in the possession of that which they have. It also enables those that have not, to produce that which they need. It would make obvious the absurdity of the idea that the only possible solution is the dishonest concept of "distribution of wealth", which in ultimate analysis is merely a distribution of poverty. It eliminates the idea that accumulations of reserves or wealth are a menace to the nation. It does this by eliminating the only real danger of such accumulations, which is the paralysis of the currency system resulting from irrational restriction of currency.

At the same time it would dispel forever that irrational attitude which demands security, and at the same time decries the setting up of savings and reserves of the necessities of life, which alone offer real security. The current idea that bookkeeping balances offer security is absurd. Above all else it would eliminate the real basis for strife between the "haves" and "have-nots", whether those groups be within the same community or in different nations.

It is only such a plan that could make the United States the capitalist state that many folks falsely fancy that it is. It obviously is not "capitalist" in the sense of making the private ownership of property secure, for there has been no real security in ownership, especially during the past decade. Ours has been a speculative economy that is as much the antithesis of true capitalism as are the theories of Communism or National Socialism. Communism in its ultimate development assumes the form of a super-capitalistic super-dictatorship. The only difference between these rival and supposedly antagonistic economies is the name of their masters.

Capitalism, it is safe to predict, is the only form of social organization that ever will be secure. For it is rooted in the very trait of possessiveness inherent in human nature which theorizing radicals have pretended it is possible to root out, merely to find that it had mastered themselves. If a form of social organization that is rooted in human nature cannot succeed, certainly no other has any chance whatsoever.

It is as absurd to say that "democracy (or republicanism) is a failure" as it is to say that "capitalism is a failure". The U. S. has never had either of them, in the correct sense of the terms. The nation has never carried out the blueprint of human organization drawn up by the wisest group of men that ever assembled for that purpose —the Constitution. They defined democracy in terms of *"freedom of life, liberty and pursuit of happiness"*. These are the goals that man has striven for from time immemorial.

The authors of the Constitution were close enough to slavery and feudalism to keenly appreciate the value of freedom and the attributes of democracy. Unfortunately the present generation are so hedonic and lacking in insight that they fail to realize the meaning of slavery though they have witnessed it in the concentration camps of Nazi Germany and of Russia. They are willing to surrender, and have surrendered, "freedom" for the bait of slave-masters—a *mirage of "security"*,—even before they have attained the measure of freedom called for by the Constitution. They actually believe the shibboleth "Democracy is a failure", though the nation has never attained it.

Democracy has not been attained in the U. S. because it has never created the basic freedom—absolute freedom to earn a living, or freedom of employment. This freedom was taken for granted by the framers of the Constitution. Frontiers, all about them, provided freedom of employment for anyone who cared to work. It was implied in the expression "freedom of life . . .".

For there can be no "freedom of life" if there is no freedom to earn the wherewithal to live.

Likewise, a true capitalism is a form of social and economic organization which makes the private ownership of property secure. The speculative gold standard scarcity economy, latterly replaced in part by a "managed" scarcity economy, offers no security in the private ownership of property. The experiences of 1929 attest to that. It is reasonable to assume, in view of the experience of the Colony of Massachusetts Bay, that if the development of our economy had been untrammeled by treacherous Tories who were in a position to impose their will, the Yankee surplus economy plan, which is the only possible basis for a true capitalism, would have been adopted as the pattern intended by the framers of the Constitution. It would have made the world a happier place to live in.

The Yankee surplus economy plan would eliminate the fear of starvation and want that results today from either under- or over-production, both at home and abroad. The adoption of the plan by any one nation would force its adoption throughout the world. For if any one nation offered, for instance, to pay three dollars a bushel for any wheat that might be turned over to its Treasury, every other country would have to do the same, or else lose the wheat its people require for their existence. No matter how high the barriers that might be set up to prevent the outflow of the wheat, it would be sure to make its way to the highest market. This would imply eventually an equally high standard of living in all lands.

When staples sell at the same level in all lands and the standard of living become equally high, barriers which are set up to prevent impairment of living standards, or jeopardy of employment, would disappear. Free trade on a world-wide basis would become possible and desirable. Such a plan offers the only practical solution of the impasse created by the breakdown of the gold standard system in international trade. It would eliminate the struggle for raw materials which underlies wars and alone could make possible international amity by making trade barriers unnecessary and anachronistic.

Fear of starvation and want would vanish rapidly in a world placed on a surplus economy basis. Humans would no longer be regarded by nations as liabilities, to be avoided—by race suicide, by retarding the younger generation in its start in life, by immigration barriers, by labor unionism, by DP camps, and by the massacres of the concentration camps which are the most eloquent expressions of the ultimate in scarcity economy.

This age-old solution of the problems of economic organization has been adopted, as in Massachusetts, whenever emergency brought to the fore the realization that the real basis of wealth is not gold but the necessities of life. In the story of Joseph and Pharaoh, it is one of the most important lessons the Bible has to offer, but one which our "economists" and "men of learning" refuse to learn.

The question arises: Why has not the Yankee plan been adopted during the decade and a half of absurd scarcity economy experiments of the New Deal? Foreign ideas are as popular and fashionable in the "social sciences" (made in Germany) as are the French gowns among the fair sex. And homely, commonsense American ideas on economics, are as deprecated as domestic gowns.

The state of the world, however, has become so critical, and the impasse so absurd, that mayhap folks will stop, look and listen long enough to adopt the sound idea and rational solution of the Yankee plan. In garbled form it has been advocated in recent years by diverse characters. Thus Sir Maynard Keynes was chief Bank of England propagandist for forcing the gold standard, scarcity economic concepts on the New Deal. In his "Treatise On Money" and in his address before the British Association for Advancement of Science in August 1938, he belied the scarcity propaganda he was paid to foist on the U. S. by urging the adoption of the staple product plan in England. Father Coughlin advocated a garbled form of the plan, as it was described in an article by this author, and made it the basis of his Social Justice plan; but he unfortunately confused it with the highly speculative Irving Fisher gold-index dollar, which is the exact antithesis. Wise and scholarly Senator Robert Owens, author of the Federal Reserve Act, attempted to introduce the Yankee staple product dollar into that Act; but Irving Fisher and Senator Carter Glass frustrated his plan. Had Senator Owens succeeded, the Federal Reserve Act would have served the interests of the nation instead of merely the Dynastic bankers and their allies; and World War I might have been averted.

If the U. S. and the world can be shifted onto a surplus economy base, the destruction of democracy and human freedom, the advance of Communism, managed economies and other forms of dictatorships and slave states, and the further advance of World War III can be averted. The drive behind the Dynasty and the Rockefeller Empire for an American monarchy can be checked; and the fear that filled the world and motivated John D. Rockefeller and other monopolists could be completely dispelled. With this out of the way the Napoleonic complex will fail to gain support.

To put the Yankee plan into operation in the U. S. will require another amendment to the Currency Act widening the monetary base to comply with existent realities; a change in the policy of the Interior Department with regard to public lands; supplanting Relief and bonus measures by a plan to finance folks who desire to produce, with loans to be repaid out of production; and enlargement of elevator and storage facilities to the point of adequacy.

The value to be given in the base to staple products should be the average historic value multiplied by the same factor as the price of gold has been increased. The advantage of the plan to the farmer and the other producers of staples are obvious. The fabricator would benefit from the stable value of raw materials and the enlarged market created by the high stable earnings of the producers of staples. The worker would benefit by earning all that he produces, or else by stabilization of his wage at the level of his ability to earn if he wished to resort to production of staples; and he would be free to earn as much as he is willing to work for. The rich would be secure in their wealth because their holdings would not constitute a barrier to others acquiring as much as they are willing to work for. Banking and industry would benefit from the liquidity of wealth and from the general prosperity. The nation and the world would benefit from the stabilization of its economy and the accumulation of the unlimited riches that Nature has to offer. These things could be accomplished in the brief period of six months, *if there is a will to accomplish them.*

This solution would defeat the purposes of the Dynasty to destroy democracy and freedom, and would render fruitless the martial plans for world conquest of both Russia and the Rockefeller Empire.

ACKNOWLEDGMENT: "THE ROYAL FAMILY" on pages 10-11, tracing THE ROOSE-VELT-DELANO DYNASTY, is reprinted from the ROOSEVELT OMNIBUS, edited by Don Wharton, by permission of Alfred A. Knopf, Inc. Copyright by Alfred A. Knopf, Inc. 1934.